muhammad in the bible

اَلَّذِينَ اٰتَيْنَاهُمُ الْكِتَابَ يَعْرِفُونَهُ كَمَا يَعْرِفُونَ اَبْنَاءَهُمْ اَلَّذِينَ خَسِرُوٓا اَنْفُسَهُمْ فَهُمْ لَا يُؤْمِنُونَ (الأنعام. الآية ٢٠)

Published by
Angkatan Nahdhatul-Islam Bersatu
(BINA)
SARAWAK

From Islamic Series No. 2
Abbas Manzil Library
Allahabad

Printed in Singapore
Kyodo-Shing Loong Printing Industries Pte Ltd)

MUHAMMAD IN THE BIBLE

by

PROF. 'ABDU 'L-AHAD DAWUD
(*Former Bishop of Uramiah*)

Angkatan Nahdhatul-Islam Bersatu
(BINA)
SARAWAK,

Professor 'Abdu 'l-Ahad Dawud, B.D., the writer of the present series of articles is the former Reverend David Benjamin Keldani, B.D., a Roman Catholic priest of the Uniate-Chaldean sect. A brief sketch of his biography appears elsewhere.

When asked how he came to Islam he wrote:

"My conversion to Islam cannot be attributed to any cause other than the gracious direction of the Almighty Allah. Without this Divine guidance all learning, search and other efforts to find the Truth may even lead one astray. The moment I believed in the Absolute Unity of God His Holy Apostle Muhammad became the pattern of my conduct and behaviour."

اَلَّذِينَ يَتَّبِعُونَ الرَّسُولَ النَّبِيَّ الْأُمِّيَّ الَّذِي يَجِدُونَهُ مَكْتُوبًا عِنْدَهُمْ فِي التَّوْرَاةِ وَالْإِنْجِيلِ يَأْمُرُهُمْ بِالْمَعْرُوفِ وَيَنْهَاهُمْ عَنِ الْمُنْكَرِ وَيُحِلُّ لَهُمُ الطَّيِّبَاتِ وَيُحَرِّمُ عَلَيْهِمُ الْخَبَائِثَ وَيَضَعُ عَنْهُمْ إِصْرَهُمْ وَالْأَغْلَالَ الَّتِي كَانَتْ عَلَيْهِمْ فَالَّذِينَ آمَنُوا بِهِ وَعَزَّرُوهُ وَنَصَرُوهُ وَاتَّبَعُوا النُّورَ الَّذِي أُنْزِلَ مَعَهُ أُولَٰئِكَ هُمُ الْمُفْلِحُونَ (الأعراف. الآية ١٥٧)

"Those who follow the Apostle, Prophet, the 'Ummi' whom they find written down with them in the Torah and the Gospel (who) enjoins them good, and forbids them evil, and makes lawful to them the good things and makes unlawful to them impure things, and removes from them their burden and the Shackles which were upon them; So (as for) those who believe in him and honour him and help him, and follow the light which has been sent down with him, these it is that are the successful." (Al Quran, VII, 157).

بِسْمِ اللهِ الرَّحْمٰنِ الرَّحِيْمِ

On behalf of Angkatan Nahdhatul-Islam Bersatu (B.I.N.A.), Sarawak, and on my own behalf, I wish to express our deepest and most profound gratitude to the Government of Qatar which demonstrated their extraordinary generosity and kindness towards BINA and its many activities in advancing the cause of Islam in Sarawak, by financing the publication by BINA of the book "MUHAMMAD IN THE BIBLE", which is of such great value to all those who are interested in discovering the truth of the religion of Islam.

I have personal knowledge of some people, including my wife who was formerly a Catholic, who discovered the religion of Islam after reading and studying this particular book. I myself have deepened my understanding of both the Christian and Islamic religions from reading and studying this book.

I pray to Allah Subhanahu Wataala to bless us all in our sacred undertaking to spread the understanding and acceptence of Islam throughout the world.

Wabillahit-Taufiq-Walhidayah.

(Datuk Patinggi Tan Sri Haji Abdul Rahman Ya'kub)

Kuching, SARAWAK
1st April, 1978

Yang Di Pertua
Angkatan Nahdhatul Islam Bersatu (BINA),
Sarawak.

اڠكاتن نهضة الإسلام برساتو

Angkatan Nahdhatul-Islam Bersatu
(BINA)
SARAWAK,

بِسْمِ اللهِ الرَّحْمَنِ الرَّحِيمِ

Bagi pihak Angkatan Nahdhatul-Islam Bersatu (BINA), Sarawak dan juga bagi pihak diri saya sendiri, saya ucapkan setinggi-tinggi terima kasih kepada Kerajaan Negeri Qatar yang telah bermurah hati membiayai perbelanjaan BINA bagi mencetak buku "Muhammad In The Bible" yang sangat besar faedahnya bagi sekalian yang mencari kebenaran Ugama.

2.   Ingin saya nyatakan bahawa beberapa orang rakan-rakan saya, termasuk isteri saya sendiri, yang dahulunya berugama Catholic, telah memeluk Ugama Islam setelah membaca buku ini. Saya sendiri telah mendapat pengetahuan yang luas dan berguna mengenai ajaran-ajaran Ugama Keristian dan Ugama Islam dari buku ini.

3.   Saya bermohon semoga Allah Subhanahu Wata'ala senantiasa memberkati usaha-usaha kita bersama untuk memperkembang luas syiar Islam di bumi ini.

Wabillahit-Taufiq-Walhidayah.

(Datuk Patinggi Tan Sri Haji Abdul Rahman Ya'kub)
Yang Di Pertua
Angkatan Nahdhatul Islam Bersatu (BINA),
Sarawak.

Kuching, SARAWAK.
1hb. April, 1978.

بِسْمِ اللهِ الرَّحْمٰنِ الرَّحِيمِ

In The name of Allah, Most Gracious, Most Merciful

On behalf of Presidency of Shariyah Courts And Religious Affairs in Qatar-Arabian Gulf, it pleases me very much to introduce "MUHAMMAD IN THE BIBLE" in this edition for the benefit of all Muslims.

I Pray to Almighty Allah to bless all Muslims and spread Islam in the world.

Abdul Rahman Bin Abdullah Al-Mahmoud
Vice-President,
Presidency of Shariyah Courts And Religious Affairs.
DOHA — QATAR
ARABIAN GULF

Doha,
9th Rajab 1398
14th JUNE 1978

FOREWORD

THE PROPHET OF ARABIA AS SPOKEN OF
IN THE BIBLE

"The Burden Upon Arabia" — isaiah xxi. 13.

The present barren period of classical scholarship, together with the increasing paucity of our knowledge of ancient languages, has crippled modern taste in its efforts to appreciate any such attempts as I intend to make in that direction. The following pages have produced a series of most able articles from the pen of the Rev. Professor 'Abdu 'l-Ahad Dāwūd, but I wonder if there are many, even among the hierarchy of the Christian Church, who could follow the erudite exposition of the learned Professor. All the more do I wonder when he seeks to carry his readers into a labyrinth of languages, dead and done with thousands of years ago. What about Aramaic, when very few even among the Clergy are able to understand the Vulgate and the original Greek version of the New Testament? More especially when our researches are based simply upon Greek and Latin etymology! Whatever may be the value of such dissertations in the enemy's eye we, nowadays, are absolutely incapable of appreciating them from the angle of erudition; for the oracular ambiguity attached to the prophetic utterances to which I allude makes them elastic enough to cover any case. The "least" in the prophecy of St. John the Baptist may not be the son of Mary, though he was looked upon as such contemptuously by his own tribe. The Holy Carpenter came from humble parentage. He was hooted down, mocked and discredited; he was belittled and made to appear the "least" in the public estimation fy the Scribes and Pharisees. The excess of zeal displayed by his followers in the second and third centuries A.D., which was ever prone to jump at anything in the form of a prophecy in the Bible, would naturally induce them to believe that their Lord was the person alluded to by the Baptist.

However, there is another difficulty in the way. How can a person rely on the testimony of a book admittedly filled up with folk-lore? The genuineness of the Bible has universally been questioned. Without going into the question of its genuineness, we may at least say that we cannot depend on its statements concerning Jesus and his miracles. Some even go so far as to assert that his existence as an historical person is questionable, and that on the authority of the Gospels it would be dangerous to arrive at any apparently safe conclusion in this matter. A Christian of the Fundamentalist type cannot well say anything against my statement of the case. If "stray sentences" and detached words in the Old Testament can be singled out by synoptic writers as applicable to Jesus, the comments of the learned writer of these erudite and absorbing articles must command every respect and appreciation even from the Clergy. I write in the same strain, but I have tried to base my arguments on portions of the Bible which hardly allow of any linguistic dispute. I would not go to Latin, Greek, or Aramaic, for that would be useless: I just give the following quotation in the very words of the Revised Version as published by the British and Foreign Bible Society.

We read the following words in the Book of Deuteronomy, chapter xviii. verse 18: "I will raise them up a prophet from among their brethren, like unto thee; and I will put my words in his mouth." If these words do not apply to Muhammad, they still remain unfulfilled. Jesus himself never claimed to be the Prophet alluded to. Even his disciples were of the same opinion: they looked to the second coming of Jesus for the fulfilment of the prophecy.[1] So far it is undisputed that the first coming of Jesus was not the advent of the "prophet like unto thee," and his second advent can hardly fulfil the words. Jesus, as is believed by his Church, will appear as a Judge and not as a law-giver; but the promised one has to come with a "fiery law" in "his right hand."

In ascertaining the personality of the promised prophet the other prophecy of Moses is, however, very helpful where it speaks of the shining forth of God from Paran, the Mecca mountain. The words in the Book of Deuteronomy, chapter xxxiii. verse 2, run as follows: "The Lord came from Sinai, and rose up from Seir unto them; he shined forth *from mount Paran, and he came with ten thousands of saints;* from his right hand went a fiery law for them."

In these words the Lord has been compared with the sun. He comes from Sinai, he rises from Seir, but he shines in his full glory from Paran, where he had to appear with ten thousands of saints with a fiery law in his right hand. None of the Israelites, including Jesus, had anything to do with Paran. Hagar, with her son Ishmael, wandered in the wilderness of Beersheba, who afterwards dwelt in the wilderness of Paran (Gen. xxi. 21). He married an Egyptian woman, and through his firstborn, Kedar, gave descent to the Arabs who from that time till now are the dwellers of the wilderness of Paran. And if Muhammad admittedly on all hands traces his descent to Ishmael through Kedar and he appeared as a prophet in the wilderness of Paran and re-

---

1. "21 Whom the heaven must receive until the times of restitution of all things, which God hath spoken by the mouth of all His holy prophets since the world began. 22 For Moses truly said unto the fathers, A prophet shall the Lord your God raise up unto you of your brethren, like unto me; him shall ye hear in all things whatsoever he shall say unto you." (Acts iii.)

entered Mecca with ten thousand saints and gave a fiery law
to his people, is not the prophecy above-mentioned fulfilled
to its very letter?   The words of the prophecy in Habakkuk
are especially noteworthy.   His (the Holy One from Paran)
glory covered the heavens and the earth was full of his praise.
The word "praise" is very significant, as the very name
Muhammad literally means "the praised one."   Besides the
Arabs, the inhabitants of the wilderness of Paran had also
been promised a Revelation: "Let the wilderness and the
cities thereof lift up their voice, the villages that Kedar doth
inhabit: let the inhabitants of the rock sing, let them shout
from the top of the mountains.   Let them give glory unto
the Lord, and declare his praise in the islands.   The Lord
shall go forth as a mighty man, he shall stir up jealousy like
a man of war, he shall cry, yea, roar; he shall prevail against
his enemies" (Isa. xlii. 11.).

In connection with it there are two other prophecies
worthy of note where references have been made to Kedar.
The one runs thus in chapter lx. of Isaiah: "Arise, shine for
thy light is come, and the glory of the Lord is risen upon
thee......The multitude of camels shall cover thee, the
dromedaries of Midian and Ephah; all they from Sheba shall
come.......All the flocks of Kedar shall be gathered together
unto thee, the rams of Nebaioth shall minister unto thee: they
shall come up with acceptance on mine altar, and I will
glorify the house of my glory" (1-7).   The other prophecy
is again in Isaiah xxi.:   "The burden upon Arabia.   In the
forest in Arabia shall ye lodge, O ye travelling companies of
Dedanim.   The inhabitants of the land of Tema brought
water to him that was thirsty, they prevented with their bread
him that fled.   For they fled from the swords......and from
the bent bow, and from the grievousness of war.   For thus
hath the Lord said unto me, Within a year, according to the

years of an hireling, and all the glory of Kedar shall fail:
And the residue of the number of archers, the mighty men
of the children of Kedar, shall be diminished" (13-17).
Read these prophecies in Isaiah in the light of one in Deuteronomy which speaks of the shining forth of God from Paran.
If Ishmael inhabited the wilderness of Paran, where he gave
birth to Kedar, who is the ancestor of the Arabs; and if the
sons of Kedar had to receive revelation from God; if the
flocks of Kedar had to come up with acceptance to a Divine
altar to glorify "the house of my glory" where the darkness
had to cover the earth for some centuries, and then that very
land had to receive light from God; and if all the glory of
Kedar had to fail and the number of archers, the mighty men
of the children of Kedar, had to diminish within a year after
the one fled from the swords and from the bent bows — the
Holy One from Paran (Hab. iii 3) is no one else than
Muhammad. Muhammad is the holy offspring of Ishmael
through Kedar, who settled in the wilderness of Paran.
Muhammad is the only Prophet through whom the Arabs
received revelation at the time when the darkness had covered
the earth. Through him God shone from Paran, and Mecca
is the only place where the house of God is glorified and
the flocks of Kedar come up with acceptance on its altar.
Muhammad was presecuted by his people and had to leave
Mecca. He was thirsty and fled from the drawn sword and
the bent bow, and within a year after his flight the descendants of Kedar meet him at Badr, the place of the first battle
between the Meccans and the Prophet, the children of Kedar
and their number of archers diminish and all the glory of
Kedar fails. If the Holy Prophets is not to be accepted as
the fulfilment of all these prophecies they will still remain
unfulfilled. "The house of my glory" referred to in Isaiah lx.
is the house of God at Mecca and not the Church of Christ

as thought by Christian commentators. The flocks of Kedar, as mentioned in verse 7, have never come to the Church of Christ; and it is a fact that the villages of Kedar and their inhabitants are the only people in the whole world who have remained impenetrable to any influence of the Church of Christ. Again, the mention of 10,000 saints in Deuteronomy xxxiii. is very significant. He (God) shined forth from Paran, and he came with 10,000 of saints. Read the whole history of the wilderness of Paran and you will find no other event but when Mecca was conquered by the Prophet. He comes with 10,000 followers from Medina and re-enters "the house of my glory." He gives the fiery law to the world, which reduced to ashes all other laws. The Comforter — the Spirit of Truth — spoken of by Jesus was no other than Muhammad himself. It cannot be taken as the Holy Ghost, as the Church theology says. "It is expedient for you that I go away," says Jesus, "for if I go not away the Comforter will not come unto you, but if I depart I will send him unto you." The words clearly show that the Comforter had to come after the departure of Jesus, and was not with him when he uttered these words. Are we to presume that Jesus was devoid of the Holy Ghost if his coming was conditional on the going of Jesus: besides, the way in which Jesus describes him makes him a human being, not a ghost. "He shall not speak of himself, but whatsoever he shall hear that he shall speak." Should we presume that the Holy Ghost and God are two distinct entities and that the Holy Ghost speaks of himself and also what he hears from God? The words of Jesus clearly refer to some messenger from God. He calls him the Spirit of Truth, and so the Qur-án speaks of Muhammad, "Nay, he has come with the Truth and verified the apostles."

"X. X."

A SHORT BIOGRAPHICAL SKETCH OF PROFESSOR 'ABDU 'L-AHAD DAWUD, B.D.

'Abdu 'l-Ahad Dáwúd is the former Rev. David Benjamin Keldani, B.D., a Roman Catholic priest of the Uniate-Chaldean sect. He was born in 1867 at Urmia in Persia; educated from his early infancy in that town. From 1886-89 (three years) he was on the teaching staff of the Archbishop of Canterbury's Mission to the Assyrian (Nestorian) Christians at Urmia. In 1892 he was sent by Cardinal Vaughan to Rome, where he underwent a course of philosophical and theological studies at the Propaganda Fide College, and in 1895 was ordained Priest. In 1892 Professor Dáwúd contributed a series of articles to *The Tablet* on "Assyria, Rome and Canterbury"; and also to the *Irish Record* on the "Authenticity of the Pentateuch." He has several translations of the *Ave Maria* in different languages, published in the *Illustrated Catholic Missions*. While in Constantinople on his way to Persia in 1895, he contributed a long series of articles in English and French to the daily paper, published there under the name of *The Levant Herald,* on "Eastern Churches." In 1895 he joined the French Lazarist Mission at Urmia, and published for the first time in the history of that Mission a periodical in the vernacular Syriac called *Qala-La-Shárá, i.e.* "The Voice of Truth." In 1897 he was delegated by two Uniate-Chaldean Archbishops of Urmia and of Salmas to represent the Eastern Catholics at the Eucharistic Congress held at Paray-le-Monial in France under the presidency of Cardinal Perraud. This

was, of course, an official invitation.   The paper read at the
Congress by "Father Benjamin" was published in the *Annals*
of the Eucharistic Congress, called "Le Pellerin" of that year.
In this paper, the Chaldean Arch-Priest (that being his official
title) deplored the Catholic system of education among the
Nestorians, and foretold the imminent appearance of the
Russian priests in Urmia.

In 1888 Father Benjamin was back again in Persia.   In
his native village, Digala, about a mile from the town, he
opened a school *gratis*.   The next year he was sent by the
Ecclesiastical authorities to take charge of the diocese of
Salmas, where a sharp and scandalous conflict between the
Uniate Archbishop, Khudabásh, and the Lazarist Fathers for
a long time had been menacing a schism.   On the day of
New Year 1900, Father Benjamin preached his last and
memorable sermon to a large congregation, including many
non-Catholic Armenians and others in the Cathedral of
St. George's Khorovábád, Salmas.   The preacher's subject
was "New Century and New Men."   He recalled the fact
that the Nestorian Missionaries, before the appearance of
Islam, had preached the Gospel in all Asia; that they had
numerous establishments in India (especially at the Malabar
Coast), in Tartary, China and Mongolia; and that they
translated the Gospel to the Turkish Uighurs and in other
languages; that the Catholic, American and Anglican Missions, in spite of the little good they had done to the Assyro-
Chaldean nation in the way of preliminary education, had
split the nation — already a handful — in Persia, Kurdistan
and Mesopotamia into numerous hostile sects; and that their
efforts were destined to bring about the final collapse.   Consequently he advised the natives to make some sacrifices in
order to stand upon their own legs like *men,* and not to
depend upon the foreign missions, etc.

The preacher was perfectly right in principle; but his remarks were unfavourable to the interests of the Lord's Missionaries. This sermon hastily brought the Apostolique Delegate, Mgr. Lésné, from Urmia to Salmas. He remained to the last a friend of Father Benjamin. They both returned to Urmia. A new Russian Mission had already been established in Urmia since 1899. The Nestorians were enthusiastically embracing the religion of the "holy" Tsar of All Russias!

Five big and ostentatious missions — Americans, Anglicans, French, Germans and Russians — with their colleges, Press backed up by rich religious societies, Consuls and Ambassadors, were endeavouring to convert about one hundred thousand Assyro-Chaldeans from Nestorian heresy unto one or another of the five heresies. But the Russian Mission soon outstripped the others, and it was this mission which in 1915 pushed or forced the Assyrians of Persia, as well as the mountaineer tribes of Kurdistan, who had then immigrated into the plains of Salmas and Urmia, to take up arms against their respective Governments. The result was that half of his people perished in the war and the rest expelled from their native lands.

The great question which for a long time had been working its solution in the mind of this priest was now approaching its climax. Was Christianity, with all its multitudinous shapes and colours, and with its unauthentic, spurious and corrupted Scriptures, the *true* Religion of God? In the summer of 1900 he retired to his small villa in the middle of vineyards near the celebrated fountain of Cháli-Boulaghi in Digala, and there for a month spent his time in prayer and meditation, reading over and over the Scriptures in their original texts. The crisis ended in a formal resignation sent in to the Uniate Archbishop of Urmia, in which he frankly explained to Mar (Mgr.) Touma Audu the reasons for abandoning his sacerdotal functions. All attempts made by the ecclesiastical authorities to withdraw his decision were of no avail. There was no personal quarrel or dispute between Father Benjamin and his superiors; it was all question of conscience.

For several months Mr. Dáwúd — as he was now called — was employed in Tabriz as Inspector in the Persian Service of Posts and Customs under the Belgian experts. Then he was taken into the service of the Crown Prince Muhammad 'Alí Mirzá as teacher and translator. It was in 1903 that he again visited England and there joined the Unitarian Community. And in 1904 he was sent by the British and Foreign Unitarian Association to carry on an educational and enlightening work among his country people. On his way to Persia he visited Constantinople; and after several interviews with the Sheikhu 'l-Islám Jemálu 'd-Dín Effendi and other Ulémas, he embraced the Holy Religion of Islam.

MUHAMMAD IN THE OLD TESTAMENT

I. PREFATORY REMARKS

I propose through this article and the ones which will follow to show that the doctrine of Islam concerning the Deity and the last great messenger of Allah is perfectly true and conforms to the teachings of the Bible.

I shall devote the present article to discussing the first point, and in a few other papers I shall attempt to show that Muhammad is the real object of the Covenant and in him, and him alone, are actually and literally fulfilled all the prophecies in the Old Testament.

I wish to make it quite clear that the views set out in this article and those which will follow it are quite personal, and that I am alone responsible for my personal and unborrowed researches in the Hebrew Sacred Scriptures. I do not, however, assume an authoritative attitude in expounding the teachings of Islam.

I have not the slightest intention nor desire to hurt the religious feelings of Christian friends. I love Christ, Moses and Abraham, as I do Muhammad and all other holy prophets of God.[1]

My writings are not intended to raise a bitter and therefore useless dispute with the Churches, but only invite them to a pleasant and friendly investigation of this all-important question with a spirit of love and impartiality. If the Chris-

---

1. Qur-án, iii. 83. "Say: We believe in Allah and what has been revealed to us and what was revealed to Abraham and Ishmael and Isaac and Jacob and the tribes, and what was given to Moses and Jesus and to the Prophets from their Lord; we do not make any distinction between any of them, and to Him do we submit."

tians desist from their vain attempt of defining the essence of the Supreme Being, and confess His absolute Oneness, then a union between them and the Muslims is not only probable but extremely possible. For once the unity of God is accepted and acknowledged, the other points of difference between the two faiths can more easily be settled.

II. ALLAH AND HIS ATTRIBUTES

There are two fundamental points between Islam and Christianity which, for the sake of the truth and the peace of the world, deserved a very serious and deep investigation. As these two religions claim their origin from one and the same source, it would follow that no important point of controversy between them should be allowed to exist. Both these great religions believe in the existence of the Deity and in the covenant made between God and the Prophet Abraham. On these two principal points a thoroughly conscientious and final agreement must be arrived at between the intelligent adherents of the two faiths. Are we poor and ignorant mortals to believe in and worship one God, or are we to believe in and fear a plurality of Gods? Which of the two, Christ or Muhammad, is the object of the Divine Covenant? These two questions must be answered once for all.

It would be a mere waste of time here to refute those who ignorantly or maliciously suppose the Allah of Islam to be different from the true God and only a fictitious deity of Muhammad's own creation. If the Christian priests and theologians knew their Scriptures in the original Hebrew instead of in translations as the Muslims read their Qur-án in its Arabic text, they would clearly see that Allah is the same ancient Semitic name of the Supreme Being who revealed and spoke to Adam and all the prophets.

Allah is the only self-existing, knowing, powerful Being. He encompasses, fills every space, being and thing; and is the source of all life, knowledge and force. Allah is the unique Creator, Regulator and Ruler of the universe. He is absolutely One. The essence, the person and nature of Allah are absolutely beyond human comprehension, and therefore any attempt to define His essence is not only futile but even dangerous to our spiritual welfare and faith; for it will certainly lead us into error.

The trinitarian branch of the Christian Church, for about seventeen centuries, has exhausted all the brains of her saints and philosophers to define the Essence and the Person of the Deity; and what have they invented? All that which Athanasiuses, Augustines and Aquinases have imposed upon the Christians "under the pain of eternal damnation" — to believe in a God who is "the third of three"! Allah, in His Holy Qur-án, condemns this belief in these solemn words:—

"They are certainly unbelievers, who say God is the third of three, for there is no God but the one God; and if they refrain not from what they say, a painful chastisement shall surely be inflicted on such of them as are unbelievers" (Qur-án, V. 73).

The reason why the orthodox Muslim scholars have always refrained from defining God's Essence is because His Essence transcends all attributes in which it could only be defined. Allah has many names which in reality are only adjectives derived from His essence through its various manifestations in the universe which He alone has formed. We call Allah by the appellations Almighty, Eternal, Omnipresent, Omniscient, Merciful, and so forth, because we conceived the eternity, omnipresence, universal knowledge, mercifulness, as emanating from His essence, and belonging to Him alone and absolutely. He is alone the infinitely Knowing, Powerful, Living, Holy, Beautiful, Good, Loving, Glorious, Terrible, Avenger, because it is from Him alone that emanate and flow the qualities of knowledge, power, life, holiness, beauty and the rest. God has no attributes in the sense we understand them. With us an attribute or a property is common to many individuals of a species, but what is God's is His alone, and there is none other to share it with Him. When we say, "Solomon is wise, powerful, just and beautiful," we do not ascribe exclusively to him all wisdom, power, justice and beauty. We only mean to say that he is relatively wise as compared with others of his species, and that wisdom too is relatively his attribute in common with the individuals belonging to his class.

To make it more clear, a divine attribute is an emana- tion of God, and therefore an activity. Now every divine action is nothing more or less than a creation.

It is also to be admitted that the divine attributes, inas- much as they are emanations, posit time and a beginning; consequently when Allah said *Kun fakána* — i.e. "Be, and it became" — or He uttered, pronounced His word in time and in the beginning of the creation. This is what the Sūfees term *'aql-kull,* or universal intelligence, as the emana- tion of the *'aql awwal,* namely, the "first intelligence." Then the *nafs-kull,* or the "universal soul" that was the first to hear and obey this divine order, emanated from the "first soul" and transformed the universe. Of course, these mystic views of the Sūfees are not to be considered as dogmas of Islam; and if we deeply penetrate into these occult doctrines, we may involuntarily be led into Pantheism which is destructive of a practical religion.

This reasoning would lead us to conclude that each act of God displays a divine emanation as His manifestation and particular attribute, but it is *not* His Essence or Being.   God is Creator, because He created in the beginning of time, and always creates.   God spoke in the beginning of time just as He speaks in His own way always.   But as His creation is not eternal or a divine person, so His Word cannot be considered eternal and a divine Person.   The Christians proceed further, and make the Creator a divine father and His Word a divine son; and also, because He breathed life into His creatures, He is surnamed a divine Spirit, forgetting that logically He could not be father before creation, nor "son" before He spoke, and neither "Holy Ghost" before He gave life.   I can conceive the attributes of God through His works at manifestations a *posteriori,* but of his eternal and *a priori* attributes I posses no conception whatever, nor do I imagine any human intelligence to be able to comprehend the nature of an eternal attribute and its relationship to the essence of God.   In fact, God has not revealed to us the nature of His Being in the Holy Scriptures nor in the human intellect.

The attributes of God are not to be considered as distinct and separate divine entities or personalities, otherwise we shall have, not one trinity of persons in the Godhead, but several dozen of trinities.   An attribute until it actually emanates from its subject has no existence.   We cannot qualify the subject by a particular attribute before that attribute has actually proceeded from it and is seen.   Hence we say "God is Good" when we enjoy His good and kind action; but we cannot describe Him—properly speaking—as "God is Goodness," because goodness is not God, but His action and work.   It is for this reason that the Qur-án always attributes to Allah the adjectival appellations, such as the Wise, the Knowing, the Merciful, but never with such descriptions as "God is love, knowledge, word," and so forth;

for love is the action of the lover and not the lover himself, just as knowledge or word is the action of the knowing person and not himself.

I particularly insist on this point because of the error into which have fallen those who maintain the eternity and distinct personality of certain attributes of God. The Verb or the Word of God has been held to be a distinct person of the Deity; whereas the word of God can have no other signification than an expression of His Knowledge and Will. The Qur-án, too, is called "the word of God," and some early Muslim doctors of law asserted that it was eternal and un-created. The same appellation is also given to Jesus Christ in the Qur-án—*Kalimatun minho,* i.e. "the Word from Him" (iii.44). But it would be very unreligious to assert that the Word or Logos of God is a distinct person, and that it as-sumed flesh and became incarnate in the shape of a man of Nazareth or in the form of a book, the former called "the Christ" and the latter "the Qur-án"!

To sum up this subject, I insistently declare that the Word or any other imaginable attribute of God, not only is it not a distinct divine entity or individuality, but also it could have no actual (*in actu*) existence prior to the be-ginning of time and creation.

The first verse with which St. Johns Gospel commences was often refuted by the early Unitarian writers, who rendered its true reading as follows: "In the beginning was the Word; and the Word was with God; and the Word was God's."

It will be noticed that the Greek form of the genitive case "Theou," i.e. "God's"[1] was corrupted into "Theos";

1. Concerning the Logos, ever since the second century a very fierce controversy about it arose among the "Fathers" of the Church, especially in the East, and it continued until the Unitarians were utterly crushed and their literature destroyed. To-day, unfortunately, there remains hardly any portion *intact* or an unaltered fragment from

that is, "God," in the nominative form of the name! It is also to be observed that the clause "In the beginning was the word" expressly indicates the origin of the word which *was not before the beginning!* By the "word of God" is not meant a separate and distinct substance, coeval and co-

the "Gospels" and "Commentaries" as well as the controversial writings belonging to the Unitarians, except what has been quoted from them in the writings of their opponents, such as the learned Greek Patriarch Photius and those before him.

Among the "Fathers" of the Eastern Christians, one of the most distinguished is St. Ephraim the Syrian. He is the author of many works, chiefly of a commentary on the Bible which is published both in Syriac and in Latin, which latter edition I had carefully read in Rome. He has also homilies, dissertations called "mādrāshi" and "contra Haeretici," etc. Then there is a famous Syrian, author Bār Dīsān (generally written Bardisanes) who flourished in the latter end of the second and the first of the third century A.D. From the writings of Bār Dīsān nothing in the Syriac is extant except what Ephraim, Jacob of Nesibin and other Nestorians and Jacobites have quoted for refutation, and except what most of the Greek Fathers employed in their own language. Bār Dīsān maintained that Jesus Christ was the seat of the temple of the Word of God, but both he and the Word were created. St. Ephraim, in combating the "heresy" of Bār Dīsān, says:—

(Syriac) :

> "Wai lakh O, dovya at Bār Dīsān
> Dagreit l'Milta eithrov d'Āllāhā.
> Baram kthabha la kthabh d'akh hākhān
> Illa d'Miltha eithov Āllāhā."

(Arabic)

> "Wailu 'l-laka yá anta' s-Safíl Bár Disán
> Li-anna fara'aita kána 'l-kalámo li 'l-Láhi
> Lá-kina 'l-Kitábo má Kataba Kazá
> Illa 'l-Kalámo Kána 'l-Láh."

(English translation) :

> "Woe unto thee O miserable Bár Dísán,
> That thou didst read the "word was God's"!
> But the Book [Gospel] did not write likewise,
> Except that "the Word was God."

Almost in all the controversies on the Logos the Unitarians are "branded" with the heresy of denying the eternality and divine personality of it by having "corrupted" the Gospel of John, etc. These imputations were returned to the Trinitarians by the true Nasára — Unitarians. So one can deduct from the patristic literature that the Trinitarians were always reproached with having corrupted the Scriptures.

existent with the Almighty, but an expression and proclama-
tion of His knowledge and will when He uttered the word
Kun, namely, "Be." When God said *Kun,* for the first time,
the worlds became; when He said *Kun,* the Qur-án was
created and written on the *"Lowḥ"* or "Table"; and when He
pronounced the word "Be," Jesus was created in the womb of
the Blessed Virgin Mary; and so on—whenever He wills to
create, His order "Be" is sufficient.

The Christian auspicatory formula: "In the name of
the Father, and of the Son, and of the Holy Ghost," does
not even mention the name of God! And this is the Christian
God! The Nestorian and Jacobite formula, which consists
of ten syllables exactly like the Muslim "Bismillahi," is
thus to be transliterated: Bshim Abhā wō-Bhrā ou-Ruḥā
d-Qudshā, which has the same meaning as that contained
in all other Christian formulas. The Qur-ánic formula, on
the other hand, which expresses the foundation of the Islamic
truth is a great contrast to the Trintarians' formula: Bis-
milláhi 'r-Rahmáni 'r-Raḥím; that is: "In the name of the
Most Merciful and Compassionate Allah."

The Christian Trinity—inasmuch as it admits a plurality
of persons in the Deity, attributes distinct personal properties
to each person; and makes use of family names similar to
those in the pagan mythology—cannot be accepted as a true
conception of the Deity. Allah is neither the father of a son
nor the son of a father. He has no mother, nor is He self-
made. The belief in "God the Father and God the Son and
God the Holy Ghost" is a flagrant denial of the unity of God,
and an audacious confession in three imperfect beings who,
unitedly or separately, cannot be the true God.

Mathematics as a positive science teaches us that a unit
is no more nor less than one; that one is never equal to one
plus one plus one; in other words, one cannot be equal to

three, because one is the third of the three. In the same way, one is not equal to a third. And *vice versa,* three are not equal to one, nor can a third be equal to a unit. The unit is the basis of all numbers, and a standard for the measurements and weights of all dimensions, distances, quantities and time. In fact, all numbers are aggregates of the unit 1. Ten is an aggregate of so many equal units of the same kind.

Those who maintain the unity of God in the trinity of persons tell us that "each person is omnipotent, omnipresent, eternal and perfect God; yet there are not three omnipotent, omnipresent, eternal and perfect Gods, but one omnipotent . . . God!" If there is no sophistry in the above reasoning then we shall present this "mystery" of the churches by an equation:—

1 God = 1 God + 1 God + 1 God; therefore: 1 God = 3 Gods. In the first place, one god cannot equal three gods, but only one of them. Secondly, since you admit each person to be perfect God like His two associates, your conclusion that $1 + 1 + 1 = 1$ is not mathematical, but an absurdity!

You are either too arrogant when you attempt to prove that three units equal one unit; or too cowardly to admit that three ones equal three ones. In the former case you can never prove a wrong solution of a problem by a false process; and in the second you have not the courage to confess your belief in three gods.

Besides, we all—Muslims and Christians—believe that God is Omnipresent, that He fills and encompasses every space and particle. Is it conceivable that all the three persons of the Deity at the same time and separately encompass the universe, or is it only one of them at the time? To say "the Deity does this" would be no answer at all. For Deity is not God, but the state of being God, and therefore a quality.

Godhead is the quality of *one* God; it is not susceptible of plurality nor of diminution. There are no godheads but one Godhead, which is the attribute of one God alone.

Then we are told that each person of the trinity has some particular attributes which are not proper to the other two. And these attributes indicate—according to human reasoning and language—priority and posteriority among them. The Father always holds the first rank, and is prior to the Son. The Holy Ghost is not only posterior as the third in the order of counting but even inferior to those from whom he proceeds. Would it not be considered a sin of heresy if the names of the three persons were conversely repeated? Will not the signing of the cross upon the countenance or over the elements of the Eucharist be considered impious by the Churches if the formula be reversed thus: "In the name of the Holy Ghost, and of the Son, and of the Father"? For if they are absolutely equal and coeval, the order of precedence need not be so scrupulously observed.

The fact is that the Popes and the General Councils have always condemned the Sabelian doctrine which maintained that God is one but that He manifested Himself as the Father or as the Son or as the Holy Spirit, being always one and the same person. Of course, the religion of Islam does not endorse or sanction the Sabelian views. God manifested His *Jamāl* or beauty in Christ, *His jelāl* or glory and majesty in Muhammad, and His wisdom in Solomon, and so on in many other objects of Nature, but none of those prophets is any more God than the vast ocean or the majestic sky.

The truth is that there is no mathematical exactitude, no absolute equality between the three persons of the Trinity. If the Father were in every respect equal to the Son or the Holy Spirit, as the unit I is positively equal to another

figure 1, then there would necessarily be *only one* person of
God and not three, because a unit is not a fragment or
fraction nor a multiple of itself. The very difference and
relationship that is admitted to exist between the persons of
the Trinity leaves no shadow of doubt that they are neither
equal to each other nor are they to be identified with one
another. The Father begets and is not begotten; the Son
is begotten and not a father; the Holy Ghost is the issue of
the other two persons; the first person is described as creator
and destroyer; the second as saviour or redeemer, and the
third as life-giver. Consequently none of the three is *alone*
the Creator, the Redeemer and the Life-giver. Then we are
told that the second person is the Word of the first Person,
becomes man and is sacrificed on the cross to satisfy the
justice of his father, and that his incarnation and resurrection
are operated and accomplished by the third person.

In conclusion, I must remind Christians that unless they
believe in the absolute unity of God, and renounce the belief
in the three persons, they are certainly unbelievers in the
true God. Strictly speaking, Christians are polytheists, only
with this exception, that the gods of the heathen are false and
imaginary, whereas the three gods of the Churches have a
distinct character, of whom the Father—as another epithet
for Creator—is the One true God, but the son is only a prophet and servant of God, and the third person one of the
innumerable holy spirits in the service of the Almighty God.

In the Old Testament, God is called Father because of
His being a loving creator and protector, but as the Churches
abused this name, the Qurán has justly refrained from
using it.

The Old Testament and the Qur-án condemn the doctrine of three persons in God; the New Testament does not
expressly hold or defend it, but even if it contains hints and

traces concerning the Trinity, it is no authority at all, because it was neither seen nor written by Christ himself, nor in the language he spoke, nor did it exist in its present form and contents for—at least—the first two centuries after him.

It might with advantage be added that in the East the Unitarian Christians always combated and protested against the Trinitarians, and that when they beheld the utter destruction of the "Fourth Beast" by the Great Messenger of Allah, they accepted and followed him. The Devil, who spoke through the mouth of the serpent to Eve, uttered blasphemies against the Most High through the mouth of the "Little Horn" which sprang up among the "Ten Horns" upon the head of the "Fourth Beast" (Dan. viii.), was none other than Constantine the Great, who officially and violently proclaimed the Nicene Creed. But, Muhammad has destroyed the "Iblis" or the Devil from the Promised Land for ever, by establishing Islam there as the religion of the one true God.

I

"And the Ahmed of all nations will come." — HAGGAI, ii.7.

Some two centuries after the idolatrous and impenitent Kingdom of Israel was overthrown, and the whole population of the ten tribes deported into Assyria, Jerusalem and the glorious temple of Solomon were razed to the ground by the Chaldeans, and the unmassacred remnant of Judah and Benjamin was transported into Babylonia. After a period of seventy years' captivity, the Jews were permitted to return to their country with full authority to build again their ruined city and the temple. When the foundations of the new house of God were being laid, there arose a tremendous uproar of joy and acclamation from the assembly; while the old men and women who had seen the gorgeous temple of Solomon before, burst into a bitter weeping. It was on this solemn occasion that the Almighty sent His servant the Prophet Haggai to console the sad assembly with this important message:—

"And I will shake all nations, and the *Himada* of all the nations will come; and I will fill this house with glory, says the Lord of hosts. Mine is the silver, mine is the gold, says the Lord of hosts, the glory of my last house shall be greater than that of the first one, says the Lord of hosts; and in this place I will give *Shalom,* says the Lord of hosts" (Haggai, ii. 7-9).

I have translated the above paragraph from the only copy of the Bible at my disposal, lent to me by an Assyrian lady cousin in her own vernacular language. But let us consult the English versions of the Bible, which we find have rendered the original Hebrew words *himda* and *shalom* into "desire" and "peace" respectively.

Jewish and Christian commentators alike have given the utmost importance to the double promise contained in the above prophecy. They both understand a messianic prediction in the word *Himda.* Indeed, here is a wonderful prophecy confirmed by the usual biblical formula of the divine oath, "says the Lord Sabaoth," four times repeated. If this prophecy be taken in the abstract sense of the words *himda* and *shalom* as "desire" and "peace," then the prophecy *becomes* nothing more than an unintelligible aspiration. But if we understand by the term *himda* a concrete idea, a person and reality, and in the word *shalom,* not a condition, but a living and active force and a definitely established religion, then this prophecy must be admittedly true and fulfilled in the person of Aḥmed and the establishment of Islam. For *himda* and *shalom*—or shlama have precisely the same significance respectively as Aḥmed and Islam.

Before endeavouring to prove the fulfilment of this prophecy, it will be well to explain the etymology of the two words as briefly as possible:—

(a) *Himda.* Unless I am mistaken, the clause in the original Hebrew text reads thus. "ve yavu ḥimdath kol haggoyim," which literally rendered into English would be "and will come the Himda of all nations." The final *hi* in Hebrew, as in Arabic, is changed into *th,* or *t* when in the genitive case. The word is derived from an archaic Hebrew—or rather Aramaic—root *ḥmd* (consonants pronounced *hemed*). In Hebrew *hemed* is generally used in the sense of great desire, covet, appetite and lust. The ninth command of the Decalogue is: "Lo *taḥmod* ish reïkha" ("Thou shalt not covet the wife of thy neighbour"). In Arabic the verb *hemida,* from the same consonants *hmd,* means "to praise," and so on. What is more praised and illustrious than that which is most craved for, coveted, and desired? Whichever of the two meanings be adopted, the fact that Aḥmed is the Arabic form of *Himda* remains indisputable and decisive. The Holy Qur-án (chap. lxi.) declares that Jesus announced unto the people of Israel the coming of an "Apostle from God whose name was to be Aḥmed." The Gospel of St. John, being written in Greek, uses the name *Paracletos,* a barbarous form unknown to classical Greek literature. But *Periclytos,* which coressponds exactly with Aḥmed in its signification of "illustrious," "glorious" and "praised," in its superlative degree, must have been the translation into Greek of *Himda* or probably *Hemida* of the Aramaic form, as uttered by Jesus Christ. Alas! there is no Gospel extant in the original language spoken by Jesus!

(*b*) As to the etymology and signification of the words *shalom, shlama,* and the Arabic *salám, Islam,* I need not detain the reader by dragging him into linguistic details. Any Semitic scholar knows that *Shalom* and *Islam* are derived from one and the same root and that both mean peace, submission, and resignation.

This being made clear, I propose to give a short exposition of this prophecy of Haggai.   In order to understand it better, let me quote another prophecy from the last book of the Old Testament called Mallachai, or Mallakhi, or in the Authorized Version, Malachi (chap. iii. I):

"Behold I will send my messenger, and he shall prepare the way before me: suddenly he will come to his temple. He is the Adonai (i.e. the Lord) whom you desire, and the Messenger of the Covenant with whom you are pleased. Lo he is coming, says the Lord of hosts."   Then compare these mysterious oracles with the wisdom embodied in the sacred verse of the Qur-án: "Praise be unto Him Who instantly transported His servant by night from the sacred temple (of Mecca) to the farther temple (of Jerusalem), the circuit of which We have blessed" (chap. xvii.).

That by the person coming suddenly to the temple, as foretold in the two biblical documents above mentioned, Muhammad, and not Jesus, is intended the following arguments must surely suffice to convince every impartial observer:—

1.   The kinship, the relation and resemblance between the two tetrograms *Himda* and *Ahmd,* and the identity of the root *hmd* from which both substantives are derived, leave not a single particle of doubt that the subject in the sentence "and the Himda of all nations will come" is Ahmed; that is to say, Muhammad.   There is not the remotest etymological

connection between *himda* and any other names of "Jesus," "Christ," "Saviour," not even a single consonant in common between them.

2. Even if it be argued that the Hebrew form *Hmdh* (read *himdah*) is an abstract substantive meaning "desire, lust, coveteousness, and praise," the argument would be again in favour of our thesis; for then the Hebrew form would, in etymology, be exactly equivalent in meaning and in similarity to, or rather identity with, the Arabic form *Himdah*. In whatever sense you wish to take the tetrogram *Hmdh*, its relation to Aḥmed and Aḥmedism is decisive, and has nothing to do with Jesus and Jesuism! If St. Jerome, and before him the authors of the Septuagint, had preserved intact the Hebrew form *Hmdh*, instead of putting down the Latin "cupiditas" or the Geek "euthymia," probably the translators appointed by King James I would have also reproduced the original form in the Authorized Version, and the Bible Society have followed suit in their translations into Islamic languages.

3. The temple of Zorobabel was to be more glorious than that of Solomon because, as Mallakhi prophesied, the great Apostle or Messenger of the Covenant, the "Adonai" or the Seyid of the messengers was to visit it *suddenly,* as indeed Muhammad did during his miraculous night journey, as stated in the Qur-án! The temple of Zorobabel was repaired or rebuilt by Herod the Great. And Jesus, certainly on every occasion of his frequent visits to that temple, honoured it by his holy person and presence. Indeed, the presence of every prophet in the house of God had added to the dignity and sanctity of the sanctuary. But this much must at least be admitted, that the Gospels which record the visitations of Christ to the temple and his teachings therein fail to make mention of a single conversion among his

audience. All his visits to the temple are reported as ending in bitter disputes with the unbelieving priests and Pharisees! It must also be concluded that Jesus not only did not bring "peace" to the world as he deliberately declared (Matt. xxiv. Mark xiii., Luke xxi.), but he even predicted the total destruction of the temple (Matt. x. 34, etc.), which was fulfilled some forty years afterwards by the Romans, when the final dispersion of the Jews was completed.

4. Aḥmed, which is another form of the name Muhammad and of the same root and signification, namely, the "most glorious," during his night journey visited the sacred spot of the ruined temple, as stated in the Holy Qur-án, and there and then, according to the sacred tradition uttered repeatedly by himself to his companions, officiated the divine service of prayer and adoration to Allah in the presence of all the Prophets; and it was then that Allah "blessed the circuit of the temple and showed His signs" to the Last Prophet. If Moses and Elias could appear in bodily presence on the mount of transfiguration, they and all the thousands of Prophets could also appear in the circuit of the temple at Jerusalem; and it was during that "sudden coming" of Muhammad to "his temple" (Mal. iii. 1) that God did actually fill it "with glory" (Hag. ii.).

That Emina, the non-Muslim widow of Abdullah, should name her orphan son "Aḥmed," the first proper noun in the history of mankind, is, according to my humble belief, the greatest miracle in favour of Islam. The second Khaliph, Hezret Omar, rebuilt the temple, and the majectic Mosque at Jerusalem remains, and will remain to the end of the world, a perpetual monument of the truth of the covenant which Allah made with Abraham and Ishmael (Gen. xv.-xvii.).

II

THE QUESTION OF THE BIRTHRIGHT
AND THE COVENANT

There is a very, very ancient religious dispute between the Ishmaelites and the Israelites about the questions concerning the Birthright and the Covenant. The readers of the Bible and the Qur-án are familiar with the story of the great Prophet Abraham and his two sons Ishmael (Ismá'íl) and Isaac (Isḥáq). The story of Abraham's call from the Ur of the Chaldees, and that of his descendants until the death of his grandson Joseph in Egypt, is written in the Book of Genesis (chapters xi.-1). In his genealogy as recorded in Genesis, Abraham is the twentieth from Adam, and a contemporary of Nimrod, who built the stupendous Tower of Babel.

The early story of Abraham in the Ur of Chaldea, though not mentioned in the Bible, is recorded by the famous Jewish historian Joseph Flavius in his *Antiquities* and is also confirmed by the Qur-án. But the Bible expressly tells us that the father of Abraham, Terah, was an idolater (Jos. xxiv. 2, 14). Abraham manifested his love and zeal for God when he entered into the temple and destroyed all the idols and images therein, and thus he was a true prototype of his illustrious descendant Muhammad. He came out unhurt and triumphantly from the burning furnace wherein he was cast by the order of Nimrod. He leaves his native land for Hārān in the company of his father and his nephew Lot. He was seventy-five years old when his father died at Hārān. In obedience and absolute resignation to the divine call, he leaves his country and starts on a long and varied journey to the land of Canaan, to Egypt and to Arabia. His wife Sáráh is barren; yet God announces to him that he is destined to become the father of many nations, that all the territories he is to traverse shall be given as an inheritance to his descendants, and that, "by his Seed all the nations of the earth shall be blessed"! This wonderful and unique promise in the history of religion was met with an unshaken faith on the part of Abraham, who had no issue, no son. When he was led out to look at the sky at night and told by Allah that his posterity would be as numerous as the stars, and as innumerable as the sand which is on the shores of the sea, Abraham believed it. And it was this belief in God, that "was counted righteousness," as the Scripture says.

A virtuous poor Egyptian girl, Hagar by name, is a slave and a maid in the service of Sáráh. At the bidding and consent of the mistress the maidservant is duly married by the Prophet, and from this union Ishmael is born, as foretold by the Angel. When Ishmael is thirteen years old, Allah again appears to Abraham through His Angel and revelation; the same old promise is repeated to Abraham; the rite of Circumcision is formally instituted and immediately executed. Abraham, at his ninetieth year of age, Ishmael, and all the male servants, are circumcised; and the "Covenant" between God and Abraham with his only begotten son is made and sealed, as if it were with the blood of circumcision. It is a kind of treaty concluded between Heaven and the Promised Land in the person of Ishmael as the only offspring of the nonagenarian Patriarch. Abraham promises allegiance and fealty to his Creator, and God promises to be forever the Protector and God of the posterity of Ishmael.

Later on — that is to say, when Abraham was ninety-nine years old and Sáráh ninety, we find that she also bears a son whom they name Isaac according to the divine promise.

As no chronological order is observed in the Book of Genesis, we are told that after the birth of Isaac, Ishmael and his mother are turned out and sent away by Abraham in a most cruel manner, simply because Sáráh so wished. Ishmael and his mother disappear in the desert, a fountain bursts out when the youth is on the point of death from thirst; he drinks and is saved. Nothing more is heard of Ishmael in the Book of Genesis except that he married an Egyptian woman, and when Abraham died he was present together with Isaac to bury their dead father.

Then the Book of Genesis continues the story of Isaac, his two sons, and the descent of Jacob into Egypt, and ends with the death of Joseph.

The next important event in the history of Abraham as recorded in Genesis (xxii.) is the offering of "his only son" a sacrifice to God, but he was ransomed with a ram which was presented by an angel. As the Qur-án says, "this was a manifest trial" for Abraham (Qur-án, xxxvii.), but his love for God surpassed every other affection; and for this reason he is surnamed "the Friend of Allah" (Qur-án, iv).

Thus runs the brief account of Abraham in connection with our subject of the Birthright and the Covenant.

There are three distinct points which every true believer in God must accept as truths. The first point is that Ishmael is the legitimate son of Abraham, his firstborn, and therefore his claim to birthright is quite just and legal. The second point is that the Covenant was made between God and Abraham as well as his only son Ishmael before Isaac was born. The Covenant and the institution of the Circumcision would have no value or signification unless the repeated promise contained in the divine words, "Throughout thee all the nations of the earth shall be blessed," and especially the expression, the Seed "that shall come out from the bowels, *he* will inherit thee" (Gen. xv. 4). This promise was fulfilled when Ishmael was born (Gen. xvi.), and Abraham had the consolation that his chief servant Eliezer would no longer be his heir. Consequently we must admit that Ishmael was the real and legitimate heir of Abraham's spiritual dignity and privileges. The prerogative that "by Abraham all the generations of the earth shall be blessed, "so often repeated — though in different forms — was the heritage by birthright, and was the patrimony of Ishmael. The inheritance to which Ishmael was entitled by birthright was not the tent in which Abraham lived or a certain camel upon which he used to ride, but to subjugate and occupy forever all the territories extending from the Nile to the Euphrates, which were inhabited by some ten different nations (xvii. 18-21). These lands have never been subdued by the descendants of Isaac, but by those of Ishmael. This is an actual and literal fulfilment of one of the conditions contained in the Covenant.

The third point is that Isaac was also born miraculously and specially blessed by the Almighty, that for his people the land of Canaan was promised and actually occupied under Joshua. No Muslim does ever think of disparaging the sacred and prophetical position of Isaac and his son Jacob; for to disparage or to lower a Prophet is an impiety. When we compare Ishmael and Isaac, we cannot but reverence and respect them both as holy servants of God. In fact, the people of Israel, with its Law and sacred Scriptures, have had a unique religious history in the Old World. They were indeed the Chosen People of God. Although that people have often rebelled against God, and fallen into idolatry, yet they have given to the world myriads of prophets and righteous men and women.

So far there could be no real point of controversy between the descendants of Ishmael and the people of Israel. For if by "Blessing" and the "Birthright" it meant only some material possessions and power, the dispute would be settled as it has been settled by sword and the accomplished fact of the Arab occupation of the promised lands. Nay, there is a fundamental point of dispute between the two nations now existing for nearly four thousand years; and that point is the question of the Messiah and Muhammad. The Jews do not see the fulfilment of the so-called Messianic prophecies either in the person of Christ or in that of Muhammad. The Jews have always been jealous of Ishmael because they know very well that *in him* the Covenant was made and with his circumcision it was concluded and sealed. and it is out of this rancour that their scribes or doctors of law have corrupted and interpolated many passages in their Scriptures. To efface the name "Ishmael" from the second, sixth, and seventh verses of the twenty-second chapter of the Book of Genesis and to insert in its place "Isaac," and to leave the descriptive epithet "thy only begotten son" is to deny the existence of the former and to violate the Covenant made between God and Ishmael. It is expressly said in this chapter by God: "Because thou didst not spare thy only begotten son, I will increase and multiply thy posterity like the stars and the sands on the seashore," which word "multiply" was used by the Angel to Hagar in the wilderness: I will multiply thy offspring to an innumerable multitude, and that Ishmael "shall become a fruitful man" (Gen. xvi. 12). Now the Christians have translated the same Hebrew word, which means "fruitful" or "plentiful" from the verb *para* — identical with the Arabic *wefera* — in their versions "a wild ass"! Is it not a shame and impiety to call Ishmael "a wild ass" whom God styles "Fruitful" or "Plentiful"?

It is very remarkable that Christ himself, as reported in the Gospel of St. Barnabas, reprimanded the Jews who said that the Great Messenger whom they call "Messiah" would come down from the lineage of King David, telling them plainly that he could not be the son of David, for David calls him "his Lord," and then went on to explain how their fathers had altered the Scriptures, and that the Covenant was made, not with Isaac, but with Ishmael, who was taken to be offered a sacrifice to God, and that the expression "thy only begotten son" means Ishmael, and not Isaac.   St. Paul, who pretends to be an apostle of Jesus Christ, uses some irreverent words about Hagar (Gal. vi. 21-31 and elsewhere) and Ishmael, and openly contradicts his Master.   This man has done all he could to pervert and mislead the Christians whom he used to persecute before his conversion; and I doubt very much that the Jesus of Paul may not be a certain Jesus, also son of Mary, who was hanged on a tree about a century or so before Christ, for his Messianic pretentions. In fact, the Epistles of St. Paul as they stand before us are full of doctrines entirely repugnant to the spirit of the Old Testament, as well as to that of the humble Prophet of Nazareth.   St. Paul was a bigoted Pharisee and a lawyer. After his conversion to Christianity he seems to have become even more fanatical than ever.   His hatred to Ishmael and his claim to the birthright makes him forget or overlook the Law of Moses which forbids a man to marry his own sister under the pain of capital penalty.   If Paul were inspired by God, he would have either denounced the Book of Genesis as full of forgeries when it says twice (xii. 10-20, xx. 2-18) that Abraham was the husband of his own sister, or that he would have exposed the Prophet to be a liar!   (God forbid.)

But he believes in the words of the book, and his con-

science does not torment him in the least when he identifies
Hagar with the barren desert of the Sinai, and qualifies Sáráh
as the Jerusalem above in heaven! (Gal. iv. 25, 26). Did
ever St. Paul read this anathema of the Law:—

> "Cursed be he that lieth with his sister, the
> daughter of his father, or the daughter of his mother.

And all the people say: Amen"? (Duet. xxvii. 22).
Is there a human or divine law that would consider more
legitimate one who is the son of his own uncle and aunt than
he whose father is a Chaldean and his mother an Egyptian?
Have you anything to say against the chastity and the piety
of Hagar? Of course not, for she was the wife of a Prophet
and the mother of a Prophet, and herself favoured with divine
revelations.

The God who made the Covenant with Ishmael thus
prescribes the law of inheritance, namely: If a man has two
wives, one beloved and the other despised, and each one has
a son, and if the son of the despised wife is the first-born,
that son, and *not* the son of the beloved wife, is entitled to
the birthright. Consequently the firstborn shall inherit twice
that of his brother (Duet. xxi. 15-17). Is not, then, this law
explicit enough to put to silence all who dispute the just claim
of Ishmael to birthright?

Now let us discuss this question of the birthright as
briefly as we can. We know that Abraham was a nomad
chief as well as an Apostle of God, and that he used to live
in a tent and had large flocks of cattle and great wealth.
Now the nomad tribesmen do not inherit lands and pastures,
but the prince assigns to each of his sons certain clans or
tribes as his subjects and dependents. As a rule the youngest
inherits the hearth or the tent of his parents, whereas the
elder — unless unfit — succeeds him to his throne. The

great Mongol Conqueror Jenghiz Khan was succeeded by Oghtai, his eldest son, who reigned in Pekin as Khāqān, but his youngest son remained in his father's hearth at Qārā-qōrum in Mongolia. It was exactly the same with Abraham's two sons. Isaac, who was the younger of the two, inherited the tent of his father and became, like him, a nomad living in tents. But Ishmael was sent to Hijáz to guard the House of Allah which he, together with Abraham, had built (Qur-án, ii.). Here he settled, became Prophet and Prince among the Arab tribes who believed in him. It was at Mecca, or Becca, that the Ka'aba became the centre of the pilgrimage called *al-hajj*. It was Ishmael that founded the religion of one true Allah and instituted the Circumcision. His offspring soon increased and was multiplied like the stars of the sky. From the days of Ishmael to the advent of Muhammad, the Arabs of Hijáz, Yemen and others have been independent and masters of their own countries. The Roman and Persian Empires were powerless to subdue the people of Ishmael. Although idolatry was afterwards introduced, still the names of Allāh, Abraham, Ishmael, and a few other Prophets were not forgotten by them. Even Esau, the elder son of Isaac, left his father's hearth for his younger brother Jacob and dwelt in Edom, where he became the chief of his people and soon got mixed with the Arab tribes of Ishmael, who was both his uncle and father-in-law. The story of Esau's selling his birthright to Jacob for a dish of pottage is foul trick invented to justify the ill-treatment ascribed to Ishmael. It is alleged that "God hated Esau and loved Jacob," while the twins were in their mother's womb; and that the "elder brother was to serve his younger one" (Gen. xxv., Rom. ix. 12, 13). But, strange to say, another report, probably from another source, shows the case to be just the reverse of the above-mentioned prediction. For the thirty-third chapter of Genesis clearly admits that Jacob *served* Esau, before whom he seven times prostrates in homage, addressing him "My Lord," and declaring himself as "your slave."

Abraham is reported to have several other sons from Qitura and "the concubines," to whom he gave presents or gifts and sent them towards the East. All these became large and strong tribes. Twelve sons of Ishmael are mentioned by name and described, each one to be a prince with his towns and camps or armies (Gen. xxv.). So are the children from Qitura, and others, as well as those descended from Esau mentioned by their names.

When we behold the number of the family of Jacob when he went to Egypt, which hardly exceeded seventy heads, and when he was met by Esau with an escort of four hundred armed horsemen, and the mighty Arab tribes submitted to the twelve Emirs belonging to the family of Ishmael, and then when the Last Messenger of Allah proclaims the religion of Islam, all the Arab tribes unitedly acclaim him and accept his religion, and subdue all the lands promised to the children of Abraham, we must indeed be blind not to see that the Covenant was made with Ishmael and the promise accomplished in the person of Muhammad (upon whom be peace).

Before concluding this article I wish to draw the attention of the students of the Bible, especially that of the Higher Biblical Criticism, to the fact that the so-called Messianic Prophecies and Passages belong to a propaganda in favour of the Davidic Dynasty after the death of King Solomon when his kingdom was split into two. The two great Prophets Elias and Elisha, who flourished in the Kingdom of Samariah or Israel, do not even mention the name of David or Solomon.

Jerusalem was not longer the centre of religion for the Ten Tribes, and the Davidic claims to a perpetual reign was rejected.

But Prophets like Ishaia and others who were attached to the Temple of Jerusalem and the House of David have foretold the coming of a great Prophet and Sovereign.

As it was said in the first article, there are certain manifest marks with which the coming Last Prophet will be known. And it is these marks that we shall attempt to study in the future articles.

III

THE MYSTERY OF THE "MISPA"

In this article, as the title shows, I shall try to give an exposition of the ancient Hebrew Cult of Stone, which they inherited from Abraham, their great progenitor, and to show that this Stone-Cult was instituted at Mecca by that Patriarch and his son Ishmael; in the land of Canaan by Isaac and Jacob; and in Moab and elsewhere by the other descendants of Abraham.

By the term "Stone-Cult," let it be understood, I do not mean stone-worship, which is idolatry; by it I understand the worship of God at a specially consecrated stone meant for that purpose. In those days of yore, when the chosen family was leading a nomadic and pastoral life, it had no settled habitation where to build a house, especially dedicated to the worship of God; it used to erect a particular stone around which it used to make a *hajj;* that is to say, to turn round seven times in the form of a dancing-ring. The word *hajj* might frighten the Christian readers and they might shrink at its sight because of its Arabic form and because of its being at present a Muslim religious performance. The word *hajj* is exactly identical in meaning and etymology with the same in the Hebrew and other Semitic languages. The Hebrew verb *hagag* is the same as the Arabic *hajaj*, the difference being only in the pronunciation of the third letter of the Semitic alphabet *gamal*, which the Arabs pronounce as *j*. The Law of Moses uses this very word *hagag* or *haghagh*.[1] when it orders the festival ceremonies to be performed. The word signifies to compass a building, an altar or a stone by running round it at a regular and trained pace with the purpose of performing a religious festival of rejoicing and chanting. In the East the Christians still practise what they call *higga* either during their festival days or at weddings. Consequently, this word has nothing to do with pilgrimage, which is derived from the Italian *pellegrino,* and this also from the Latin *peregrinus* — meaning a "foreigner."

Abraham during his sojourns frequently used to build an altar for worship and sacrifice at different places and on particular occasions. When Jacob was on his way to Padan Aram and saw the vision of that wonderful ladder, he erected a stone there, upon which he poured oil and called it Bethel, i.e. "the house of God"; and twenty years later he again visited that stone, upon which he poured oil and "pure wine," [!] as recorded in Genesis xxviii. 10-22; xxxv. A special

---

1. Unlike the Arabs, both the Hebrew as well as the Aramaic peoples have no *j* sound in their alphabet; their third letter, *gamal,* when hard has *g* sound and when soft or aspirate becomes guttural and sounds *gh*.

stone was erected as a monument by Jacob and his father-in-law upon a heap of stones called *Gal'ead in* Hebrew, and *Yaghar sahdutha* by Laban in his Aramaic language, which means "a heap of witness." But the proper noun they gave to the erected stone was *Mispa* (Gen. xxxi. 45-55), which I prefer to write in its exact Arabic form, *Mispha,* and this I do for the benefit of my Muslim readers.

Now this *Mispha* became later on the most important place of worship, and a centre of the national assemblies in the history of the people of Israel. It was here that Naphthah — a Jewish hero — made a vow "before the Lord," and after beating the Ammonites, he is supposed to have offered his only daughter as a burnt offering (Judges xi.). It was at *Mispha* that four hundred thousand swordsmen from the eleven tribes of Israel assembled and "swore before the Lord" to exterminate the tribe of Benjamin for an abominable crime committed by the Benjamites of Geba' and succeeded (Judges xx., xxi.). At *Mispha* all the people were summoned by the Prophet Samuel, where they "swore before the Lord" to destroy all their idols and images, and then were saved from the hands of the Philistines (1 Sam. vii.). It was here that the nation assembled and Saul was appointed king over Israel (1 Sam. x.). In short, every national question of great moment was decided at this *Mispha* or at Bethel. It seems that these shrines were built upon high places or upon a raised platform, often called *Ramoth,* which signifies a "high place." Even after the building of the gorgeous Temple of Solomon, the *Misphas* were held in great reverence. But, like the *Ka'aba* at Mecca, these *Misphas* were often filled with idols and images. After the destruction of Jerusalem and the Temple by the Chaldeans, the

Mispha still maintained its sacred character as late as the time of the Maccabees during the reign of King Antiochus.[1]

Now, what does the word *Mispa* mean? It is generally translated into a "watch-tower." It belongs to that class of Semitic nouns — *Asmá Zarf* — which take or drive their name from the thing that they enclose or contain. *Mispa* is the place or building which derives its name from *săphă,* an archaic word for "stone." The usual word for stone in Hebrew is *iben,* and in Arabic *hajar.* The Syriac for stone is *kipa.* But *safa* or *sapha* seems to be common to them all for some particular object or person when designated as a "stone." Hence the real meaning of *Mispa* is the locality or place in which a *sapha* or stone is set and fixed. It will be seen that when this name, *Mispa,* was first given to the stone erected upon a heap of stone blocks, there was no edifice built around it. It is the spot upon which a sapha rests, that is called *Mispa.*

Before explaining the signification of the noun *sapha* I have to tax again the patience of those of my readers who are not acquainted with the Hebrew. The Arabic language lacks the *p* sound in its alphabet just as much as do the Hebrew and other Semitic languages, in which the letter *p,* like *g,* is sometimes soft and is pronounced like *f* or *ph.* In English, as a rule, the Semitic and Greek words containing *f* sound are transliterated and written by the insertion of "ph" instead of "f," e.g. *Seraph, Mustapha,* and *Philosophy.* It

1. The Bible which I consult does not contain the so-called deutro-canonical or Apocryphal books of the Old Testament. This Bible is published by the American Bible Society (New York, 1893). The title runs thus *Kthabhi Qaddishi Dadiathiqi Wadiathiqi Khadatt An S'had-watha Poushaqa dmin lishani qdimaqi. Matba 'ta d'dasta. Biblioneta d'America* [The Holy Books of the Old Testament and of the New Covenant (Testament), with the concordance or witnesses. Trans. from the ancient languages. Published at the Press of the American Bible Society].

is in accordance with this rule that I prefer to write this word *sapha* to *safa.*

When Jesus Christ surnamed his first disciple Shim'on (Simon) with the significant title of "Petros" (Peter), he must evidently have had in his mind this ancient sacred *Sapha* which had been lost long ago! But, alas! we cannot positively set out the exact word which he expressed in his own language. The Greek form *Petros* in the masculine gender — *Petra* in the feminine — is so unclassical and un-Greek, that one is astonished at its being ever adopted by the Churches. Did Jesus or any other Jew ever dream of calling the fisherman Bar Yona, *Petros?* Decidedly not. The Syriac version called *Pshitta* has frequently rendered this Greek form into *Kipha (Kipa).* And the very fact that even the Greek text has preserved the original name "Kephas," which the English versions have reproduced in the shape of "Cephas," shows that Christ spoke the Aramaic language and gave the surname "Kipha" to his principal disciple.

The old Arabic versions of the New Testament have frequently written St. Peter's name as "Sham'un' as-Saphā"; that is to say, "Simon the Stone." The words of Christ: "Thou art Peter," etc., have their equivalent in the Arabic version in the form of "Antas-Saphā" (Matt. xvi. 18; John i. 42, etc.).

It follows, therefore, that if Simon be the *Sapha,* the Church which was to be built on it would naturally be the *Mispha.* That Christ should liken Simon to *Sapha* and the Church to *Mispha* is very remarkable; but when I come to divulge the mystery hidden in this similitude and the wisdom embodied in the *Sapha,* then it must be accepted as the most marvellous truth of Muhammad's merit to his glorious title:

"THE MUSTAPHA"!

From what has been stated above, our curiosity would naturally lead one to ask the following questions:—

(*a*) Why did the Muslims and Unitarian descendants of Abraham choose a stone to perform their religious service on or around it? (*b*) Why should this particular stone be named *sapha?* (*c*) What is the writer driving at? And so on — perhaps several others.

The stone was selected as the best suitable material upon which a travelling devotee offered his sacrifice, poured his pure oil and wine,[1] and performed his religious services around it. It was more than this; this stone was erected to commemorate the vows and certain promises which a prophet or righteous man made to his Creator, and the revelation he received from God. Consequently, it was a sacred monument to perpetuate the memory and the sacred character of a great religious event. For such a purpose no other material could surpass the stone. Not only does the solidity and durability of the stone make it suitable for that purpose, but its mere simplicity, cheapness, worthlessness in a lonely place would guarantee it against any attraction of human avarice or enmity to steal or destroy it. As is well known, the Law of Moses strictly forbids to hew or carve the stones of the altar. The stone called *Sapha* was to be absolutely left natural; no images, inscriptions, or engravings were to be wrought upon it, lest any one of these should be worshipped in time to come by the ignorant people. Gold, iron silver, or any other metal, could not answer all these qualities required in the simple stone. It will be understood, therefore, that the *purest,* the *most durable, eligible,* and the *safest* ma-

---

1. Wine was not forbidden to the people of Israel.

terial for a religious and sacred monument could be none other than the stone.

The molten bronze statue of the Jupiter worshipped by the heathen Roman Pontifex Maximus, was taken away from the Pantheon and recast into the image of St. Peter by order of a Christian Sovereign Pontiff; and indeed, the wisdom embodied in the *Sapha* is admirable and worthy of all those who worship no other object besides God.

It should also be remembered that not only is the erected *Sapha* a sacred monument, but the very spot and the circuit in which it is situated as well. And it is for this reason that the Muslim *hajj,* like the Hebrew *higga,* is performed round the building where the Sacred Stone is fixed. It is known fact that the Karamatians who carried the Black Stone from the *Ka'aba* and kept it in their own country for some twenty years, were obliged to bring and put it back in its former place because they could not draw the pilgrims from Mecca. If it had been gold or other precious object, it could not have existed, at least, for some five thousand years; or even if it had had on it some carvings or images of art, it would have been destroyed by the Prophet Muhammad himself.

As to the meaning — or rather meanings — of the *Sapha,* I have already referred to them as qualities of the stone.

The word consists of the consonants "sādi" and "pi" ending with the vowel "hi" both as a verb and noun. It means, in its *qal* form, "to purify, to watch, to gaze from distance, and to choose." It also has the meanings of "to be firm and sound"; in its *pi'el* paradigm, which is causative, it simply means "to make a choice, to cause to elect," and so on.

A man who watched from a tower was called *Sophi* (2 Kings ix. 17, etc.). In ancient times — that is, before the building of the Temple of Solomon — the Prophet or the

"Man of God" was called *Roï* or *Hozi,* which means the "seer" (1 Sam. ix. 9). The Hebrew scholars are, of course, familiar with the word *Msaphpi,* or rather *Msappi,* which is equivalent in orthography to the Arabic *musaphphi,* which signifies "one who endeavours to elect that which is pure, sound, firm," and so forth. The watchman on the Tower of Yizrael, as quoted above, was gazing and watching sharply from a great distance to distinguish a company of persons coming on towards the town. He saw the first messenger of the King who arrived and joined the group but did not return. The same was the case with the second and the third envoy. It was later on that the *Sophi* could distinguish the chief of the group as Jehu. Now, what then was the business and the office of that watchman? It was to look out sharply from some distance to distinguish one among the others with a view to understanding his identity and his movements, if at all possible, and then to inform his king. If you ask: What was the business and the office of the solitary *Sophi* of the *Mispa*? the *answer* — which would merely be that he used to watch from the minaret of the *Misppha* (*Mispa*) in order to distinguish the identity of the pilgrims in the desert, or that he used to keep watch against some danger — could not satisfy an eager inquirer. If so, the *Mispha* would lose its religious and sacred character, and would rather seem to assume that of a military wachtower. But the case with the *Sophi* of the *Mispha* was quite different. Originally the *Mispha* was only a simple shrine on a solitary high place in Gal'ead where the *Sophi* with his family or attendants used to live. After the conquest and occupation of the land of Canaan by Israel, the number of the *Misphas* increases, and they soon become great religious centres and develop into institutions of learning and confraternities. They seem to be like the Islamic Mevlevi, Bektashi, Neqshbendi, and other religious confraternities, each one of them being under its own *Sheikh* and *Murshid*. They had schools attached to the *Mispha,* where the Law, the religion, the Hebrew literature and other branches of knowledge were taught. But over and above this educational work, the *Sophi* was the supreme head of a community of initiates whom he used to instruct and teach the esoteric or mystic religion which we know under the name of *Sophia.* Indeed, what we term to-day *Súphees* (*súfees* or *sufís*) were then called *nbiyim* or "prophets," and what is called, in Islamic *takkas, zikr* or invocation in prayer, they used to term "prophesying." In the time of the Prophet Samuel, who was the head of the State as well as that of the *Mispha* institutions, these disciples and initiates had become very numerous; and when Saul was anointed and crowned, he joined the *zikr* or religious practice of invocation with the initiates and was announced everywhere: "Behold Saul also among the Prophets." And this saying became a proverb; for he was also "prophesying" with the group of prophets (1 Sam. x. 9-13). The Suphism among the Hebrews continued to be an esoteric religious confraternity under the supremacy of the Prophet of the time until the death of King Solomon. After the division of the kingdom into two, it appears that a great schism had taken place among the *Sophis* too. In the time of the Prophet Elias, about 900 B.C., we are told that he was the only true Prophet left and that all others were killed; and that there were eight hundred and fifty prophets of the Baal and Ishra who "ate at the table of Queen Izabel" (1 Kings xviii. 19). But only a few years later, Elias's disciple and successor, the Prophet Elisha, at Bethel and at Jericho is met by scores of the "sons of Prophets" who foretell him about the imminent ascension of his master Elias (2 Kings ii.).

Whatever may have been the real position of the Hebrew *Sophis* (or *Sophees*) after the great religious and national schism, one thing is certain, namely, that the true knowledge of God and the esoteric science of religion was preserved until the appearance of Jesus Christ, who built his Community of the Initiates in the Inner Religion upon Simon the *Sapha,* and that the true *Sophis* or seers of the Christian *Mispha* perpetuated this knowledge and watched over it until the appearance of the Elect of Allah, Muhammad *al-Mustapha* — the Hebrew "Mustaphi"!

The Bible mentions — as I said above — numerous prophets attached to the *Misphas;* but we must well understand that, as the Qur-an clearly declares, "God best knows whom He shall appoint for His Messenger";[1] that He does not bestow the gift of prophecy on a person on account of his nobility, riches, or even piety, but for His own pleasure. The faith and all works of piety, meditations, spiritual exercises, prayers, fasting, and divine knowledge may raise a novice to become a spiritual *murshid* or guide, or to the rank of a saint, but never to the status of a prophet; for prophecy is not procured by effort, but is a gift of God. Even among the Prophets there are only a few who were Apostles or Messengers favoured with a special book and commissioned to direct a certain people or with a particular mission. Therefore the term "prophets" as used in the Hebrew Scriptures is often ambiguous.

I must also remark in this connection that probably the majority of the material of the Bible was the work or production of these *Misphas* before the Babylonian Captivity or even earlier, but afterwards has been revised by unknown hands until it has taken the shape which we nowadays have.

1. Chapter vi.

It now remains to say few words about the Muslim *Sufism* and the Greek word *Sophia* (wisdom); and a discussion of these two systems of high knowledge does lie outside the scope of this article.   Philosophy, in the wider sense of the term, is the study or science of the first principles of being; in other words, it transcends the limits of physics to study the pure being, and leaves behind the study of causes or laws of that which happens or is seen in Nature.   It takes the greatest pains to find the truth.   The Muslim Sufism is the contemplation on Allah and self, and takes the greatest pains to achieve a union between the two.   The superiority of the Islamic Sophia to the Greek philosophy is manifest from the object it views at.   And it is decidedly superior to the Christian celibacy and monasticism in its indifference towards the consciences and the beliefs of other people. A Muslim *Sophi* (úfí) always entertains respect for other religious, laughs at the idea of "heresy" and abhors all persecutions and oppressions.   Most of the Christian Saints were either persecutors of or the persecuted by heretics, and their celebrity consists in their excess of intolerance.   This is, alas, but only too true.

As a secondary remark I should like to add that the Muslim authors have always written the Greek word "philosophy" in the form of *Phelsepha* with *sin* instead of *sadi or tzadi,* which is one of the constituent letters in the Hebrew and Arabic words *Sapha* and *Sophi.*   I think this form was introduced into the Arabic literature by the Assyrian translators who formerly belonged to the Nestorian sect.   The Turks write the name St. Sophia of Constantinople with *sadi,* but philosophy with *sin,* like the *samekh* of the Hebrews.   I believe that the Greek *Sophia* is to be identified etymologically with the Hebrew word; and the idea that the Muslim word *sophia* (*sowfiya*) is derived from the *soph,* which means "wool," ought to be abandoned.

The true *Sophia* — or wisdom — the true knowledge of God, the true science of religion and morality, and the infallible selection of the Last Apostle of Allah from among all His Messengers, belonged to the ancient institution of Israel called *Mispha,* until it was transformed into the *Mispha* of the *Nassara* or Christian. It is indeed marvellous to see how complete is the analogy and how the economy of God concerning His dealings with man is carried on with absolute uniformity and order. The *Mispha* is the filter where all the data and persons are filtered and strained by the *Musaphphi* (Hebrew, *Mosappi*) as by a colander (for such is the meaning of the word); so that the genuine is distinguished and separated from the false, and the pure from the impure; yet centuries succeed each other, myriads of Prophets come and go, still the *Mustapha,* the Elected One, does not appear. Then comes the Holy Jesus; but he is rejected and persecuted, because there existed no longer in Israel that official *Mispha* which would have recognized and announced him as a true Messenger of God who was sent to bear witness to the *Mustapha* that was the Last Prophet to follow him. The "Grand Assembly of the Synagogue" convoked and instituted by Ezra and Nehemiah, the last member of which was "Simeon the Just" (*ob* 310 B.C.), was succeeded by the Supereme Tribunal of Jerusalem, called the "Sahedrin"; but this latter Assembly, whose President was the *Nassi* or the "Prince," condemned Jesus to death because it did not recognize his person and the nature of his divine mission. A few Sophis, however, knew Jesus and believed in his prophetical mission; but the crowds at one time mistook him for the *Mustapha* or the "elected" Apostle of Allah, and seized and acclaimed him king, but he vanished and disappeared from among them. He was *not* the *Mustapha,* otherwise it would be ridiculous to make Simon the *Sapha* and his Church the Mispha; for the office and the duty of the *Mispha* was to *watch* and *look for* the Last Apostle, so that when he came he would be proclaimed as the Elected and Chosen One — the *Mustapha.* If Jesus were the *Mustapha,* there would be no need for the institution of the *Mispha* any longer. This is a very deep and interesting subject; it deserves patient study. Muhammad al-Mustapha is the mystery of the *Mispha,* and the treasure of the *Sophia.*

IV

MUHAMMAD IS THE "SHILOH"

Jacob, the grandson of Abraham, is lying sick in bed; he is in his one hundred and forty-seventh year, and the end is approaching rapidly. He summons his twelve sons and their families to his bedroom; and he blesses each son and foretells the future of his tribe. It is generally known as the "Testament of Jacob," and is written in an elegant Hebrew style with a poetic touch. It contains a few words which are unique and never occur again in the Bible. The Testament recalls the varied events in the life of a man who has had many ups and downs. He is reported to have taken advantage of his brother's hunger and bought his right of birth for a dish of pottage, and deceived his blind old father and obtained the blessing which by birthright belonged to Esau. He served seven years to marry Rachel, but was deceived by her father, being married to her elder sister Liah;

so he had to serve another term of seven years for the former. The massacre of all the male population by his (Jacob's) two sons Simon and Livi for the pollution of his (Jacob's) daughter Dina by Schechim, the prince of that town, had greatly grieved him. The shameful conduct of his first-born, Reubin, in defiling his father's bed by lying with his concubine was never forgotten nor forgiven by him. But the greatest grief that befell him after the loss of his beloved wife Rachel was the disappearance for many years of his favourite son Joseph. His descent into Egypt and his meeting with Joseph caused him great joy and the recovery of his lost sight. Jacob was a Prophet, and surnamed by God "Israel," the name which was adopted by the twelve tribes that descended from him.

The policy of usurpation of the birthright runs through the records of the Book of Genesis, and Jacob is represented as a hero of this violation of the rights of other persons. He is reported to give the birthright of his grandson Manashi to his younger brother Ephraim, in spite of the remonstrances of their father Joseph (chap. xlviii.). He deprives his first-born son of his birthright and accords the blessing to Judah, his fourth son, because the former had lain with Bilha, Jacobs's "concubine," who is the mother of his two sons Dan and Nephthali; and deprives the latter because he was no better than the other, inasmuch as he committed adultery with his own daughter-in-law Thamar, who bore a son who became an ancestor of David and of Jesus Christ (chap. xxv. 22, chap. xxxviii.)!

It is indeed incredible that the author, or at least the final editor, of this book was "inspired by the Holy Spirit," as the Jews and Christians allege. Jacob is reported to have married two sisters simultaneously, an action condemned by

God's law (Lev. xviii. 18). In fact, with the exception of Joseph and Benjamin, his other sons are described as rough shepherds, liars (to their father and to Joseph), murderers, adulterers, which means it was a family not becoming a Prophet at all. Of course, the Muslims cannot accept any calumny against a Prophet or a righteous man unless it be expressly recorded or mentioned in the Qur-án. We do not believe the sin attributed to Judah to be true (cf. chap. xxxviii.), otherwise the blessing accorded to him by Jacob would be a contradiction; and it is this very blessing that we propose to study and discuss in this article.

Jacob could not have blessed his son Judah if the latter was really the father of his own daughter-in- law's son, Peres, for both adulterers would be condemned to death by the Law of God, Who had given him the gift of prophecy (Lev. xx 12). However, the story of Jacob and that of his not very exemplary family is to be found in the Book of Genesis (chaps. xxv. — 1.).

The famous prophecy, which may be considered as the nucleus of this testament, is contained in the tenth verse of the forty-ninth chapter of Genesis as follows:—

> "The Sceptre shall not depart from Judah,
> And the Lawgiver from between his feet,
> Until the coming of Shiloh,
> And to him belongeth the obedience of peoples."

This is the literal translation of the Hebrew text as much as I can understand it. There are two words in the text which are unique and occur nowhere else in the Old Testament. The first of these words is "Shilōh," and the other "yiqha" or "yiqhath (by construction or contraction).

Shilōh is formed of four letters, *shín, yod, lámed and hi.* There is a "Shiloh," the proper name of a town in Ephraim,

(1 Sam. i., etc.), but there is no *yod* in it. This name cannot be identical with, or refer to, the town where the Ark of the Covenant or the Tabernacle was; for until then no sceptre or lawgiver had appeared in the tribe of Judah. The word certainly refers to a person, and not to a place.

As far as I can remember, all the versions of the Old Testament have preserved this original *Shiloh* without giving it a rendering. It is only the Syriac *Pshiṭṭa* (in Arabic called *al-Bessiṭa*) that has translated it into "He to whom it belongs." It is easy to see how the translator has understood the word as composed of *"sh"* abridged form of *āsher* = "he, that," and *lōh* (the Arabic *lehu*) = "is his." Consequently, according to the Pshiṭṭa, the clause will be read in the following manner: "Until he to whom it belongeth come, And," etc. The personal pronoun "it" may refer to the sceptre and the lawgiver separately or collectively, or perhaps to the "obedience" in the fourth clause of the verse, the language being poetic. According to this important version the sense of the prediction would appear to be plainly this:—

> "The royal and prophetic character shall not pass away from Judah until he to whom it belongs come, for his is the homage of people."

But apparently this word is derived from the verb *shalah* and therefore meaning "peaceful, tranquil, quiet and trust-worthy."

It is most likely that some old transcriber or copyist *currente calamo* and with a slip of pen has detached the left side of the final letter *ḥeṭ*, and then it has been transformed into *hi;* for the two letters are exceedingly alike being only very slightly different on the left side. If such an error has been transmitted in the Hebrew manuscript — either intentionally or not — then the word is derived from *shălăḥ*, "to send, delegate," the past participle of which would be *shăluḥ* — that is, "one who is sent, apostle, messenger."

But there appears no reasonable cause for a deliberate change of *ḥeṭ* for *hi,* since the *yod* is preserved in the present shape of Shiloh, which has no *vaw* that would be necessary for the past participle Shălūḥ. Besides, I think the Septuagint has retained the Shiloh as it is. The only possible change, therefore, would be of the final letter *ḥeṭ* into *hi*. If such be the case, then the word would take the form of Shilūăḥ and correspond exactly to the "Apostle of Yah," the very title given to Muhammad alone *"Răsūl Allah,"* i.e. "the Apostle of God." I know that the term "shiluah" is also the technical word for the "letter of divorce," and this because the divorced wife is "sent" away.

I can guess of no other interpretation of this singular name besides the three versions I have mentioned.

Of course, it goes without saying that both the Jews and Christians believe this blessing to be one of the foremost Messianic prophecies. That Jesus, the Prophet of Nazareth, is a Christ or Messiah no Muslim can deny, for the Qur-án does acknowledge that title. That every Israelite King and High Priest was anointed with the holy oil composed of olive oil and various spices we know from the Hebrew Scriptures (Lev. xxx. 23-33). Even the Zardushti Koresh King of Persia is called God's Christ: "Thus says the Lord to His Christ Cyrus," etc. (Isa. xlv. 1-7).

It would be superfluous here to mention that although neither Cyrus nor Jesus were anointed by the sacred anointment, yet they are called Messiahs.

As to Jesus, even if his prophetic mission were recognized by the Jews, his Messianic office could never be

accepted by them.   For none of the marks or characteristics
of the Messiah they expect are to be found in the man whom
they attempted to crucify.   The Jew expects a Mesiah with
the sword and temporal power, a conqueror who would
restore and extend the kingdom of David, and a Messiah who
would gather together the dispersed Israel unto the land of
Canaan, and subdue many nations under his yoke; but they
could never acclaim as such a preacher upon the Mount of
Olives, or one born in a manger.

To show that this very ancient prophecy has been practically and literally fulfilled in Muhammad the following arguments can be advanced.   By the allegorical expressions "the
Sceptre" and "Law-giver" it is unanimously admitted by the
commentators to mean the royal authority and the prophecy
respectively.   Without stopping long to examine the root and
derivation of the second singular word "yiqha," we may adopt
either of its two significations, "obedience" or "expectation."

Let us follow the first interpretation of Shiloh as given
in the Pshiṭta version: "he to whom it belongs."   This practically means "the owner of the sceptre and the law," or "he
who possesses the sovereign and legislative authority, and
his is the obedience of nations."   Who, then, can this mighty
Prince and great Legislator be?   Certainly not Moses, for
he was the first organizer of the Twelve Tribes of Israel, and
before him there never appeared a king or prophet in the
tribe of Judah.   Decidedly not David, because he was the
first king and prophet descended from Judah.   And evidently
not Jesus Christ, because he himself repudiated the idea that
the Messiah whom Israel was expecting was a son of David
(Matt. xxii. 44, 45; Mark xii. 35-37; Luke xx. 41-44).   He
has left no written law, and never dreamt of assuming the
royal sceptre; in fact, he advised the Jews to be loyal to

Cæsar and pay him tribute, and on one occasion the crowds attempted to make him a king, but he escaped and hid himself. His Gospel was written on the tablet of his heart, and he delivered his message of "good news," not *in scripto,* but orally. In this prophecy there is no question of the salvation from original sin by the blood of a crucified person, nor of a reign of a god-man over human hearts. Besides, Jesus did not abrogate the Law of Moses, but he distinctly declared that he had come to fulfil it; nor was he the last Prophet; for after him St. Paul speaks of many "prophets" in the Church.

Muhamad came with military power and the Qur-án to replace the old Jewish worn-out sceptre and the impracticable and old-fashioned law of sacrifices and of a corrupt priesthood. He proclaimed the purest religion of the one true God, and laid down the best practical precepts and rules for morals and conduct of men. He established the religion of Islam which has united into one real brotherhood many nations and peoples who associate no being with the Almighty. All Muslim peoples obey the Apostle of Allah, love and reverence him as the founder of their religion, but never worship him or give him divine honour and attributes. He crushed and put an end to the last vestiges of the Jewish principality of Qureihda and Khaibar, having destroyed all their castles and fortifications.

The second interpretation of the tetragram "Shilh," pronounced Shiloh, is equally important and in favour of Muhammad. As it was shown above, the word signifies "tranquil, peaceful, trustworthy, quiet" and so forth. The Aramaic form of the word is *Shilya,* from the same root *Shala* or *shla.* This verb is not used in Arabic.

It is a well-known fact in the history of the Prophet of Arabia that, previous to his call to the Apostleship, he was

extremely quiet, peaceful, trustworthy, and of a contempla-
tive and attractive character; that he was surnamed by the
people of Mecca "Muhammad al-Emīn." When the Meccans
gave this title "Emīn" or "Amīn" to Muhammad they had
not the remotest idea of "Shiloh," yet the ignorance of the
idolatrous Arabs was made use of by God to confound the
unbelieving Jews, who had scriptures and knew their contents.
The Arabic verb *amana,* like the Hebrew aman, to be "firm,
constant, secure," and therefore "to be tranquil, faithful and
trustworthy," shows that "amin" is precisely the equivalent
of Shiloh, and conveys all the significations contained in it.

Muhammad, before he was called by God to preach the
religion of Islam and to abolish the idolatry which he success-
fully accomplished, was the most quiet and truthful man in
Mecca; he was neither a warrior nor a legislator; but it was
after he assumed the prophetical mission that he became the
most eloquent speaker and the best valiant Arab.   He fought
with the infidels sword in hand, not for his own personal
interest, but for the glory of Allah and for the cause of His
religion — Al-Islam.   He was shown by God the keys of
the treasures of the earth, but he did not accept them, and
when he died he was practically a poor man.   No other
servant of God, whether a king or a prophet, has rendered
such an admirably great and precious service to God and to
man as Muhammad has done: to God in eradicating the
idolatry from a large part of the globe, and to man by having
given the most perfect religion and the best laws for his
guidance and security.   He seized the sceptre and the law
from the Jews; fortified the former and perfected the latter.
If Muhammad were permitted to reappear to-day in Mecca
or Medina, he would be met by the Muslims with the same
affection and "obedience" as he saw there during his earthly

life.   And he would see with a deep sense of pleasure that the holy Book he had left is the same without the least alteration in it, and that it is chanted and recited exactly as he and his companions did.   He would be glad to congratulate them on their fidelity to the religion and to the unity of Allah; and to the fact that they have not made of him a god or son of a god.

As to the third interpretation of the name "Shiloh" I remarked that it might possibly be a corruption of "Shāluah," and in that case it would indisputably correspond to the Arabic title of the Prophet so often repeated in the Qur-án, namely, "Rasūl" which means exactly the same as Shaluah does, i.e. "an Apostle" or "Messenger." "Shaluah Elohim" of the Hebrews is precisely the "*Rasūl Allah*" which phrase is chanted five times a day by the Crier to the Prayers from the minaret of all mosques in the world.

In the Qur-án several prophets, particularly those to whom a sacred scripture has been delivered, are mentioned as Rasūl; but nowhere in the Old Testament do we come across Shiloh or Shālūăh except in the Testament of Jacob.

Now from whatever point of view we try to study and examine this prophecy of Jacob, we are forced, by the reason of its actual fulfilment in Muhammad, to admit that the Jews are vainly expecting the coming of another Shiloh, and that the Christians are obstinately persisting in their error in believing that it was Jesus who was intended by Shiloh.

Then there are other observations which deserve our serious consideration.   In the first place it is very plain that the sceptre and the legislator would remain in the tribe of Judah so long as the Shiloh does not appear on the scene. According to the Jewish claim, Shiloh has not come yet.   It would follow, therefore, that both the Royal Sceptre and the

Prophetical Succession were still in existence and belonged to that tribe. But both these institutions have been extinct for over thirteen centuries.

In the second place it is to be observed that the tribe of Judah also has disappeared together with its royal authority and its sister — the prophetical succession. It is an indispensable condition for the maintenance of a tribal existence and identity to show that the tribe as a whole lives either in its own fatherland or elsewhere *collectively* and speaks its own language. But with the Jews the case is just the reverse. To prove yourself to be an Israelite, you need hardly trouble yourself about it; for anybody will recognize you, but you can never prove yourself to belong to one of the twelve tribes. You are dispersed and have lost your very language.

The Jews are forced to accept one or the other of the two alternatives, namely, either to admit that Shiloh has come already, but that their forefathers did not recognize him, or to accept the fact that there exists no longer a tribe of Judah from which Shiloh will have to descend.

As a third observation it is to be remarked that the text clearly implies, and much against the Judæo-Christian belief, that Shiloh is to be a total stranger to the tribe of Judah, and even to all the other tribes. This is so evident that a few minutes of reflection are sufficient to convince one. The prediction clearly indicates that when Shiloh comes the sceptre and the lawgiver will pass away from Judah; this can only be realized if Shiloh be a stranger to Judah. If Shiloh be a descendant of Judah, how could those two elements cease to exist in that tribe? It could not be a descendant of any of the other tribes either, for the sceptre and the lawgiver were for all Israel, and not for one tribe only. This observation explodes the Christian claim as well. For Jesus is a descendant of Judah — at least from his mothers side.

I very often wonder at these itinerant and erring Jews. For over twenty-five centuries they have been learning a hundred languages of the peoples whom they have been serving.   Since both the Ishmaelites and the Israelites are the offspring of Abraham, what does it matter to them whether Shiloh comes from Judah or Zebulun, from Esau or Isachar, from Ishmael or Isaac, as long as he is a descendant of their father Abraham?   Obey the Law of Muhammad, becomes Muslims, and then it will be that you can go and live in your old fatherland in peace and security.

V

MUHAMMAD AND CONSTANTINE
THE GREAT

The most wonderful and, perhaps, the most manifest prophecy about the divine mission of the greatest man and the Apostle of God, contained in the seventh chapter of the Book of the Prophet Daniel, deserves to be seriously studied and impartially considered.   In it great events in the history of mankind, which succeed each other within a period of more than a thousand years, are represented by the figures of four formidable monsters in a prophetical vision to Daniel. "Four winds of heaven were roaring against the great sea." The first beast that comes out from the deep sea is a winged lion; then comes forth the second beast in the shape of a bear holding three ribs between its teeth.   This is succeeded by the third terrible beast in the form of a tiger having four wings and four heads.   The fourth beast, which is more formidable and ferocious than the former ones, is a monster with ten horns upon its head, and has iron teeth in its mouth. Then a little horn shoot up amidst the others, before which three horns break down. Behold, human eyes and mouth appear upon this horn, and it begins to speak great things against the Most High. Suddenly, in the midst of the firmament the vision of the Eternal is seen amidst a resplendent light, seated upon His tribune (Arabic: *Korsí*) of the flames of light whose wheels were of shining light.[1] A river of light is flowing and going forth before Him; and millions of celestial beings are serving Him and tens and tens of thousands of them are standing before Him. The Judgment Court is, as it were, holding its extraordinary session; the books are opened. The body of the beast is burnt with fire, but the blaspheming Horn is left alive until a "Bar Nasha" — that is, a "Son of Man" — is taken up on the clouds and presented to the Eternal, from whom he receives power, honour and kingdom for ever. The stupefied Prophet approaches one of those standing by and beseeches him to explain the meaning of this wonderful vision. The good Angel gives the interpretation of it in such a manner that the whole mystery enveloped in the figurative or allegorical language and image is brought to light.

Being a prince of the royal family, Daniel was taken, together with three other Jewish youths, to the palace of the King of Babylon, where he was educated in all the knowledge of the Chaldeans. He lived there until the Persian Conquest and the fall of the Babylonian Empire. He prophesied under Nebuchadnezzar as well as under Darius. The Biblical critics do not ascribe the authorship of the entire

---

1. The original word is *núr,* and, like the Arabic word, it means "light" rather than "fire," which is represented in the text by "ish."

Book to Daniel, who lived and died at least a couple of centuries before the Greek Conquest, which he mentions under the name of "Yavan = Ionia." The first eight chapters — if I am not mistaken — are written in the Chaldean and the latter portion in the Hebrew. For our immediate purpose it is not so much the date and the authorship of the book that forms the important question as the actual fulfilment of the prophecy, contained in the Septuagint version, which was made some three centuries before the Christian era.

According to the interpretation by the Angel, each one of the four beasts represents an empire. The eagle-winged lion signifies the Chaldean Empire, which was mighty and rapid like an eagle to pounce upon the enemy. The bear represents the "Mádaí-Páris," or the Medo-Persian Empire, which extended its conquests as far as the Adriatic Sea and Ethiopia, thus holding with its teeth a rib from the body of each one of the three continents of the Eastern Hemisphere. The third beast, from its tigrish nature of swift bounds and fierceness, typifies the triumphant marches of Alexander the Great, whose vast empire was, after his death, divided into four kingdoms.

But the Angel who interprets the vision does not stop to explain with details the first three kingdoms as he does when he comes to the fourth beast. Here he enters with emphasis into details. Here the scene in the vision is magnified. The beast is practically a monster and a huge demon. This is the formidable Roman Empire. The ten horns are the ten Emperors of Rome who persecuted the early Christians. Turn the pages of any Church history for the first three centuries down to the time of the so-called conversion of Constantine the Great, and you will read nothing but the horrors of the famous "Ten Persecutions."

So far, all these four beasts represent the "Power of Darkness," namely, the Kingdom of Satan, idolatry.

In this connection let me divert your attention to a luminous truth embodied in that particularly important article of the Faith of Islam: "The Good and Evil are from Allah." It will be remembered that the old Persians believed in a "Duality of Gods," or, in other words, the Principle of Good and Light, and the other the Principle of Evil and Darkness; and that these eternal beings were eternal enemies.   It will be observed that among the four beasts the Persian Power is represented by the figure of a bear, less ferocious than, and not so carnivorous as, the other three; and what is more: inasmuch as it can roam upon its hind legs it resembles man — at least from some distance.

In all the Christian theological and religious literature I have read, I have never met with a single statement of phrase similar to this article of the Muslim Faith: God is the real author of good and evil.   This article of the Muslim Faith, as the contrary, is extremely repugnant to the Christian religion, and a source of hatred against the religion of Islam.   Yet this very doctrine is explicitly announced by God to Cyrus, whom He calls His "Christ."   He wants Cyrus to know that there is no god besides Him, and declares:—

"I am the fashioner of the light, and the creator of the darkness; the maker of peace, and *the creator of evil;* I am the Lord who does all these" (Isa. xlv. 1-7).

That God is the author of evil as well as of good is not in the least repulsive to the idea of God's goodness.   The very denial of it is opposed to the absolute unity of the Almighty.   Besides, what we term or understand as "evil" only affects the created beings, and it is for the development and the improvement of the creatures; it has not in the least any effect on God.

Leaving this digression, I hasten to say that all these wild beasts were the enemies of the "holy people of God," as the old Israel and the early followers of the Gospels were called.   For they alone had the true knowledge, the scriptures and the revelation of God.   These wild beasts persecuted and massacred the people of God.   But the nature and the character of the Little Horn which sprang up on the head of the fourth monster was so different from that of the other animals, that God Himself had, as it were, to come down and establish His throne in the firmament, to judge and condemn to destruction the fourth animal; to summon to His presence the Bar Nasha — "Son of Man" — and to make him the Sultan of men; for the words *sholṭana, yaqar, malkutha,* which signify respectively the "empire, honour, kingdom" of all the peoples and nations, were granted to him (verse 14) and to the "people of the Saints of the Most High" (verse 27).

It will be noticed that as the Son of Man is nobler than, and superior to, the beasts, so the religion which he professed and established is infinitely holier than that of the Little Horn.

Now let us examine and find out who the Little Horn is. Having once definitely ascertained the identity of this eleventh king, the identity of the Bar Nasha will be settled *per se.* The Little Horn springs up after the Ten Persecutions under the reigns of the emperors of the Roman Power.   The empire was writhing under four rivals, Constantine being one of them. They were all struggling for the purple; the other three died or fell in battle; and Constantine was left alone as the supreme sovereign of the vast empire.

The earlier Christian commentators have in vain laboured to identity this ugly Little Horn with the Anti-Christ, with the Pope of Rome by Protestants, and with the Founder of Islam.   (God forbid!)   But the later Biblical critics are at a loss to solve the problem of the fourth beast which they wish to identify with the Greek Empire and the Little Horn with Antiochus. Some of the critics, e.g. Carpenter, consider the Medo-Persian Power as two separate kingdoms. But this empire was not more two than the late Austro-Hungarian Empire was. The explorations carried on by the Scientific Mission of the French savant, M. Morgan, in Shúshan (Susa) and elsewhere leave no doubt on this point. The fourth beast can, therefore, be no other than the old Roman world.

To show that the Little Horn is no other than Constantine the Great, the following arguments can safely be advanced:—

(a) He overcame Maximian and the other two rivals and assumed the purple, and put an end to the persecution of Christianity. Gibbon's *The Decline and Fall of the Roman Empire* is, I think, the best history that can instruct us about those times. You can never invent four rivals after the Ten Persecutions of the Church, other than Constantine and his enemies who fell before him like the three horns that fell before the little one.

(b) All the four beasts are represented in the vision as irrational brutes; but the Little Horn possessed a human mouth and eyes which is, in other words, the description of a hideous monster endowed with reason and speech. He proclaimed Christianity as the true religion, left Rome to the Pope and made Byzantium, which was named Constantinople, the seat of the empire. He pretended to profess Christianity but was never baptized till a little before his death, and even this is a disputed question. The legend that his conversion was due to the vision of the Cross in the sky has long since — like the account about Jesus Christ inserted in the *Antiquities* of Josephus — been exploded as another piece of forgery.

The enmity of the beasts to the believers in God was

brutal and savage, but that of the rational Horn was diabolical and malignant. This enmity was most noxious and harmful to the religion, because it was directed to pervert the truth and the faith. All the previous attacks of the four empires were pagan; they persecuted and oppressed the believers but could not pervert the truth and the faith. It was this Constantine who entered in the fold of Jesus in the shape of a believer and in the clothes of a sheep, but inwardly he was not a true believer at all. How poisonous and pernicious this enmity was will be seen from the following:—

(c) The Horn-Emperor speaks "big things" or "great words" (*rōrbhān* in the Chaldean tongue) against the Most High. To speak blasphemous words about God, to associate with Him other creatures, and to ascribe to Him foolish names and attributes, such as the "begetter" and "begotten," "birth" and "procession" (of the second and the third person), "unity in the trinity" and "incarnation," is to deny His unity.

Ever since the day when God revealed Himself to Abraham in Ur of the Chaldees until the Creed and the Acts of the Council of Nicea were proclaimed and enforced by an imperial edict of Constantine amidst the horror and protests of three-fourths of the true believing members in A.D. 325, never has the unity of God so officially and openly been profaned by those who pretended to be His people as Constantine and his gang of the unbelieving ecclesiastic! In the first article of this series I have shown the error of the Churches concerning God and His attributes. I need not enter into this unpleasant subject again; for it gives me great pain and grief when I see a holy prophet and a holy spirit, both God's noble creatures, associated with Him by those who ought to know better.

If Brahma and Osiris, or if Jupiter and Vesta were associated with God, we would simply consider this to be a pagan belief; but when we see Jesus the Prophet of Nazareth and one of the millions of the holy spirits in the service of the Eternal raised equal to the dignity of God, we cannot find a name for those who so believe other than what the Muslims have always been obliged to use — the epithet "Gāwun."

Now, since this hideous Horn speaking great words, uttering blasphemies against God, is a king — as the Angel reveals it to Daniel, and since the king was the eleventh of the Cæsars who reigned in Rome and persecuted the people of God, he cannot be other than Constantine, because it was his edict that proclaimed the belief in the Trinity of persons in the Deity, a creed which the Old Testament is a living document to condemn as blasphemy, and which both the Jews and Muslims abhor. If it be other than Constantine, then the question arises, who is he? He has already come and gone, and not an imposter or the Anti-Christ hereafter to apepar, that we may be unable to know and identify. If we do not admit that the Horn in question has come already, then how are we to interpret the four beasts, the first of which is certainly the Chaldean Empire, the second the Medo-Persian, and so forth? If the fourth beast does not represent the Roman Empire, how can we interpret the third, with its four heads, as the Empire of Alexander, split into four kingdoms after his death? Is there any other Power succeeding the Greek Empire before the Roman Empire with its ten potentates persecuting the believers in God? Sophistry and illusion are of no use. The "Little Horn" is decidedly Constantine, even if we may deny the prophecy of Daniel. It is immaterial whether a prophet, priests or a sorcerer wrote the seventh chapter of the Book of Daniel. One thing is certain, that its predictions and descriptions of the events, some twenty-four centuries ago, are found to be exact, true, and have been fulfilled in the person of Constantine the Great, whom the Church of Rome has always very wisely abstained from beatifying as a Saint, as the Greek Church has done.

(d) Not only does the "Little Horn," which grew into something of a more "formidable vision" than the rest, speak impious words against the Most High, but also it wages war against the "Saints of the Most High, and vanquishes them" (verse 25). In the eyes of a Hebrew Prophet the people who believed in one God was a *separate* and *holy people*. Now it is indisputably true that Constantine persecuted those Christians who, like the Jews, believed in the absolute Unity of God and courageously declared the Trinity to be a false and erroneous conception of the Deity. More than a thousand ecclesiastics were summoned to the General Council at Nicea (the modern Izmid), of whom only three hundred and eighteen persons subscribed to the decisions of the Council, and these too formed three opposite factions with their respective ambiguous and unholy expressions of "homousion" or "homoousion," "consubstantial," and other terms utterly and wholly strangers to the Prophets of Israel, but only worthy of the "Speaking Horn."

The Christians who suffered persecutions and martyrdoms under the pagan emperors of Rome because they believed in One God and in His servant Jesus were now doomed by the imperial edict of the "Christian" Constantine to even severer tortures because they refused to adore the servant Jesus as consubstantial and coeval with his Lord and Creator! The Elders and Ministers of the Arian Creed, i.e. *Qăshīshi and Mshămshāni* — as they were called by the early Jewish Christians — were deposed or banished, their religious books suppressed, and their churches seized and handed over to the Trinitarian bishops and priests. Any historical work on the early Christian Church will give us ample information about the service rendered by Constantine to the cause of the Trinitarian Creed, and tyranny to those who opposed it. The merciless legions in every province were placed at the disposal of the ecclesiastical authorities. Constantine personifies a régime of terror and fierce war against the Unitarians, which lasted in the East for three centuries and a half, when the Muslims established the religion of Allah and assumed the power and dominion over the lands trodden and devastated by the four beasts.

(e) The "Talking Horn" is accused of having contemplated to change "the Law and the times."   This is a very serious charge against the Horn. Its blasphemies or "great words against the Most High" may or may not affect other people, but to change the Law of God and the established holy days or festivals would naturally subvert the religion altogether. The first two commandments of the Law of Moses, concerning the absolute Oneness of God — "Thou shalt have no other gods besides Me" — and the strict prohibition of making images and statues for worship were directly violated and abrogated by the edict of Constantine. To proclaim three personal beings in the Deity and to confess that the Eternal Almighty was conceived and born of the Virgin Mary is the greatest insult to the Law of God and the grossest idolatry. To make a golden or wooden image for worship is abominable enough, but to make a mortal an object of worship, declare him God(!), and even adore the bread and the wine of the Eucharist as "the body and blood of God," is an impious blasphemy.

Then to every righteous Jew and to a Prophet like Daniel, who from his youth was a most devoted observer of the Mosaic Law, what could be more repugnant than the substitution of the Easter for the Paschal Lamb of the great feast of the Passover and the sacrifice of the "Lamb of God" upon the cross, and upon thousands of altars every day? The abrogation of the Sabbath day was a direct violation of the fourth command of the Decalogue, and the institution of Sunday instead was as arbitrary as it is inimical. True, the Qur-án abrogated the Sabbath day, not because the Friday was a holier day, but simply because the Jews made an abuse of it by declaring that God, after the labour of six days, reposed on the seventh day, as if He were man and was fatigued. Muhammad would have destroyed any day or object, however holy or sacred, if it were made an object of worship intending to deal a blow or injury to God's greatness and glory. But the abrogation of the Sabbath by the decree of Constantine was for the institution of the Sunday on which Jesus is alleged to have risen from the sepulchre. Jesus himself was a strict observer of the Sabbath day, and reprimanded the Jewish leaders for their objection to his doing the deeds of charity on it.

(f) The "Horn" was allowed to make war against the Saints of the Most High for a period of some three centuries and a half; it only "weakened" them, made "them languid" — but could not extinguish and entirely root them out. The Arians, who believed in one God alone, sometimes, e.g. under the reign of Constantius (the son of Constantine), of Julian and others who were more tolerant, strongly defended themselves and fought for the cause of their faith.

The next important point in this wonderful vision is to identify the "Bar Nasha," or the Son of Man, who destroyed the Horn; and we shall undertake to do this in the next article.

VI

MUHAMMAD IS THE SON-OF-MAN

In the previous discourse we perused and commented upon the marvellous vision of the Prophet Daniel (Dan. vii.). We saw how the four beasts that represented the four kingdoms succeeding one another were the Powers of Darkness and how they persecuted the Jews and the early Church of Jesus, which was constituted of true believers in the One God. We also remarked that those Powers were pagan and allegorically described as ferocious brutes. Further, we saw that the "Eleventh Horn," which had eyes and mouth, which uttered blasphemies against the Most High had fought and overcome His Saints had changed the times and the Law of God, could be no other than Constantine the Great, who in A.D. 325, promulgated his imperial rescript proclaiming the creed and the decisions of the Nicene General Council.

In this article let us follow our researches patiently with regard to the glorious BARNASHA, or the "Son-of-Man," who was presented upon the clouds to the Most High, to whom was given the *Sultaneh* (Sholtānā in the original text, i.e. "dominion" or "empire") honour and kingdom for ever, and who was commissioned to destroy and annihilate the terrible Horn.

Now let us proceed forthwith to establish the identity of this "Barnasha."

Before finding out who this Son-of-Man is, it is but essential that we should take into consideration the following points and observations:—

(*a*) When a Hebrew Prophet predicts that "all the nations and peoples of the earth shall serve him" (i.e. the Barnasha) or "the people of the Saints of the Most High."

we must understand that he means thereby the nations mentioned in Genesis xv. 18-21, and not the English, the French, or the Chinese nations.

(*b*) By the phrase "the people of the Saints of the Most High" it is understood to mean first the Jews and then the Christians who confessed the absolute unity of God, fought and suffered for it until the appearance of the Barnasha and the destruction of the Horn.

(*c*) After the destruction of the Horn the people and the nations that will have to serve the Saints of God are the Chaldeans, Medo-Persians, Greeks, and the Romans — the four nations represented by the four beasts that had trod upon and invaded the Holy Land.

From the Adriatic to the Walls of China all the various nations have either as Muslims received the homage or as unbelievers served the Muslims, who are the only true believers in the One God.

(*d*) It is remarkable to realize the significant fact that God often allows the enemies of His true religion to subdue and persecute His people because of two purposes. First, because he wants to punish His people for their lethargy, drawbacks and sins. Secondly, because He wishes to prove the faith, the patience and the indestructibility of His Law and Religion, and thus to allow the infidels to continue in their unbelief and crime until their cup is full. God in due time Himself intervenes on behalf of the believers when their very existence is on its beam-ends. It was a terrible and most critical time for all Muslims when the Allied Forces were in Constantinople during those awful years of the Armistice. Great preparations were made by the Greeks and their friends to take back the Grand Mosque of Aya Sophia; the Greek Patriarch of Constantinople went to London carrying with him a precious ancient patriarchal cope set in gems and pearls for the Archbishop of Canterbury, who was strenuously advocating the restoration of Constantinople and the grand edifice of St. Sophia to the Greeks. On the eve of the Prophet's night journey to Heaven — called *al-mi'rāj* — the sacred building was crammed with a great multitude of the suppliant faithful who till the dawn most earnestly supplicated the Almighty Allah to deliver Turkey, and particularly the Sacred House, from those who "would fill it with ugly idols and images as before!" In connection with that patriarchal mantle or cope, I wrote an article in the Turkish paper the *Aqshām,* showing the existence of a schism between the Greek Orthodox and the Protestant Anglican Churches. I pointed out that the cope was not meant as a pallium of investiture and recognition of the Anglican orders, and that a reunion between the two Churches could never be accomplished unless one or the other of the parties should renounce and abjure certain articles of faith as heretical and erroneous. I also pointed out that the cope was a diplomatic bribe on behalf of Greece and its Church. The letter ended with these works: "All depends upon the grace and miracle which this *bakhshish* of a pontifical cope is expected to work!"

The result is too well known to be repeated here. Suffice it to say that the Patriarch died in England, and the Almighty, who sent the Barnasha to crush the Horn and chase out the legions of Rome from the East, raised Mustaphā Kamāl, who saved his country and restored the honour of Islam!

(*e*) It is to be noted that the Jews were the chosen people of God until the advent of Jesus Christ. In the eyes of the Muslims neither the Jews nor the Christians have a right to claim the title of "the People of the Saints of the Most High," because the former reject Jesus altogether, while the latter insult him by deifying him. Moreover, both are equally unworthy of that title because of their refusing to recognize the Last Prophet who has completed the list of the Prophets.

We shall now proceed to prove that the Barnasha — the Son-of-Man — who was presented to the "Ancient of Days" and invested with power to kill the monster, was no other than Muhammad, whose very name literally means "the Praised and Illustrious." Whatever other person you may try to invent in order to deprive the august Apostle of Allah of this unique glory and majesty bestowed on him in the Divine Court, you will only make yourselves ridiculous; and this for the following reasons:—

1. We know that neither Judaism nor Christianity has any particular name for its faith and its system. That is to say, neither the Jews nor the Christians have any special name for the doctrines and forms of their faith and worship. "Judaism" and "Christianity" are not Scriptural nor authorized either by God of the founders of those religions. *In fact, a religion, if true, cannot properly be named after its second founder, for the real author and founder of a true religion is God, and not a Prophet.* Now the proper noun for the laws, doctrines, forms and practices of worship as revealed by Allah to Muhammad is "Islām," which means "making peace" with Him and among men. "Muhammadanism" is not the proper appellation of Islam. For Muhammad, like Abraham and all other Prophets, was himself a Muslim, and not a Muhammadan! Judaism means the religion of Judah, but what was Judah himself? Surely not a Judaist! And similarly was Christ a Christian or a Jesuit? Certainly neither of them! What were, then, the names of these two distinct religions? No names at all!

Then we have the barbarous Latin word "religion,"

meaning "the fear of the gods." It is now used to express "any mode of faith and worship." Now what is the equivalent word for "religion" in the Bible? What expression did Moses or Jesus use to convey the meaning of religion? Of course, the Bible and its authors make no use of this word at all.

Now the Scriptural term used in the vision of Daniel is the same as applied repeatedly by the Qur-án to Islām, namely, "Dīn" (and in the Qur-án, "Dīn"), which means "judgment." God on His "Korsiya" or tribune is the "Dayyana" or the "Judge." Let us read the description of this celestial Court of Judgment: "the tribunes are set, the books are opened, and the 'Dina' — judgment — is established." By the "Books" is to be understood the "Preserved Table" wherein the decrees of God are inscribed from which the Qur-án was transcribed and revealed by the Angel Gabriel to Muhammad; and also the books of accounts of every man's actions. It was according to the decrees and laws of God contained in that "Preserved Table," and the wicked actions of the Horn, that the Great "Dayyana" — the Judge condemned it to death and appointed Muhammad to be "Adon," i.e. "Commander" or "Lord," to destroy the monster. All this language of Daniel is extremely Qur-ánic. The religion of Islam is called "Dīnu 'l-Islām." It was according to the decrees and laws of this "Dīna" that the "Barnasha" destroyed the Devil's religion and his lieutenant the Horn. How can it, then, be at all possible that any man other than Muhammad could be meant by the appearance of a "Son-of-Man" in the presence of the Most High? Islām is, indeed, a "judgment of peace," because it possesses an authenticated Book of Law, with which justice is administered and iniquity punished, the truth discerned and the falsehood condemned; and above all, the unity of God, the eternal rewards for good deeds, and eternal damnation for wicked actions are clearly stated and defined.   In English a magistrate is called "Justice of Peace;" that is to say, a "judge of peace." Now this is in imitation of a Muslim Judge, who settles a quarrel, decides a case, by punishing the guilty and rewarding the innocent, thus restoring peace.   This is Islām and the law of the Qur-án.   It is not Christianity nor the Gospel, for the latter absolutely forbids a Christian to appeal to a judge, however innocent and oppressed he may be (Matt. v. 25, 26, 38-48).

2.   The Son-of-Man, or Barnasha, is certainly Muhammad.   For he came after Constantine, and not before him as Jesus or any other Prophet did.   The Trinitarian régime in the East represented by the Horn, which we rightly identify with Constantine the Great, was permitted to fight with the Unitarians and vanquish them for a period described in the figurative, prophetical language as "time, times and half a time," which phrase signifies three centuries and a half, at the end of which all the power of idolatry on the one hand and the Trinitarian dominion and tyranny on the other were eradicated and swept away entirely.   There is nothing more absurd than the assertion that Judah the Maccabæus (Maqbhaya) was the Barnasha on the clouds, and the Horn Antiochus.   It is alleged that (if I remember aright) Antiochus, after desecrating the Temple of Jerusalem, lived only three years and a half — or three days and a half — at the end of which time he perished.   In the first place, we know that Antiochus was a successor of Alexander the Great and King of Syria, consequently one of the four heads of the winged Tiger and not the eleventh Horn of the fourth Beast as stated in the vision.   In the eighth chapter of the Book of Daniel, the Ram and the He-goat are explained by a Saint as representing the Persian and the Greek Empires respectively.   It is expressly explained that the Greek Empire

immediately succeeded the Persian and that it was divided into four kingdoms, as stated in the first vision.   Secondly, the Horn with the speech indicates that the person who blasphemed and changed the Law and holy days could not be a pagan, but one who knew God and associated with Him purposely the other two persons whom he had equally known, and perverted the faith.   Antiochus did not pervert the faith of the Jews by instituting a trinity or plurality of Gods, nor did he change the Law of Moses and its festival days.   Thirdly, it is childish to give such a magnitude and importance to local and insignificant events which took place between a petty king in Syria and a small Jewish chief, so as to compare the latter with the glorious man who received the homage of the millions of angels in the presence of the Almighty.   Moreover, the prophetical vision describes and depicts the Barnasha as the greatest and the noblest of all men, for no other human being is reported in the Old Testament to have been the object of such honour and grandeur as Muhammad.

3.   It is equally futile to claim for Jesus Christ this celestial honour given to the Son-of-Man.   There are two main reasons to exclude Jesus from this honour; (a) If he is purely a man and prophet, and if we consider his work a success or failure, then he is certainly far behind Muhammad.   But if he is believed to be the third of the three in the Trinity, then he is not to be enlisted among men at all.   You fall into a dilemma, and you cannot get out of it; for in either case the Barnasha could not be Jesus.   (b) If Jesus was commissioned to destroy the fourth Beast, then instead of paying poll-tax or tribute to Cæsar and submitting himself to be bastinadoed or whipped by the Roman governor Pilate, he would have chased away the Roman legions from Palestine and saved his country and people.

4.   There has never lived upon this earth a Prince-

Prophet like Muhammad, who belonged to a dynasty that reigned for a long period of about 2,500 years, was absolutely independent and never bent its neck under a foreign yoke. And certainly there has never been seen on earth another man like Muhammad, who has rendered more material and moral service to his own nation in particular and to the world in general. It is impossible to imagine another human being so dignified and so worthy as Muhammad for such a magnificent glory and honour as depicted in the prophetical vision. Let us just compare the great Prophet Daniel with the Barnasha he was beholding with awe and wonder. Daniel was a slave or captive, though raised to the dignity of a vizier in the courts of Babylon and Susa; he worshipped an angel, but was forbidden. What would, in the presence of the Almighty, be his position when compared with Muhammad, who would be crowned as the Sultan of the Prophets, the Leader of mankind, and the object of the angels' homage and admiration? Small wonder that the Prophet David calls Muhammad "My Lord" (Psa, c. 10).

5.   It is no wonder to find that on his night-journey to Heaven Muhammad was received with the highest honours by the Almighty and invested with power to extirpate idolatry and the blasphemous Horn from countries given by God to him and to his people as an everlasting heritage.

6.   Another most amazing feature in this prophetical vision is, according to my humble belief, that the sight of a Barnasha upon the clouds and his presentation to the Almighty corresponds with and is simultaneous with the Mi'rāj — or night journey of the Prophet Muhammad; in other words, this second part of the vision of Daniel is to be identified with the Mi'rāj! There are, indeed, several indications both in the language of Daniel and in the Sacred "Hadīth" — or traditions of the Apostle of Allah — which lead me to

this belief. The Qur-án declares that during that night-journey God transported His servant from the Sacred Mosque at Mecca to the Father Temple of Jerusalem. He blessed the precincts of that Temple, then in ruins, and showed him His signs (chap. xvii.).

It is related by the Holy Prophet that at the Temple of Jerusalem he officiated in his capacity of the Imam, and conducted the prayers with all the company of the Prophets following him. It is further related that it was from Jerusalem that he was carried up unto the Seventh Heaven, being accompanied by the spirits of the Prophets and Angels until he was taken to the presence of the Eternal. The modesty of the Prophet which forbade him to reveal all that he saw, heard and received from the Lord of Hosts is made good by Daniel, who narrates the decision of Gods judgement. It appears that the Spirit which interpreted the vision to Daniel was not an Angel, as thoughtlessly remarked by me elsewhere, but the Spirit or the Soul of a Prophet, for he calls "Qāddīsh" (in the masculine gender) and "Qaddush" (iv. 10; viii. 13), which means a Saint or a Holy Man — a very usual name of the Prophets and Saints. How glad must have been the holy souls of the Prophets and the Martyrs who had been persecuted by those four beasts especially more so when they saw the decree of death being pronounced by the Almighty against the Trinitarian régime of Constantine and the Seal of the Prophets being commissioned to kill and annihilate the uttering Horn! It will also be remembered that this vision was seen as well during the same night in which took place the journey of the Barnasha from Mecca to the heavens!

From the testimony of Daniel we, as Muslims, must admit that Muhammad's journey was corporeally performed — a thing of no impossibility to the Omnipotent. There must exist a law in physics according to which a body is not controlled by the main body to which it belongs, or by the law of gravitation, but by the law of velocity. A human body belonging to the earth cannot escape from it unless a superior force of velocity should detach it from the force of gravitation. Then there must also exist another law in physics according to which a light body can penetrate into a thick one and a thick body into an even still thicker or harder one through the means of a superior force, or simply through the force of velocity. Without entering into the details of this subtle question, suffice it to say that before the force of velocity the weight of a solid body, whether moved or touched, is of no concern. We know the rate of the velocity of the light from the sun or a star. If we discharge a bullet at the rate, say, of 2,500 metres a second, we know it penetrates and pierces a body of iron plate which is several inches thick. Similarly, an angel, who can move with an infinitely greater velocity than that of the light of the sun and even the thought in the mind, could, of course, transport the bodies of Jesus, Muhammad and Elijah with an astounding facility and rapidity, and set at nought the law of gravitation of the globe to which they belonged.

St. Paul also mentions a vision he had seen fourteen years before of a man who had been taken up into the third heaven and then unto Paradise, where he heard and saw words and objects that could not be described. The Churches and their commentators have believed this man to be St. Paul himself. Although the language is such as to convey to us the idea that he himself is the man, yet out of modesty it is that he keeps it a secret lest he should be considered a proud man (2 Cor. xii. 1-4). Although the Qur-án teaches us that the Apostles of Jesus Christ were all holy and inspired men, yet their writings cannot be relied upon, because the wrangling and disputant Churches have subjected them to interpolations. The Gospel of St. Barnabas states that Paul afterwards fell into an error and misled many of the believers.

That Paul does not reveal the identity of the person seen by him in the vision, and that the words which he heard in Paradise "cannot be spoken and no man is permitted to speak them," shows that Paul was not himself the person who was taken up to Heaven. To say that Paul, for reason of humility and out of modesty, does not praise himself is simply to misrepresent Paul. He boasts of having rebuked St. Peter to his face, and his epistles are full of expressions about himself which do rather confirm the idea that Paul was neither humble nor modest.

Besides, we know from his writings to the Galatians and the Romans what a prejudiced Jew he was against Hagar and her son Ishmael. The glorious person he saw in his vision could be no other than the person seen by Daniel! It was Muhammad that he saw, and durst not report the words which were spoken to him by the Almighty because on the one hand he was afraid of the Jews, and because on the other he would have contradicted himself for having glorified himself so much with the Cross and the Crucified. I am half convinced that Paul was allowed to see the Barnasha whom Daniel had seen some six centuries before, but "the angel of Satan who was continually pouring blows upon his head" (2 Cor. xii. 7) forbade him to reveal the truth! It is an admission by Paul that "the angel of Satan," as he calls him, prohibited him from revealing the secret of Muhammad, whom he had seen in his vision. If Paul was a true righteous servant of God, why was he delivered into the hands of the "angel of the Devil" who was continually beating him on the head? The more one reflects on the teachings of Paul, the less one doubts that he was the prototype of Constantine the Great!

In conclusion, I may be permitted to draw a moral for the non-Muslims from this wonderful vision of Daniel. They should take to heart a lesson from the fate which befell the four beasts, and particularly the Horn, and to reflect that Allah alone is the One True God; that the Muslims alone faithfully profess His absolute Unity; that He is aware of their oppressions, and that they have their Sultan of the Prophets near to the Throne of the Most High.

VII

KING DAVID CALLS HIM: "MY LORD"

The history of David, his exploits and prophetical writings, are found in two books of the Old Testament, Samuel and the Psalms. He was the youngest son of Yishai (Jessie) from the tribe of Judah. While still a young shepherd, he had killed a bear and torn into halves a lion. The valiant young man swung a small stone right through the forehead of Goliath, an armed Philistine champion and saved the army of Israel. The highest reward for a successful feat displaying valour was the hand of Michal, a daughter of King Saul. David played on harp and flute, and was a good singer. His flight from his jealous father-in-law, his adventures and exploits as a bandit, are well known. On the death of Saul, David was invited by the people to assume the reins of the kingdom, for which he had long before been anointed by the Prophet Samuel. He reigned for some seven years at Hebron. He took Jerusalem from the Jebusites and made it the capital of his kingdom. Its two hills, or mounts, were named "Moriah" and "Sion." Both these words have the same signification and import as the famous "Marwa" and "Sapha" at Mecca, which words respectively mean "the place of the vision of the Lord," and "the rock" or "stone." David's wars, his very grave family troubles, his sin against the faithful soldier, Uriah, and his wife, Bathsheba, was not left with impunity. He reigned forty years; his life was marked with wars and family griefs. There are some contradictory accounts about him which are evidently to be ascribed to the two opposite sources.

The crime of David in connection with Uriah and his wife (2 Sam. xi.) is not even alluded to in the Qur-án (Sura xxxviii.). It is one of the superiorities of the Holy Qur-án that it teaches us that all prophets are born sinless and die sinless. It does not, like the Bible, impute to them crimes and sins — e.g. the double crime of David, mentioned in the Bible, which, according to the Law of Moses, is punishable by death — which, let alone a prophet who is a chosen servant of God the Almighty, we would not even think of attaching to the name of an ordinary human being.

The story of David committing adultery and two angels having come to him thus to remind him of the sin is a puerile falsehood — wherever it may be found. It has been repudiated by the best Muslim opinion. Rāzī says: "Most of the learned, and those who have searched for the truth among them, declare this charge false and condemn it as a lie and a mischievous story. The words *istaghfora* and *ghafarana* occurring in the text of verse 24, chap. xxxviii. of the Holy Qur-án by no means indicate that David had committed a sin, for *istighfār* really signifies the seeking of protection; and David sought Divine protection when he saw that his enemies had grown so bold against him; and by *ghafarana* is meant the rectification of his affairs; for David, who was a great ruler, could not succeed in keeping his enemies under complete control.

The Old Testament does not mention the time when the gift of prophecy was granted to David. We read that after David had committed the two sins it was Nathan the Prophet who was sent by God to chastise David. Indeed, until late in his life we find him always having recourse to other prophets. According to the Biblical accounts, therefore, it would seem that the gift of prophecy came to him after he had thoroughly repented of his sin.

In one of the previous articles I remarked that after the split of the Kingdom into two independent States which were often at war with each other, the ten tribes which formed the Kingdom of Israel were always hostile to the dynasty of David and never accepted any other portion of the Old Testament except the Torah — or the Law of Moses as contained in the Pentateuch. This is evident from the Samaritan version of the first five books of the Old Testament. We do not meet with a single word or prophecy about David's posterity in the discourses of the great prophets, like Elijah, Elisha, and others, who flourished in Samariah during the reigns of the wicked kings of Israel. It is only after the fall of the Kingdom of Israel and the transportation of the ten tribes into Assyria that the Prophets of Judeah began to predict the advent of some Prince from the House of David who was soon to restore the whole nation and subdue its enemies. There are several of these abscure and ambiguous sayings in the writings or discourses of these later prophets which have given a rapturous and exotic exultation to the Fathers of the Church; but in reality they have nothing to do with Jesus Christ. I shall briefly quote two of these prophecies. The first is in Isaiah (Chap. vii., verse 14), where that Prophet predicts that "a damsel already pregnant with child shall bear forth a son, and thou shalt name him Emmanuel." The Hebrew word *a'lmāh* does not mean "virgin," as generally interpreted by the Christian theologians and therefore applied to the Virgin Mary, but it signifies "a marriageable woman, maiden, damsel." The Hebrew word for "virgin" is *bthulah*. Then the child's name is to be Emmanuel, which means "God-is-with-us." There are hundreds of Hebrew names which are composed of "el" and another noun, which forms either the first or the last syllable of such compound nouns. Neither Isaiah, nor King Ahaz, nor any Jew, ever thought that the newly born infant would be himself "God-with-us." They never thought anything else but that his name only would be as such. But the text expressly says that it was Ahaz (who seems to have known the maiden with child), that would give the boy that name. Ahaz was in danger, his enemies were pressing hard against Jerusalem, and this promise was made to him by showing him a *sign,* namely, a pregnant maiden, and not a Virgin Mary, that would come into the world more than seven hundred years later! This simple prediction of a child that would be born during the reign of Ahaz was equally misunderstood by the writer of the Gospel of Matthew (Matt. i. 23). The name "Jesus" was given by the Angel Gabriel (Matt. i. 21), and he was never called "Emmanuel." Is it not scandalous to take this name as an argument and proof of the Christian doctrine of the "Incarnation"?

The other strange interpretation of a prophetic prediction is from Zachariah (ix. 9), which is misquoted and utterly misunderstood by the writer of the first Gospel (xxi. 5). The Prophet Zachariah says: "Rejoice much, O daughter of Sion; shout, O daughter of Jerusalem: behold, thy King is coming unto thee; righteous and with salvation is he; meek and mounted upon an ass; and upon a colt, son of a she-ass."

In this poetical passage the poet simply wishes to describe the male ass — upon which the King is seated — by saying that it was a young ass, and this colt, too, is described as the son of a female ass. It was only one male colt or young donkey. Now Matthew quotes this passage in the following way:—

> "Tell the daughter of Sion,
> Behold, thy King is coming unto thee;
> Meek, and mounted on a female ass,
> And on a colt, the son of a female ass."

Whether or not the person who wrote the above verse did really believe that Jesus, when making his triumphal entry into Jerusalem by mounting or sitting at the same time both upon the mother ass and her young colt, worked a miracle is not the question; nevertheless it is true to say that the majority of the Christian Fathers so believed; and it never occurred to them that such a show would look rather a comedy than a royal and pompous procession. Luke, however, is careful, and has not fallen into Matthew's mistake. Were these authors both inspired by the same Spirit?

Zachariah foretells in Jerusalem, after the return of the Jews from captivity, the coming of a king. Though meek and humble, mounted upon a colt of an ass, still he is coming with salvation and would rebuild the house of God. He prophesies this at a time when the Jews are endeavouring to rebuild the Temple and the ruined town; their neighbouring peoples are against them; the work of building is stopped until Darius, King of Persia, issues a firman for the construction. Although no Jewish king had ever appeared since the sixth century before Christ, nevertheless they had had autonomous governments under foreign sovereigns. The salvation here promised, be it noted, is *material* and *immediate,* and *not* a salvation to come five hundred and twenty years afterwards, when Jesus of Nazareth would ride upon two asses simultaneously and enter into Jerusalem, already a large and wealthy city with a magnificent temple, simply to be captured and crucified by the Jews themselves and by their Roman masters, as the present Gospels tell us! This would be no solace at all for the poor Jews surrounded with enemies in a ruined city. Consequently, by the word "king" we may understand one of their chief leaders — Zerobabel, Ezra, or Nehemiah.

These two examples are intended to show chiefly to my Muslim readers — who may not be well acquainted with the Jewish Scriptures — how the Christians have been misguided by their priests and monks in giving stupid interpretations and meanings to the prophecies contained therein.

Now I come to David's prophecy:—

"Y*a*HW*a*H said to my ADON,

Sit at my right until I place

Thine enemies a footstool under thy feet."

This verse of David is written in Psalm cxi, and quoted by Matthew (xxii. 44), Mark (xii. 36), and Luke (xx 42). In all languages the two names contained in the first distich are rendered as "The Lord said unto my Lord." Of course, if the first Lord is God, the second Lord is also God; nothing more convenient to and suitable an argument for a Christian priest or pastor than this, namely, the speaker is God, and also the spoken to is God; therefore David knows two Gods! Nothing more logical than this reasoning! Which of these two *Domini* is "the Lord" of David? Had David written, *"Dominus meus dixit Domino meo,"* he would have made himself ridiculous, for then he would have admitted himself to be a slave or servant of two Lords, without even mentioning their proper names. The admission would go even farther than the existence of two Lords; it would mean that

David's second Lord had taken refuge with his first Lord, who ordered him to take a seat on his right side until he should put his enemies a footstool under his feet. This reasoning leads us to admit that, in order to understand well your religion, you are obliged to know your Bible or Qur-án in the original language in which it was written, and not to depend and rely upon a translation.

I have purposely written the original Hebrew words YaHWaH and Adon, in order to avoid any ambiguity and misunderstanding in the sense conveyed by them. Such sacred names written in religious Scripture should be *left* as they are, unless you can find a thoroughly equivalent word for them in the language into which you wish to translate them. The tetragram Yhwh used to be pronounced Yehovah (Jehovah), but now it is generally pronounced Yahwah. It is a proper name of God the Almighty, and it is held so holy by the Jews that when reading their Scriptures they never pronounce it, but read it "Adoní" instead. The other name, "Elohim," is always pronounced, but Yahwah never. Why the Jews make this distinction between these two names of the same God is a question for itself, altogether outside the scope of our present subject. It may, however, in passing, be mentioned that Yahwah, unlike Elohim, is never used with pronominal suffixes, and seems to be a special name in Hebrew for the Deity as the national God of the people of Israel. In fact, "Elohim" is the oldest name known to all Semites; and in order to give a special character to the conception of the true God, this tetragram is often conjointly with Elohim applied to Him. The Arabic form, *Rabb Allah,* corresponds to the Hebrew form, *Yahwah Elohim.*

The other word, "Ādōn," signifies a "Commander, Lord, and master," or the same as the Arabic and Turkish nouns *Amīr, Sayyid,* and *Āghā.* Ādōn stands as the opposite term of "soldier, slave, and property." Consequently the first part of the distich is to be rendered as "God said to my Lord."

David, in his capacity of a monarch, was himself the Lord and Commander of every Israelite and the Master of the Kingdom. Whose "servant" was he, then? David, being a powerful sovereign, could not be, as a matter of fact, a slave or servant of any living human being whatsoever. Nor is it imaginable that he would call "his Lord" any dead prophet or saint, such as Abraham or Jacob, for whom the usual and reasonable term was "Father." It is equally conceivable that David would not use the appellation "my Lord" for any of his own descendants, for whom, too, the usual term would be "son." There remains, besides God, no other conceivable being who could be David's Lord, except the noblest and the highest man of the race of mankind. It is quite intelligible to think that in the sight and choice of God there must be a man who is the noblest, the most praised, and the most coveted of all men. Surely the Seers and the Prophets of old knew this holy personage and, like David, called him "my Lord."

Of course, the Jewish Rabbins and commentators of the Old Testament understood by this expression the Messiah, who would descend from David himself, and so replied they to the question put to them by Jesus Christ as quoted above from Matthew (xxii.), and the other Synoptic. Jesus flatly repudiated the Jews when he asked them a second question: "How could David call him 'my Lord' if he were his son?" This question of the Master put the audience to silence, for they could find no answer to it. The Evangelists abruptly cut short this important subject of discussion. To stop there without a further explanation was not worthy either of the Master or of his reporters. For, leaving the question of his god-head, and even of his prophetical character, aside, Jesus as a teacher was obliged to solve the problem raised by himself when he saw that the disciples and the hearers were unable to know *who* then that "Lord," could be!

By his expression that the "Lord," or the "Adon," could not be a son of David, Jesus excludes himself from that title. This admission is decisive and should awaken the religious teachers of the Christians to reduce Christ to his due status of a high and holy Servant of God, and to renounce the extravagant divine character ascribed to him much to his own disgust and displeasure.

I cannot imagine a teacher who, seeing his pupils unable to answer his question, should keep silent, unless he is himself ignorant like them and unable to give a solution to it. But Jesus was not either ignorant or a malevolent teacher. He was a prophet with a burning love to God and man. He did not leave the problem unsolved or the question without an answer. The Gospels of the Churches do not report the answer of Jesus to the question: "Who was the Lord of David?" But the Gospel of Barnabas does. This Gospel has been rejected by Churches because its language is more in accordance with the revealed Scriptures and because it is very expressive and explicit about the nature of Jesus Christ's mission, and above all because it records the exact words of Jesus concerning Muhammad. A copy of this Gospel can easily be procured. There you will find the answer of Jesus himself, who said that the Covenant between God and Abraham was made on Ishmael, and that "the most glorious or praised" of men is a descendant of Ishmael and not of Isaac through David. Jesus repeatedly is reported to have spoken of Muhammad, whose spirit or soul he had seen in heaven. I shall have, if God wills, an occasion to write on this Gospel later.

There is no doubt that the prophetical eye of Daniel that saw in a wonderful vision the great "Barnasha," who was Muhammad, was also the same prophetical eye of David. It was this most glorious and praised of men that was seen by the Prophet Job (xix 25) as a "Saviour" from the power of the Devil.

Was it, then, Muhammad whom David calls "my Lord" or "my Adon"?   Let us see.

The arguments in favour of Muhammad, who is styled "Sayyidu 'l-Mursalīn," the same as "Adon of the Prophets," are decisive; they are so evident and explicit in the words of the Old Testament that one is astonished at the ignorance and the obstinacy of those who refuse to understand and obey.

1.   The greatest Prophet and Adon, in the eyes of God and man, is not a great conqueror and destroyer of mankind, nor a holy recluse who spends his life in a cave or cell to meditate upon God only to save himself, but one who renders more good and service to mankind by bringing them into the light of the knowledge of the One true God, and by utterly destroying the Power of the Devil and his abominable idols and wicked institutions.   It was Muhammad who "bruised the head of the Serpent,"[1] and that is why the Qur-án rightly calls the Devil "Iblīs," namely, "the Bruised One"!   He purged the Temple of the Ka'aba and all Arabia of the idols, and gave light, religion, happiness, and power to the ignorant Arab idolaters, who in a short time spread that light into the four directions of the earth.   In the service of God, the works and the success of Muhammad are incomparable and unrivalled.

The Prophets, Saints, and Martyrs form the army of God against the Power of the Devil; and Muhammad alone

1.   See the *Islamic Review* for October 1926, my article "Why the Qur-án calls the Devil 'Iblis.' "

is decidedly the Commander-in-Chief of them all.   He is, indeed, alone the Adon and Lord not only of David but of all the Prophets, for he has purified Palestine and all the countries visited by Abraham of idolatry and foreign yoke.

2.   Since Jesus Christ admits that he himself was not the "Lord" of David, nor that the Messiah was to descend from David, there remains none other than Muhammad among the Prophets to be the Adon or Lord of David.   And when we come to compare the praiseworthy religious revolution that the Noble Son of Ishmael brought about in the world, with what all the thousands of prophets put together have achieved, we have to come to the conclusion that it is alone Muhammad who could deserve the meritorious title of Adon.

3.   How did David know that "Yahwah said to Adon, 'Sit thou at my right until I put thine enemies a footstool under thy feet'?" and *when* did David hear this word of God? Christ himself gives the answer, namely "David in spirit wrote this."   He saw the Adon Muhammad just as Daniel had seen him (Dan. vii.), and St. Paul had seen him (2 Cor. xii.), and many others had.   Of course, this mystery of "Sit thou at my right" is hidden from us.   Yet we may safely conjecture that this official investiture with the honour of seating himself at the right of the throne of God, and therefore raised to the dignity of the "Adon," not only of the Prophets but of all the Creatures, took place on the famous night of his Mi'rāj to Paradise.

4.   The only principal objection to Muhammad's divine mission and superiority is his condemnation of the doctrine of the Trinity.   But the Old Testament knows no other God besides Allah, and the Lord of David did not sit at the right hand of a triple god, but at that of the One Allah.   Hence among the Prophets who believed in and served Allah none

was so great, and accomplished such a stupendous service
for Allah and mankind, as Muhammad, upon whom be peace
and blessings.

VIII

THE LORD AND THE APOSTLE
OF THE COVENANT

The last book of the Canonical Jewish Code of the Bible
bears the name of "Malachai," which looks to be more a surname than a proper noun.   The correct pronounciation of
the name is Mālākhī, which means "my angel" or "my messenger."   The Hebrew word, "māl'àkh," like the Arabic
"malak," like the Greek term "anghelos" from which the
English name "angel" is derived, signifies "a messenger," one
commissioned with a message or news to deliver to some-
body.

Who this Mālākhī is, in what period of the Jewish history he lived and prophesied, is not known either from the
book itself or from any other portion of the Old Testament.
It begins with the words: "The 'missa' of the Word of
Yahweh the El of Israel by the hand of Mālākhī," which may
be translated: "The discourse of the Word of Yāhweh,
God of Israel, by the hand of Mālākhī."   It contains four
short chapters.

The oracle is addressed, not to a king and his courtiers,
but to a people already settled in Jerusalem with the Temple
and its services.   The sacrifices and oblations are of the
meanest and worst kind; the sheep and cattle offered at the

altars are not of the best quality; they are blind, lame, and lean animals. The tithes are not regularly paid, and if at all paid are of the inferior material. The priests, too, naturally, cannot devote their time and energy to perform their sacred duty. For they cannot chew the beefsteaks and roasted mutton-chops of the lean old, crippled sacrifices. They cannot live on the scanty tithes or insufficient stipends. Yāhweh, as usual with this incorrigible people, now threatens, now holds out promises, and at times complain.

This discourse, or oracle, seems to have been delivered by the Prophet Mālākhī in about the beginning of the fourth century before the Christian era, when the people of Israel were also tired of Yahweh; and used to say: "The Table of the Lord (Yahweh) is an abomination, and His meal is contemptible" (Mal. i. 12). "He who doeth evils is good in the eyes of Yahweh, and He is pleased with them; or, where is the God of the judgment?" (Mal. ii. 17).

The Book of Mālākhī, notwithstanding its being of a *post captivitatem* date, is, however, written in a seemly good Hebrew style. To say that this "misa," or discourse, has come down to us intact and unadulterated is to confess ignorance of the language. There are several mutilated sentences, so that it is almost impossible to understand the exact sense they intend to convey.

The subject of our discussion in this article is the famous prediction couched in Mal. iii. 1. The prophecy runs thus:—

> "Behold, I send My Messenger, and he shall prepare the way before Me; and suddenly shall come to his temple the Adon whom ye are seeking, and the Messenger of the Covenant whom ye desire. Behold, he cometh, says the Lord of Hosts" (Mal. iii. 1).

This is a well-known Messianic prophecy. All Christian

Saints, Fathers, Popes, Patriarchs, Priests, monks, nuns, and even the Sunday-school children, will tell us that the first messenger mentioned in the text is St. John the Baptist, and the second messenger, whom their vernacular versions have rendered "Angel of the Covenant," is Jesus Christ!

A definite determination of the subject of this prophecy is of extreme importance, because the Christian Churches have ever since believed that two distinct persons are indicated therein; and the author of this erroneous belief is a singularly remarkable blunder of St. Matthew's.   One of the characteristic features of the First Gospel — Matthew — is to show and prove the fulfilment of some particular statement or prediction in the Old Testament concerning nearly every event in the life of Jesus Christ.   He is very careless to guard himself against contradictions, and less scrupulous in his quotations from the Hebrew Scriptures.   He is certainly not well versed in the literature of his own language. I had occasion to refer in the preceding article of this series to one of his blunders concerning the ass upon which Jesus mounted.[1]   This is a most serious point directly touching the authenticity and the validity of the Gospels.   Is it possible that the Apostle Matthew should himself be ignorant of the true character of the prophecy of Mālākhī, and ignorantly ascribe to his master a misquotation which would naturally put to question his very quality of a divinely inspired Prophet?   Then, what should we think of the author of the Second Gospel — of St. Mark — who ascribes the passage in Mālākhī to Isaiah?   (Mark i. 2).   Jesus is reported by Matthew (xi. 1-15), and this too is followed or copied by Luke (vii. 18-28), to have declared to the multitude that John the Baptist was "more than a Prophet," that it was he "about

1. See *I.R.*, January, 1929, p. 18.

whom it was written: Behold, I am sending My Angel before thy face, and he shall prepare thy way before thee;" and that "none among those born by women was greater than John, but the least in the kingdom of heaven is greater than he." The corruption of the text of Mālākhī is plain and deliberately made.   The original text tells us that Yahweh Sabaoth, i.e. God of Hosts, is the speaker and the believers are the people addressed, as can be readily seen in the words "whom *ye* are seeking . . . whom *ye* desire."   God says: "Behold, I send My Messenger, and he shall prepare the way before *My* face."   But the Gospels have interpolated the text by effacing the personal pronoun of the first person singular, and inserted "before *thee*" (or "thy face," as in Hebrew) *twice*. It is generally believed that Matthew wrote his Gospel in the then vernacular Hebrew or Aramaic in order to prove to the Jews that God, addressing Jesus Christ, said: "Behold, I send My messenger (Angel) [such is the version in Matthew xi. 10] before thee, and he shall prepare thy way before thee;" and wishes to show that this angel or messenger was John the Baptist.   Then a contrast between John and Jesus is left to Jesus, who describes John as above every prophet and greater than the sons of all human mothers, but the least in the Kingdom of Heaven — of which Jesus is meant to be the King — is greater than John.

I do not believe for a second that Jesus or any of his disciples could have made use of such language with the object of perverting the Word of God, but some fanatical monk or an ignorant bishop has forged this text and put into the mouth of Jesus the words which no prophet would speak.

The traditional idea that the Messenger commissioned to prepare or repair the way before the "Adon" and the "Messenger of the Covenant" is a servant and subordinate of the latter, and therefore to conclude that two distinct persons are predicted is a creation of the ignorance concerning the importance of the mission and the magnitude of the work assigned to that messenger.   He is not to be supposed as a pioneer or even an engineer appointed to construct roads and bridges for the passing of a royal procession.   Let us therefore pore over this subject more deeply and in a courageous, impartial, and dispassionate manner.

1.   In the first place, we must well understand that the Messenger is a man, a creature of human body and soul, and that he is not an Angel or a superhuman being.   In the second place, we should open our eyes of wisdom and judgment to see that he is not despatched to prepare the way before another Messenger called "Adon" and the "Messenger of the Promise," but he is commissioned to *found* and *establish* a *straight, safe,* and good *Religion*.   He is commissioned to remove all the obstacles in the way between God and His creatures; and to fill up all the gaps and chasms in this grand path, so that it may be smooth, easy to walk on, well lighted, and protected from all danger.   The Hebrew phrase, "*u* pinna derekh," means to say that the Messenger "will put straight and clear the worship or the religion."   The verb "dārākh" of the same root as the Arabic "dărăka," means "to walk, reach, and comprehend;" and the substantive "derekh" signifies, "road, way, step," and metaphorically "worship and religion."   It is used in this spiritual sense all through the Psalms and the Prophets.   Surely this high Messenger of God was not coming to repair or reform a way, a religion for the benefit of a handful of Jews, but to establish a universal and an unchangeable religion for all men.   Though the Jewish religion inculcates the existence of one true God, still their conception of Him as a national Deity of Israel, their priesthood, sacrificial rites and cere-

monies, and then the non-existence of any positive articles of belief in the immortality of the soul, the resurrection of the dead, the last judgment, the eternal life in heaven or hell, and many other deficient points, make it absolutely unfit and insufficient for the peoples of diverse languages, races, climates, temperaments, and habits. As regards Christianity, it, with its meaningless seven sacraments, its beliefs in original sin, the incarnation of a god — unknown to all previous religious and mythological literature — and in a trinity of individual gods, and finally because it does not possess a *single* line *in scripto* from its supposed founder, Jesus Christ, has done no good to mankind. On the contrary, it has caused divisions and sects, all inbued with bitter feelings of hatred and rancour against each other.

The Messenger, then, was commissioned with the abrogating of both those religions and the establishing of the ancient religion of Abraham and Ishmael and the other Prophets, with new precepts for all men. It was to be the shortest road to "reach" God; the simplest religion to worship Him, and the safest Faith to remain ever pure and unadulterated with superstition and stupid dogmas. The Messenger was commissioned to prepare a road, a religion that will conduct all who wish to believe in and love the One God without having need of the leadership of hundreds of self-appointed guides and pretenders. And above all, the Messenger was to come suddenly to his temple, whether it be the one in Jerusalem or the one in Mecca; he was to root out all idolatry in those countries, not only by the destruction of idols and images, but also inculcating in their former worshippers the faith in one true Allah. And the accomplishment of this stupendous task, namely, to construct a new Path, a universal religion, that teaches that between God and man no absolute mediator, no priest, saint or sacrament, is at all permissible, has only been done by an apostle whose name is Muhammad al-Mustaphā!

2. John the Baptist was not the Messenger foretold by Mālākhī. The accounts given about him by the four Evangelists are very contradictory, but the one thing that they together agree on is that he prepared no way at all; for he was not accredited with a sacred scripture: he neither founded a religion nor reformed the old one. He is reported to have left his parents and home while still a youth; he lived in the desert on honey and the locust; and spent there his life until he was about thirty years old, when he showed himself to the multitudes on the banks of the River Jordan, where he used to baptize the penitent sinners who confessed their sins to him. While Matthew knows nothing of his relationship with Jesus, or does not care to report it, Luke, who wrote his Gospel, *not* from a revelation, but from the works of the disciples of the Master, records the homage rendered by John to Jesus when both in the wombs of their mothers (Luke i. 39-46). He baptizes Jesus in the waters of the River Jordan like everybody else, and is reported to have said that he (John) was "not worthy to bow down to untie the laces of the shoes" (Mark i. 7) of Jesus, and according to the Fourth Gospel he (John) exclaimed that Jesus was "the Lamb of God that takes away the sins of the world" (John i. 29). That he knew Jesus and recognized him to be the Christ is quite evident. Yet when he was imprisoned he sends his disciples to Jesus, asking him: "Art thou he who is to come, or should we anticipate another one?" (Matt. xi. 3, etc.). The Baptist was martyred in the prison because he reprimanded an infidel Edomite, King Herod the Tetrarch, for having married the wife of his own brother. Thus ends, according to the narrative of the Evangelists, the life of a very chaste and holy prophet.

It is strange that the Jews did not receive John as a prophet. It is also stranger still to find that the Gospel of Barnabas does not mention the Baptist; and what is more, it puts the words said to have been uttered by John concerning Christ into the mouth of the latter about Muhammad, the Apostle of Allah. The Qur-án mentions the miraculous birth of John under the name of "Yahya," but does not refer to his mission of baptism.

The description of his sermon is given in the third chapter of Matthew. He seems to have announced the approach of the Kingdom of Heaven and the advent of a Great Apostle and Prophet of God who would baptize the believers, not with *water,* "but with fire and with the holy spirit."

Now, if John the Baptist were the Messenger appointed by God to prepare the way before Jesus Christ, and if he was his herald and subordinate, there is no sense and wisdom whatever in John to go about baptizing the crowds in the waters of a river or a pond and to occupy himself with half a dozen disciples. He ought to have immediately followed and adhered to Jesus when he had seen and known him! He did nothing of the kind! Of course, a Muslim always speaks of a prophet with utmost respect and reverence, and I am not expected to comment further, as an Ernest Renan or an indifferent critic would do! But to say that a prophet whom they describe as a dervish of the wilderness clad in the skins of animals, and a dervish who comes forth and sees his "Adon" and the "Angel of the Covenant," and *then* does not follow and cleave to him, is ridiculous and incredible. To think and believe that a prophet is sent by God to prepare the way, to purify and clear the religion for the coming of his superior, and then describing him as living all his life in the desert among the animals, is to tell us that he was constructing *chaussées,* causeways or railways, *not* for men, but for beasts and genii.

3. Nor was John the Baptist the Prophet Elijah or Elias, as Christ is made to have said. The Prophet Mālākhī, in his fourth chapter (verses 5, 6), speaks of the coming of Elijah, which fact is foretold to take place some time before the day of the Resurrection and not before the Appearance of the Messenger in question. Even if Christ had said that John was Elijah, the people did not know him. What Jesus meant to say was that the two were similar in their ascetical life, their zeal for God, their courage in scolding and admonishing the kings and the hypocrite leaders of the religion.

I cannot go on discussing this untenable claim of the Churches concerning John being the Messenger "to prepare the way." But I must add that this Baptist did not abrogate one iota of the Law of Moses, nor add to it a tittle. And as to baptism, it is the old Jewish *ma'muditha* or ablution. Washing or ablution could not be considered a "religion" or "way" whose place has been taken by the famous and mysterious Church institution of the Sacrament of Baptism!

4. If I say that Jesus Christ is not intended in the prophecy of Mālākhī, it would seem that I was advancing an *argumentum in absurdum,* because nobody wil contradict or make an objection to my statement. The Churches have always believed that the "Messenger of the way" is John the Baptist, and not Jesus. The Jews, however, accept neither of the two. But as the person foretold in the prophecy is one and the same, and *not two,* I most conscientiously declare that Jesus is not, and could not be, that person. If Jesus wss a god, as he is now believed to be, then he could not be employed to prepare the way before the face of Yahweh Sabaoth! If Jesus were the Yahweh Sabaoth who

made this prophecy, then who was the other Yehweh Sabaoth before *whose face* the way was to be prepared? If he were a simple man, made of flesh and blood, and servant of the Lord of Hosts, then the claim falls to the ground. For Jesus as a simple human being and prophet could not be the founder of the trinitarian Churches. Whichever form of the Christian religion we may take, whether it be the Orthodox, Catholic, Protestant, Salvationist, Quaker, or any of the multitudinous sects and communities, none of them can be the "way," the "religion" indicated by Mālākhī; and Jesus is *not* its founder or preparer. So long as we deny the absolute Oneness of God, we are in error, and Jesus cannot be our friend nor can he help us.

5. The person indicated in the prophecy has three qualifications, namely, the Messenger of Religion, the Lord Commander, and the Messenger of the Convent. He is also described and distinguished by three conditions, namely "he is suddenly coming to his Mosque or Temple, he is looked for and sought by men, and is greatly desired and coveted."

Who can, then, be this glorious man, this Great Benefactor of humanity, and this valiant Commander who rendered noble services in the cause of Allah and His religion other than Muhammad? — upon whom may rest God's peace and blessing.

He brought to the world an unrivalled Sacred Book, Al-Qur-án, a most reasonable, simple, and beneficial religion of Islam, and has been the means of guidance and conversion of millions and millions of the heathen nations in all parts of the globe, and has transformed them all into one universal and united Brotherhood, which constitutes the true and formal "Kingdom of Allah" upon the earth announced by Jesus and John the Baptist. It is futile and childish to compare either Jesus or John with the great Apostle of Allah, when we know perfectly well that neither of these two did ever attempt to convert a single pagan nor succeeded in persuading the Jews to recognize his mission.

IX

GENUINE PROPHETS PREACH ONLY ISLAM

There is no nation known to history like the people of Israel, which during a period of less than four hundred years, was infested with myriads of false prophets, not to mention the swarms of sorcerers, soothsayers and all sorts of witchcrafts and magicians. The false prophets were of two kinds: those who professed the religion and the Torah (Law) of Yahweh and pretended to prophesy in His name, and those who under the patronage of an idolater Israelite monarch prophesied in the name of Báal or other deities of the neighbouring heathen peoples. Belonging to the former category there were several impostors as contemporaries with the true prophets like Mikha (Micah) and Jeremiah, and to the latter there were those who gave much trouble to Elijah, and caused the massacres of the true prophets and believers during the reign of Ahab and his wife Jezebel. Most dangerous of all to the cause of true faith and religion were the pseudo-prophets, who conducted the divine services in the temple as well as in the Misphas and pretended to deliver the oracles of God to the people. No prophet, perhaps, received at the hands of these impostors more of persecution and hardships than the Prophet Jeremiah.

While still a young man, Jeremiah began his prophetic mission about the latter quarter of the seventh century before the Christian era, when the Kingdom of Judah was in great danger of invasion by the armies of the Chaldeans. The Jews had entered into alliance with the Pharaoh of Egypt, but as the latter had been badly defeated by the troops of Nebuchadnezzar, Jerusalem's doom was merely a question of time. In these critical days, during which the fate of the remnant of the people of God was to be decided, the Prophet Jeremiah was stoutly advising the king and the leaders of the Jews to submit and serve the King of Babylon, so that Jerusalem might be saved from being burnt down to ashes and the people from being deported into captivity. He poured out all his eloquent and fiery discourses into the ears of the kings, the priests, and the elders of the people, but all of no avail. He delivered message after message from God, saying that the only remedy for saving the country and the people from the imminent destruction was to submit to the Chaldeans; but there was no one to lend ear to his warnings.

Nebuchadnezzar comes and takes the city, carries away with him the king, the princes, and many captives, as well as all the treasures of the temple, including the gold and silver vessels. Another prince, and a third one, is appointed by the Emperor of Babylon to reign as his vassal in Jerusalem. This king, instead of being wise and loyal to his master of Babylon, revolts against him. Jeremiah incessantly admonishes the king to remain loyal and to abandon the Egyptian policy. But the false prophets continue to harangue in the temple, saying: "Thus says the Lord of hosts, Behold, I have broken the yoke of the King of Babylon, and in two years' time all the Jewish captives and the vessels of the House of God will be returned to Jerusalem." Jeremiah makes a wooden yoke round his own neck and goes to the temple and tells the people that God has been pleased to place in this way the yoke of the monarch of Babylon upon the neck of all the

Jews. He is struck on the face by one opponent prophet, who breaks to pieces the wooden yoke from Jeremiah's neck and repeats the harangue of the false prophets. Jeremiah is thrown into a deep dungeon full of mire, and is fed only on a dry loaf of barley a day until a famine prevails in the city, which is besieged by the Chaldeans. The pseudo-prophet Hananiah dies as Jeremiah had foretold. The wall of the city is thrown down somewhere, and the victorious army rushes into the city, the fleeing King Zedekiah and his retinue are seized and taken to the King of Babylon. The city and the temple, after being pillaged, are set on fire and all the inhabitants of Jerusalem are carried into Babylonia; only the poorer classes are left to cultivate the land. By order of Nebuchadnezzar, Jeremiah is granted a favour of staying in Jerusalem, and the newly appointed governor, Gedaliah, is charged to guard and well look after the prophet. But Gedaliah is killed by the rebellious Jews, and then they all flee to Egypt, carrying Jeremiah with them. Even in Egypt he prophesies against the fugitives and the Egyptians. He must have ended his life in Egypt.

His books, as it now stands, is quite different from the text of the Septuagint; evidently the copy from which the Greek text was written by the Alexandrian translators had a different order of chapters.

The Biblical critics consider that jeremiah was the author, or, at any rate, a compiler, of the fifth book of the Pentateuch called Deuteronomy. I myself am of the same opinion. Jeremiah was a Levite and a priest as well as a prophet. There is much of Jeremiah's teachings in Deuteronomy which are unknown in the rest of the Old Testament writings. And I take one of these teachings for my present subject, which I consider as one of the gems or golden texts of the Old Testament and must be esteemed very precious and holy.

After this detailed explanation I hasten to the main point which I have selected for the topic of this article: How to distinguish a genuine prophet from a false prophet. Jeremiah has supplied us with a fairly satisfactory answer, namely:

"THE PROPHET WHO PREACHES ISLAM"

In the Book of Deuteronomy (xiii. 1 - 5, xviii. 20 - 22) God the Almightly gives some instructions concerning the false prophets who may prophesy in the name of the Lord and in such an insidious way that they could mislead His people. Further, he tells us that the best way to find out the impostor's perfidy was to anticipate the fulfilment of his predictions, and then to put him to death when his fraud was divulged. But, as is well known, the ignorant cannot well distinguish between the genuine prophet and the imposter, just as much as they to-day are unable to definitely discover which of the two, a Roman Catholic priest or a Calvinist minister, is a genuine follower of Jesus Christ! A false prophet would also foretell events, work wonders, and do other religious things similar — at least in appearance — to those performed by a true one. The competition between the Prophet Moses and the magicians of Egypt is an apt illustration of this statement. Thus it is Jeremiah who gives us the best way of testing the veracity, the genuineness, of a prophet, and that way is the sign of Islam. Please read the whole chapter xxviii. of Jeremiah, and then ponder and reflect on the ninth verse:—

"The prophet which foretells the Islam (Shālōm), at the coming of the word of the Prophet, that prophet

will be recognized to have been sent by God in truth"
(Jer. xxviii. 9).

This translation is strictly literal.   The original verb *naba*,
usually translated as "to foretell" or "to prophesy," and the
noun *nābi,* "a prophet" has given the impression that a prophet is a person who foretells the future or past events by the
aid of divine revelation.   This definition is only partially true.
The complete difinition of the word "Prophet" must be: "one
who receives oracles or messages from God, and delivers
them faithfully to the person or people intended." It is evident
that a divine message need not necessarily be a foretelling of
past and future events.   In the same way verb "prophesy"
does not necessarily mean to reveal the past or future
occurrences, but rather to preach or promulgate the message
from God.   Consequently to prophesy is to deliver and utter
a *new* oracle, its nature or charater being quite immaterial.
To read the words of a prophet would be to prophesy no
more than would a prophet *deliver an oracle* when making
a discourse or public speech of his own accord. In the
Qur-ān God orders His beloved servant Muhammad to
declare: "I   am flesh like unto yourselves; only revelation
comes to me," etc., so that we may be careful not to attribute
to any of the prophets the quality of knowing and saying
everything through the revelation.   The divine revelations
used to come at intervals, while the prophets in their personal
intercourse and knowledge might be liable to mistakes and
errors.   A prophet is not appointed by God to teach humanity
physics, mathematics, or any other positive science.   It would
be very unjust on our part to blame a prophet for a slip of
language or a mistake committed *as* a man.

A prophet, therefore, is the subject of test and examination only when he *officially* and *formally delivers* the
message he has received from his Lord. His private affairs,

his family concerns, and his personal attainments do not concern us so much as his *mission* and *office*. In order to find out whether a prophet is genuine or an impostor, it is not fair to give a verdict against his prophetical character because he is reported to have been a little harsh or rude to his mother or because he believed in the literal inspiration and the Mosaic authorship of the Pentateuch. While making this observation, I have in mind the case of Jesus Christ, and many others in the history of Israel on other points.

It is *mala fides* and illwill to accuse prophets of sensuality, rudeness, ignorance in sciences, and of other personal frailties. They were men like ourselves and subject to the same natural inclinations and passions. They were protected only from mortal sins and from the perversion of the message they had to hand further. We must be extremely careful not to exalt the prophets of God too high in our imagination, lest God be displeased with us. They are all His creatures and servants; they accomplished their work and returned to Him. The moment we forget God and concentrate our love and admiration upon the person of any of the messengers of God we are in danger of falling into the sin of polytheism.

Having so far explained the nature and the signification of the prophet and the prophecy, I shall now endeavour to prove that no prophet could be genuine unless, as Jeremiah expressly says, he preaches and propagates the religion of Islam.

In order to understand better the sense and the importance of the passage under our contemplation we should just cast a glance over the preceding verse where Jeremiah tells his antagonist Prophet Hananiah: "The prophets that have been before me and before thee from old (times) prophesied against many lands, and against great kingdoms,

concerning war and evil and pestilence." Then he proceeds:—

> "The prophet that prophesies concerning Islam as
> soon as the word of the prophet comes, that prophet is
> known to have been sent by the Lord in truth."

There can be raised no serious objection to the English
wording of this passage excepting the clause *"l shālōm"*
which I have translated as "concerning Islam." The preposition "l" before "shālōm" signifies "concerning" or "about,"
and places its subject in the objective case and not in the
dative, as it would be if the predicate were a verb like
"come," "go," or "give."

That "shālōm" and the Syriac "Shlāmā," as well as the
Arabic "salām" and "Islām," are of one and the same Semitic
root, "shālām," and mean the same thing, is an admitted
truth by all the scholars of the Semitic languages. The verb
"shālām" signifies "to submit, resign oneself to," and then "to
make peace;" and consequently "to be safe, sound, and
tranquil." No religious system in the world has ever been
qualified with a better and more comprehensive, dignified,
and sublime name than that of "Islam." The true Religion
of the True God cannot be named after the name of any of
His servants, and much less after the name of a people or
country. It is, indeed, this sanctity and the inviolability of
the word "Islam" that strikes its enemies with awe, fear, and
reverence even when the Muslims are weak and unhappy.
It is the name and title of a religion that teaches and commands an absolute submission and resignation of will and self
to the Supreme Being, and then to obtain peace and tranquillity in mind and at home, no matter what tribulations or
passing misfortunes may threaten us that fills its opponents

with awe.[1]   It is the firm and unshaking belief in the Oneness
of Allah and the unswerving confidence in His mercy and
justice that makes a Muslim distinguishable and prominent
among non-Muslims.   And it is this sound faith in Allah and
the sincere attachment to His Holy Qur-án and the Apostle
that the Christian missionaries have been desperately attack-
ing and have hopelessly failed.   Hence, Jeremiah's words
that "the Prophet who prophesies, namely, who preaches and
speaks concerning the affairs of Islam as his religion, he will
at once be known to have been sent by the Lord in truth."
Let us, therefore, take into serious consideration the following points:—

1.   The Prophet Jeremiah is the only prophet before
Christ who uses the word Shālōm in the sense of a religion.
He is the only prophet who uses this word with the object
of setting or proving the veracity of a messenger of God.
According to the Qur-ánic revelation, Abraham, Ishmael,
Isaac, Jacob, Moses, and all the prophets were Muslims, and
professed Islam as their religion.. The term "Islām" and its
equivalents, "Shālōm" and Shlāmā," were known to the Jews
and Christians of Mecca and Medina when Muhammad appeared to perfect and universalize the religion of Islam.   A
prophet who predicts "peace" as an abstract, vague and
temporary condition cannot succeed in proving his identity
thereby.   In fact, the point of dispute, or rather the critical

---

1.   It is interesting and significant to note how the observations of the
learned professor coincide with those of the ex-Kaiser of Germany
who, on the occasion of his seventieth birthday celebrations at Doorn,
Holland, was reported to have said in his speech: "And understand
this — if ever the Muhammadans should conceive the idea that it is
Allah's command to bring order into a declining West and subjugate
to His will, then — with faith in God — they will come upon the
godless Europeans like a tidal wave, against which even the reddest
Bolshevist, full of eagerness for combat, will be helpless." (*Evening
Standard,* London, January 26, 1929.)

national question, controverted by the two eminent prophets
known to the court and the nation like Jeremiah and Hananiah (Jer. xxviii.), could not be solved and definitely settled
by the affirmation of the one and the denial of the other, of
the imminent catastrophy.   To predict "peace" by Jeremiah
when he had all the time been predicting the great national
disaster — either by the submission of the King Sidaqia to
the Chaldean sovereign or by his resistance — would not
only involve his failure, not to talk of his being a success in
proving his veracity, but also it would make him even ridiculous.   For, in either case, his presumed "peace" would
mean no peace at all.   On the contrary, if the Jews resisted
the Chaldean army, it meant a complete national ruin, and if
they submitted, an unconditional servitude.   It is evident,
therefore, that Jeremiah uses the term "Shǎlōm" in the sense
of a tangible, concrete, and real religious system which Islam
comprises.   To make it more clear, we should attentively
listen to the arguments of the two opponent prophets discussing and disputing the national question in the presence of
a wicked king and his court of vile flatterers and depraved
hypocrites.   Jeremiah has at heart the cause of God and His
religion of peace, and in the vital interests of the religion
of peace, or Islam, he advises the wicked king and his courtiers to submit to the yoke of Babylon and serve the Chaldeans
and *live*.   For there was no other alternative open to them.
They had abandoned the God of their forefathers, polluted
His temple, mocked and reviled His prophets, and committed
evil and treachery (2 Chron. xxxvi., etc.).   So God had
delivered them into the hands of Nebuchadnezzar, and would,
not save them.   For a true and sincere servant of God, the
religion comes first and the nation after.   It is the government and the nation — especially when they have forsaken
God — that are to be *sacrificed* for the cause of religion, and

not *vice versa!*   The other Prophet of Gibeon, called Hananiah, sought to please his master the king; he was a courtier and favourite, rich and in splendour, whereas his antagonist was always languishing and starving in the prisons and dungeons.   He cares not a fillip for the religion and the real welfare of the people.   He is also a prophet, for so says the Book of Jeremiah, yet he is a villain, and has exchanged God for a depraved king!   He prophesies in the name of the same God as does Jeremiah, and announces the return of the booty and the captives from Babylon in two years' time.

Now, from the above imperfect description of the prophets, which of the two would you qualify as the true servant of God and as the loyal defender of God's religion?   Surely Jeremiah would at once attract your sympathy and choice.

2.   It is only the religion of Shālōm, of Islam, that can testify to the character and the office of a true prophet, Imam, or any minister of God on earth.   God is one, and His religion is one.   There is no other religion in the world like Islam, which professes and defends this absolute unity of the Deity.   He who, therefore, sacrifices every other interest, honour and love for the cause of this Holy Religion, he is undoubtedly the genuine prophet and the minister of God. But there is still one thing more worthy of our notice, and that thing is this.   If the religion of Islam be not the standard and the measure by which to test the veracity of a prophet or minister of God, then there is no other criterion to answer that purpose.   A miracle is not always a sufficient proof, for the sorcerers also work wonders.   The fulfilment of a prophecy or prediction, too, is not in itself a sufficient proof; for just as one holy Spirit reveals a future event to a true prophet, so does sometimes an evil spirit the same to an imposter.   Hence it is clear that the prophet who "prophesies concerning Shālōm — Islam — as being the name of Faith

and path of life, as soon as he receives a message from God he will be known to have been sent by Him." Such was the argument which Jeremiah had recourse to and with which he wished to convince his audience of the falsity of Hananiah. But the wicked king and his entourage would not listen to and obey the word of God.

3. As argued in the preceding paragraph, it should be noted that neither the fulfilment of a prediction nor the working of a miracle was enough to prove the genuine character of a prophet; that the loyalty and strict attachment to the religion is the best and the decisive proof for the purpose; that "Shālōm" was used to express the religion of peace. Once again we repeat the same assertion that Shālōm is no other than Islam. And we demand from those who would object to this interpretation to produce an Arabic word besides Islam and Salām as the equivalent of the Shālōm, and also to find for us another word in Hebrew besides Shālōm that would convey and express the same meaning as Islam. It is impossible to produce another such an equivalent. Therefore we are forced to admit that Shālōm is the same as "salām" or "peace" in the abstract, and "Islām" as a religion and faith in the concrete.

4. As the Qur-an in chap. ii. expressly reminds us that Abraham and his sons and grandsons were the followers of Islam; that they were neither Jews nor Christians; that they preached and propagated the worship and the faith in the one God to all the peoples among whom they sojourned or dwelt, we must admit that not only the Jews, but several other nations that descended from the other sons of Abraham and many tribes converted and absorbed by them, were also Muslims; that is to say, believers in Allah and resigned to His will. There were the people of Esau, the Edomites, the Midianites, and numerous other peoples living in Arabia, who

knew God and worshipped Him like the Israelites. These peoples had also their own prophets and religious guides like Job, Jethro (the father-in-law of the Prophet Moses), Balaam, Hud, and many others. But they, like the Jews, had taken to idolatry until it was totally eradicated by the Prince of the prophets. The Jews, in about the fifth century B.C., produced the greater portion of their canonical books of the Old Testament, when the memories of the conquest of the land of Canaan by Joshua, the temple and Jerusalem of Solomon, were events buried in the past epochs of their wondrous history. A nationalistic and Judaistic spirit of solicitude and seclusion reigned among the small remnant of Israel; the belief in the coming of a great Saviour to restore the lost throne and crown of David was regnant, and the old meaning of "Shālōm" as the name of the religion of Abraham and common to all the different peoples descended from him was no longer remembered. It is from this point of view that I regard this passage of Jeremiah as one of the golden texts in the Hebrew sacred writ.

X

ISLAM IS THE KINGDOM OF GOD ON EARTH

In examination of that marvellous vision of the Prophet Daniel (Chap. vii.) we saw[1] how Muhammad was escorted by the myriads of celestial beings and conducted to the glorious presence of the Eternal; how he heard the words of honour and affection which no creature had ever been favour-

---

1. *Vide* Articles V and VI, which appeared in the *Islamic Review* for November and December, 1928.

ed with (2 Cor. xii.); how he was crowned to the dignity of the Sultan of the Prophets and invested with power to destroy the "Fourth Beast" and the "Blasphemous Horn." Further, we saw how he was authorized to establish and proclaim the Kingdom of God on earth; how all that human genius can possibly imagine of the highest honours accorded by the Almighty to a beloved Servant and to His most worthy Apostle could be ascribed to Muhammad alone. It should be remembered that among all the Prophets and Messengers of Allah, Muhammad alone figures like a tower above all; and the grand and noble work he accomplished stands a permanent monument of his honour and greatness. One cannot appreciate the value and importance of Islam as the unique bulwark against idolatry and polytheism unless the absolute unity of God is earnestly admitted. When we fully realize that Allah is the same God whom Adam and Abraham knew, and whom Moses and Jesus worshipped, then we have no difficulty in accepting Islam as the only true religion and Muhammad as the Prince of all the Prophets and Servants of God. We cannot magnify the greatness of Allah by conceiving Him now as a "Father," now as a "Son," and now as a "Holy Ghost," or to imagine Him as having three persons that can address each other with the three singular personal pronouns: I, thou, he. By so doing we lose all the true conception of the Absolute Being, and cease to believe in the true God. In the same way, we cannot add a single iota to the sanctity of the religion by the institution of some meaningless sacraments or mysteries; nor can we derive any spiritual food for our spirits from feeding upon the corpse of a prophet or an incarnate deity; for by so doing we lose all idea of a true and real religion and cease to believe in the religion altogether. Nor can we in the least promote the dignity of Muhammad if we were to imagine him a son of God or an

incarnate deity; for by so doing we would entirely lose the
real and the historical Prophet of Mecca and 'fall uncon-
sciously into the abyss of polytheism. The greatness of
Muhammad consists in his establishing such a sound, plain,
but true religion, and in the practical application of its precepts and principles with such precision and resolution that
it has never been possible for a true Muslim to accept any
other creed or faith than that which is professed in the formula: "I believe there is no god but Allah, and that Muhammad is the Apostle of Allah." And this short creed will
continue to be the faith of every true believer in Allah to
the day of the Resurrection.

The great destroyer of the "Eleventh Horn," that personified Constantine the Great and the Trinitarian Church,
was not a *Bar Allaha* ("Son of God"), but a *Bar Nasha*
("Son of Man") and none other than Muhammad al-Mus-
ṭapha who *actually* founded and established the Kingdom of
God upon earth. It is this Kingdom of God that we are now
to examine and expound. It would be remembered that it
was during the divine audience of the Sultan of the Prophets,
as given in Daniel, that it was promised that:—

"The kingdom and the dominion and the greatness
of the kingdom under all heaven shall be given to the
people of the Saints of the Most High; its (the people's)
kingdom (shall be) a kingdom for ever, and all dominions shall serve and obey it" (Dan. vii. 22 and 27).
The expressions in this prophetical passage that the Kingdom
of God shall consist of "the People of the Saints of the Most
High," and that all other dominions or powers shall serve
and obey that people, clearly indicate that in Islam the Religion and State are one and the same body, and consequently
inseparable. Islam is not only the Religion of God, but also
His earthly empire or kingdom. In order to be able to form

a clear and true idea concerning the nature and the constitution of the "Kingdom of God on earth" it is necessary to cast a glance upon the history of the religion of Islam before it was perfected, completed, and formally established by God Himself under His Apostle Muhammad.

1. ISLAM BEFORE MUHAMMAD WAS NOT THE KINGDOM OF GOD UPON EARTH, BUT ONLY GOD'S TRUE RELIGION

Those who believe that the true religion of Allah was revealed only to Abraham and preserved by the people of Israel alone, must be very ignorant students of the Old Testament literature, and must have a very erroneous notion of the nature of that religion. Abraham himself offered tithes to the King and Imam[1] of Jerusalem and was blessed by him' (Gen. xiv. 18). The father-in-law of Moses was also an Imam and a Prophet of Allah; Job, Balaam, Ad, Hud, Loqmân, and many other prophets were not Jews. The various tribes and nations like the Ishmaelites, Moabites, Ammonites, Edomites, and others which descended from the sons of Abraham and Lot, knew God the Almighty though they too, like the Israelites, fell into idolatry and ignorance. But the light of Islam was never entirely extinguished or substituted by idolatry. Idols or images, which were considered as "sacred" and as household gods by the Jews, as well as their kindred nationalities, and usually called "Traphim" (Gen. xxxi.) in the Hebrew, were, in my humble opinion of the same nature and character as the images and idols which the Orthodox and Catholic Christians keep and worship in

---

1. In Hebrew these old Imams are called "Kōhen," and rendered by Christians as "Priest." A Jewish priest can never be identified with a Christian Sacramentarian priest.

their houses and temples. In those olden times of ignorance the idols were of the kind of "identity card" or of the nature of a passport. Is it not remarkable to find that Rachel (Rahīl), the wife of Jacob and the daughter of Laban, should steal the "traphim" of her father? (Gen. xxxi.). Yet Laban as well as her husband were Muslims, and on the same day raised the stone "Mispha" and dedicated it to God!

The Jews in the wilderness, inebriate with the wonders and miracles worked day and night — their camp shadowed by a miraculous cloud at daytime and illuminated by a pillar of fire at night, themselves fed with the "manna" and "Salwai" — as soon as the Prophet Moses disappeared for a few days on the misty top of Mount Sinai, made a golden calf and worshipped it. The history of that stubborn people from the death of Joshua to the anointment of King Saul, covering a period of more than four centuries, is full of a series of scandalous relapses into idolatry. It was only after the close of the revelation and the Canon of their holy Scriptures in the third century before Christ that the Jews ceased to worship idols, and have since remained monotheists. But their belief in the Unity of God, though it makes them Unitarians, does not entitle them to the qualification of being called "Muslims," because they have stubbornly rejected both the persons and the revelations of Jesus and Muhammad. It is only through submission to the will of God that a man can attain peace and become Muslim, otherwise the faith without obedience and submission is similar to that of the devils who believe in the existence of Allah and tremble.

As we possess no records concerning the other peoples who were favoured with divine revelations and with the Prophets and Imam sent to them by God, we shall only content ourselves with the declaration that the religion of Islam existed among Israel and other Arab peoples of old, sometimes more luminous, but mostly like a flickering wick or like a dim spark glimmering in a dark room. It was a religion professed by a people who soon forgot it, or neglected it, or transformed it into pagan practices. But all the same there were always individuals and families who loved and worshipped God.

It seems that the Jews, especially the masses, had no true conception of God and of religion as the Muslims have had of Allah and Islam. Whenever the people of Israel prospered and was successful in its wars, then Jahwah was acknowledged and worshipped; but in adverse circumstances He was abandoned and the deity of a stronger and more prosperous nation was adopted and its idol or image worshipped. A careful study of the Hebrew Scripture will show that the ordinary Jew considered his God sometimes stronger or higher, and sometimes weaker, than those professed by other nations. Their very easy and reiterated relapse into idolatry is a proof that the Israelites had almost the same notion about their El or Yahwah, as the Assyrians had of their own Ashur, the Babylonians of Mardukh, and the Phœnicians of their Ba'āl. With the exception of the Prophets and the Sophīs, the Muslims of Torah, the Israel of the Mosaic Law, never rose equal to the height of the sanctity of their religion nor of the true conception of their Deity. The faith in Allah and a firm conviction and belief in a future life was not ingrained and implanted in the spirit and in the heart of that people.

What a contrast, then, between the Muslims of the Qur-án, the believers of the Muhammadan Law,[1] and the Muslims of Torah or the Mosaic Law! Has it ever been seen and proved that a Muslim people abandoned its Mosque, Imam,

1. The term "Muhammadan" is used here to distinguish it from the Mosaic Law, which both belong to Allah.

and the Qur-án, and embraced any other religion and acknowledged that Allah was not its God? Never! It is extremely unlikely that a Muhammadan Muslim community, so long as it is provided with the Book of Allah, the Mosque and the Mullah, could relapse into idolatry or even into Christianity.

I am aware of the certain so-called Tartar families who embraced the Orthodox Christian Faith in Russia. But I can assure my readers, on authentic authority, that these "Tartars" were those Mongols who, long after the subjugation of Russia and the establishment of the "Altin Ordu" by Batu Khan, were either still pagans or newly converted to Islam and seem to have been forced or induced to join the Russian Church. And in this connection it should not be ignored that this happened after the Muslim power of the "Golden Horde" ("Altin Ordu") tumbled down at the tremendous invasion of Timur Lang (Tamerlane). On the contrary, Muslim traders and merchants, in China as well as in the dark continent of Africa, have always propagated their holy religion; and the millions of Chinese and negro Muslims are the fruit of these unpaid and unofficial Mussulman missionaries. It is evident from the above that the true religion of God before Muhammad was only in its infancy, that it remained immature and undeveloped amongst the Hebrews, although it shone brilliantly in the life of the true servants of Yahwah. Under the direction of the God-fearing Judges and the pious Kings of Israel, the government was always theocratic, and as long as the oracles of the Prophets were favourably received and their injunctions duly executed, both the religion and the nation prospered.

But the true religion of God never took the form of the Kingdom of God as it did under the Qur-ánic régime. Allah in His infinite wisdom had decreed that four great Powers of

Darkness should succeed each other before His own Kingdom was to be established. The great ancient civilizations and empires of the Assyro-Chaldeans, of the Medo-Persians, of the Greeks and of the Romans, had to appear and flourish, to persecute and oppress the people of God, and to perpetrate all the evil and wickedness that the Devil could devise. All the glory of these great Powers consisted in their worshipping the Devil; and it was this "glory" that the "Prince of the Darkness" promised to grant to Jesus Christ from the top of a high mountain if he were only to follow him and worship him.

2. CHRIST AND HIS DISCIPLES PREACHED THE KINGDOM OF GOD

They were, it is true, the harbingers of the Kingdom of God upon earth. The soul and the kernel of the Gospel of Jesus is contained in that famous clause in his prayer: "Thy Kingdom come." *For twenty centuries the Christians of all denominations and shades of belief have been praying and repeating this invocation, "Thy Kingdom come," and God alone knows how long they will continue to pray for and vainly anticipate its coming.* This Christian anticipation of the coming of the Kingdom of God is of the same nature as the anticipation of Judaism for the coming of Messiah. Both these anticipation exhibit an inconsiderate and thoughtless imagination, and the wonder is that they persistently cling to this futile hope. If you ask a Christian priest or parson what he thinks of the Kingdom of God, he will tell you all sorts of illusory and meaningless things. This Kingdom is, he will affirm, the Church to which he belongs when it will overcome and absorb all the other heretical Churches. Another parson or priest will harangue on the "millennium."

A Salvationist or a Quaker may tell you that according to his belief the Kingdom of God will consist of the new-born and sinless Christians, washed and cleansed with the blood of the Lamb; and so forth.

The Kingdom of God does not mean a triumphant Catholic Church, or a regenerated and sinless Puritan State. It is not a visionary "Royalty of the Millennium." It is not a Kingdom composed of celestial beings, including the departed spirits of the Prophets and the blessed believers, under the reign of a divine Lamb; with angels for its police and gendarmes; the Cherubs for its governors and judges; the Seraphs for its officers and commanders; or the Archangels for its Popes, Patriarchs, Bishops, and evangelical preachers. The Kingdom of God on earth *is a Religion,* a powerful society of believers in One God equipped *with faith and sword* to fight for and maintain its existence and absolute independence against the Kingdom of Darkness, against all those who do not believe that God is One, or against those who believe that He has a son, a father or mother, associates and coevals.

The Greek word *euangelion,* rendered "Gospel" in English, practically means "the enunciation of good news." And this enunciation was the tidings of the approaching Kingdom of God, the *least* among whose citizens was *greater* than John the Baptist. He himself and the Apostles after him preached and announced this Kingdom to the Jews, inviting them to *believe* and *repent* in order to be admitted into it. Jesus did not actually abrogate or change the Law of Moses, but interpreted it in such a spiritual sense that he left it a dead letter. When he declared that hatred was the root of murder, lust the source of fornication; that avarice and hypocrisy were as abominable sins as idolatry; and that mercy and charity were more acceptable than the burnt-offerings and the strict observance of the Sabbath, he practically abolished the letter of the Law of Moses in favour of its spiritual sense. These spurious and much interpolated Gospels report frequent parables and references of Christ to the Kingdom of God, and to Bar-Nasha or the Son of Man, but they are so corrupted and distorted that they have succeeded, and still succeed, in misleading the poor Christians to believe that by "Kingdom of God" Jesus only meant his Church, and that he himself was the "Son of Man."

These important points will be fully discussed, if Allah will, later on; but for the present I have to content myself with remarking that what Jesus announced was, it was Islam that was the Kingdom of God and that it was Muhammad who was the Son of Man, who was appointed to destroy the Beast and to establish the powerful Kingdom of the People of the Saints of the Most High.

The religion of God, until Jesus Christ, was consigned chiefly to the people of Israel; it was more material and of a national character. Its lawyers, priests, and scribes had disfigured that religion with a gross and superstitious literature of the traditions of their forefathers. Christ condemned those traditions, denounced the Jews and their leaders as "hypocrites" and "the children of the Devil." Although the demon of idolatry had left Israel, yet later on seven demons had taken possession of that people (Matt. xii. 43-45; Luke xi. 24-26).

Christ reformed the old religion; gave a new life and spirit to it; he explained more explicitly the immortality of the human soul, the resurrection and the life in the next world; and publicly announced that the Messiah whom the Jews were expecting was not a Jew or a son of David, but a son of Ishmael whose name was Ahmad, and that he would establish the Kingdom of God upon earth with the power of the Word of God and with sword.   Consequently, the religion of Islam received a new life, light and spirit, and its adherents were exhorted to be humble, to show forbearance and patience.   They were beforehand informed of persecutions, tribulations, martyrdoms, and prisons.   The early "Nassara," as the Qur-án calls the believers in the Gospel of Jesus Christ, suffered ten fearful persecutions under the Roman Emperors.   Then comes the great Constantine and proclaims liberty for the Church; but after the decisions and the Trinitarian Creed of the Nicene Council in 325 A.C., the Unitarian Muslims[1] were submitted to a series of new and even more cruel persecutions by the Trinitarians, until the advent of Muhammad (upon whom be peace and blessings).

3.   THE NATURE AND CONSTITUTION OF THE KINGDOM OF GOD

There is a royal Islamic anthem sung aloud five times a day from the minarets and the mosques in every part of the globe where the Muslims live.   This anthem is followed by a most solemn worship to Allah by his faithful people. This royal Muslim hymn is called Ādhān (Āzān).   This is not all; every action, enterprise and business, however important or trifling it may be, is begun with the words *bismi 'l-Lah,* which means "in the name of Allah," and ends with an *Al-Hamdu li'l-Lāh,* meaning "praise be to Allah!"   The bond of faith which binds a Muslim to his Heavenly King is so strong, and the union between the Sovereign and His subject so close, that nothing, however powerful or seductive, can separate him from Allah.   The Qur-án declares that "We

1.   *Jesus Christ has never authorized his followers to call themselves "Christians."   There is no better title for the early Unitarians than "Muslims."* — A.D.

are nearer to God than the *ḥablu 'l-Warid"* (1. 16), which means "the life-vain."

Never was there a favourite courtier who, in his sentiments of affection, devotion, obedience, and respect for his beneficent monarch, could ever equal those which a Mussulman entertains towards his Lord. Allah is the King of the Heavens and Earth, He is the King of Kings and the Lord of Lords in general. He is the King and the Lord of every Muslim in particular, for it is a Muslim alone who thanks and praises his Almighty King for all that happens and befalls him, be it prosperity or adversity.

Nearly three hundred million Muslims are endowed — more or less — with the same feelings of faith and trust in Allah.

It is evident, therefore, that the nature of Islam consists in its being the only real and truly Theocratic Kingdom on earth. Allah need no longer send Messengers or Prophets to convey His oracles and messages to the Muslims as He used to do to Israel and other Hebrew peoples; for His will is fully revealed in the Holy Qur-án and imprinted on the minds of His faithful subjects.

As to the formation and the constitution of the Kingdom of God, *inter alia,* the following points should be noted:—

(*a*) All Muslims form one nation, one family, and one brotherhood. I need not detain my readers to study the various quotations from the Qur-án and the Hădīth (Tradition of the Prophet) on these points. We must judge the Muslim society, not as it presents itself *now,* but as it *was in the time* of Muhammad and his immediate successors. Every member of this community is an honest worker, a brave soldier, and a fervent believer and devotee. All honest fruit of the toil belongs by right to him who earns it; nevertheless the law makes it impossible for a true Muslim to become

excessively wealthy.   One of the five[1] obligatory pious practices of Islam is the duty of almsgiving, which consists of
sădăqa and *zăkăt,* or the voluntary and the obligatory alms.
In the days of the Prophet and the first four Khaliphs, no
Muslim was known to be enormously rich.   The national
wealth went into the common treasury called "Baitu 'l-Māl,"
and no Muslim was left in need or want.

The very name "Muslim" signifies *literally* "a maker of
peace."   You can never find another human being more
docile, hospitable, inoffensive and peaceful a citizen than a
good Muslim.   But the moment his religion, honour, and
property are attacked, the Muslim becomes a formidable foe.
The Qur-án is very precise on this point: "Wa lā ta'tadū" —
"And you must not transgress" (or take the offensive).   The
Holy Jihād is not a war of offence, but of self-defence.
Though the robbers, the predatory tribes, the semi-barbarous
nomad Muslims, may have some religious notions and believe
in the existence of Allah, it is the lack of knowledge and of
religious training which is the root-cause of their vice and
depravity.   They are an exception.   One can never become
a good Muslim without the religious training and education.

(*b*)   According to the description of the Prophet
Daniel, the citizens of the Kingdom of God are "the People
of the Saints."   In the original Chaldish or Aramaic text,
they are described as "A'mma d' qaddīshid' l'lionin," an
epithet worthy only of the Prince of the Prophets and of his
noble army of the Muhājirīn (Emigrants) and the Ansār
(Helpers), who uprooted idolatry from a great part of Asia
and Africa and destroyed the Roman Beast.

All the Muslims, who believe in Allah, in His angels,
Books, and Apostles; in the day of the Resurrection and

1.   The Jihād or "Holy War" is also an obligatory practice of piety.
So they are *not four,* but five.

Judgment; that the good and evil are from Allah; and perform their pious practices according to their ability and with
good will, are holy saints and blessed citizens of the Kingdom.   There is no grosser religious ignorance than the belief
that there is a person called the Holy Ghost who fills the
hearts of those who are baptized in the names of three gods,
each the third of the three, or the three of the third, and
thus sanctifies the believers in their absurdities.   A Muslim
believes that there is not one Holy Spirit, but innumerable
holy spirits all created and ministers of the One Allah.   The
Muslims are sanctified, not by baptisms or ablution, but their
spirits are purified and sanctified by the light of faith and by
the fire of zeal and courage to defend and fight for that faith.
John the Baptist, or rather Christ himself (according to the
Gospel of Barnabas), said: "I baptize you with water unto
repentance, but he who comes after me, he is stronger than I;
he will baptize you with fire and with the holy spirit."   It
was this fire and this spirit with which Muhammad baptized
the semi-barbarian nomads, the heathen Gentiles, and converted them into an army of heroic saints, who transformed
the old waning synagogue and the decaying church into a
permanent and strong Kingdom of Allah in the promised
lands and elsewhere.

4.   THE PERMANENCE AND THE DIGNITY OF THE
KINGDOM OF ALLAH

is doubly assured by an Angel to Daniel.   It is stated that
"all the nations under the heaven shall serve the People of
the Saints of the Most High."   It requires no proof to say
that all the Christian Powers show a particular respect, and
even deference when necessary, not only to Muslim Powers,
to Muslim sacred places and mosques, but also to the local

institutions of their Muslim subjects. The mystery of this "service" lies in this: in the first place, the Muslims always inspire respect and fear through their dignified behaviour, attachment to their religion and obedience to just laws, and their peacefulness; and secondly, because the Christian Governments, as a rule, treat the Muslims with justice and do not interfere with their laws and religion.

Space does not permit us to extend our observations over other points of this Divine Religion and Kingdom, such as the Muslim Khaliphas, Sultans, etc. Suffice it to say that the Muslim Sovereigns are subject to the same Qur-ánic laws as their compatriots; that justice and modesty are the best safeguards for the prosperity and stability of every State, Muslim or non-Muslim; and that the spirit and the principles of the Book of Allah are the best guidance for all legislation and civilization.

MUHAMMAD IN THE NEW TESTAMENT

I

ISLAM AND AHMADIYĀT ANNOUNCED
BY ANGELS

Two very extraordinary events have been recorded by two Evangelists in connection with the birth of Sayyidinā Jesus Christ (upon whom be peace and the blessings of Allah). The Evangelist Mattai (Matthew) has left to us an account of the wonderful pilgrimage of the Magi, who were guided by a star from Persia to the manger at Bethlehem, where the new-born Jesus, whom they "worshipped" and presented with rich gifts of gold, myrrh, and incense, was lying. The condensed material in this historical event or fictitious story of the "Wise Men" from the East is in itself a plausible legend consisting of more than half a dozen miracles, which the Christian Church alone has been able to create and to believe in. The Church has preserved the very names of the Magi, who, headed by the King Caspar, were "inspired by God," and knew that the little Babe of Bethlehem was God, Lamb, and King, and therefore they offered him incense as to a deity, myrrh for his burial as a sacrifice, and gold for his royal treasury! That the Zoroastrian magicians, or the astrologian Chaldees, through the astral divination and guidance, traversed all that distance to Jerusalem, and there lost the sight of the star; that the Jewish reigning sovereign Herod and the inhabitants of Jerusalem

shook and trembled at the news of the birth of a new king;
that only an incoherent passage in the writings of the Prophet
Micah (v. 2) could solve the problem of the locality where
the nativity had taken place; and finally that the astrologers
were informed by God in a dream not to return to Herod,
are indeed some wonderful miracles which only the Christian superstition can swallow.   The royal retinue of the pilgrims proceeds to Bethlehem only at a few miles' distance
from Jerusalem, and, lo! the old guiding star again appears
and leads them on until it stops exactly above the spot where
the infant was born.   The prodigious rapidity with which
the long journey from Persia to Bethlehem was completed
while the babe was still in the stable (Luke ii. 4-7) shows
the importance of the miracle.

Another miracle connected with the birth of Christ is
the fact, or the fiction, that after all those demonstrations at
the Court of Herod and in the educated classes at Jerusalem,
nobody knew the address of the Holy Family; and that this
mystifying ignorance cost the massacre by Herod of hundreds
of infants at Bethlehem and its suburbs.   The last but not the
least miracle insinuated in this narrative is the fulfilment of
another prophecy from Jeremiah (xxxi. 15), where Rachel is
represented as weeping and lamenting over the slaughter of
the Ephraimites at Ramah *and not at Bethlehem,* and this, too,
some seven hundred years ago, when the descendants of
Rachel were deported into Assyria while she herself was dead
long before Jacob her husband descended into Egypt!   St.
Matthew, who alone among all the ancient archivists and historians knows this event, does not tell us what the impressions
of King Caspar and his astrologers after their visit of pilgrimage to the manger of Bethlehem were.   Were they convinced that the son of Mary was a king, or were they not?
If they were persuaded that Jesus was a king, why then did

Persia persecute Christianity until it was converted to Islam in the seventh century? Is it not true that the Persians received no light and information about Jesus of Nazareth from their magicians, but only from the Muslim army sent by Hazrat Omar, the second caliph?

It is not my intention to deny altogether the truth of the visit of some Eastern Magi to the crypt of Jesus, but simply to show the avidity or the ambition of the Church to exaggerate simple events in the life of Jesus Christ and to exhibit in them some supernatural characteristics.

The other equally wonderful event which concerns our present discourse is recorded by the Evangelist Luke (ii. 1-20). Some shepherds were watching their flocks in a field near Bethlehem on the very night when Jesus was born in a manger. An angel announces the birth of the "Saviour Lord," and suddenly a host of angels appear in the sky and sing aloud the following hymn:

> Glory be to God in the Highest,
> And on earth peace,
> And among men good will. [Verse 14.]

This famous angelic anthem, known as *Gloria in excelsis Deo,* and sung in all the sacerdotalist churches during their celebration of the sacraments, is, unfortunately, only a vague translation from the Greek text, which cannot be considered at all reliable or truthworthy because it does not show us the original words in the language in which the angels chanted and which the Hebrew shepherds understood. That the heavenly hosts sang their joyous song in the language of the shepherds, and that that language was *not* Greek but the vernacular Hebrew — or rather the Aramaic — is an admitted truth. All the scriptural names of Allah, angels, heaven, prophets, etc., are revealed to us in the Semitic tongues (Hebrew, Aramaic, Arabic); and to imagine that the celestial hosts sang in Greek to the ignorant Jewish shepherds in the suburbs of Bethlehem would be equivalent to the belief that such an angelic army, in the firmament above the mountains of Kurdistan, sang a similar hymn in Japanese for the digestion, or puzzle, of some Kurdish herdsmen!

The appearance of an angel to the humble shepherds of Bethlehem and the annunciation of the birth of a great Prophet that very night, and the hearing of the angelic Hallelujah (Allilujah) by *them* alone and not by the haughty priests and the scribes, is one of the innumerable miracles recorded in the history of the people of Israel. There is nothing in the story which might be considered to be such a contradictory nature as to expose the narrative to incredibility. An angel can appear to a prophet or a holy servant of God and communicate to him a message from Allah in the presence of other people, yet be quite imperceptible to them. The good shepherds had good hearts and good faith, therefore they were worthy of the divine favour. So from a religious point of view there is nothing incompatible or incredible in this wonderful event as recorded by St. Luke. The author of this narrative exhibits precision of diction, he is discreet and cautious in his statements, and throughout his Gospel he uses a very good Greek style. Considering the fact that he wrote his book long after the death of all the Apostles, and that he had "very carefully" examined numerous works concerning Jesus and his Gospel, it seems very probable that he was aware of the legend of the Magi and abstained altogether from including it in his own book.[1] It is precisely stated in the first four verses with which the third Gospel opens that the Apostles, whom he calls "the

---

1. Readers are advised to very carefully read the preface, or the introductory passage, at the beginning of St. Luke's Gospel.

eyewitnesses and the ministers of the Word," had *not* written *themselves* any account about the Master and his teachings, but only by way of tradition had delivered them orally to their followers or successors. It is also clearly stated that the sources to which St. Luke had recourse for the composition of his Gospel were various "stories" composed by persons who had heard them narrated by the Apostles and others who were the eyewitnesses of those events and doctrines, and that the author very attentively examined them all and chose only such as he considered true or trustworthy. Moreover, it is quite evident from the confession of St. Luke himself, as it may be easily deducted from his preface, that he claims no direct revelation made to himself, nor does he attribute any inspiratory character to his book. It may, too, be safely assumed that the first and the fourth Gospels were either not written when Luke compiled his own narrative, or that he had not seen them; for he could not have ventured to counterpoise or contradict the Gospels written by the two Apostles, Matthew and John.

These brief observations, which can be multiplied, must convince every impartial reader that the so-called "Four Gospels" do not exhibit the necessary features which are indispensable for any Scripture claiming a divine inspiration.

The Churches have believed that the author of the third Gospel is the Physician Luke (Col. iv. 14) who accompanied St. Paul in his missionary journeys and was with him a prisoner at Rome (2 Tim. iv. 11; Philem. 24, etc.). However, this is not the place to discuss the question of the authorship of the book, nor its other important peculiarities. Suffice it to say that St. Luke has recorded some beautiful parables and teachings of the Holy Master, such as the parable of the Good Samaritan (x. 25-37); the Avaricious Rich Man (xii. 15-21); the Self-righteous Pharisee and the

Publican (xiii. 9-18); the Perseverance in Prayer (xi. 1-13); the Lost Sheep, the Lost Coin, and the Prodigal Son (xv.); the Dives and Lazarus (xvi. 19-31); the Mite of the Poor Widow (xxi); the Wicked Husbandman (xx. 9-16); the Unjust Judge (xviii. 1-8); the Conversion of Zacchaeus (xix. 1-10); and several others. But the most important among all the contents of the third Gospel is the angelic hymn, which forms the topic of our present study and contemplation.

This hymn, like all the contents of the New Testament, is presented to us *not* in the original language in which it was sung, but only in its Greek version; and God alone knows the source from which our Evangelist copied, translated, or simply narrated it from hearsay.

Is it possible that Jesus or his Apostles did not leave a real and authentic Gospel in the language in which it was revealed? If there were such a true Gospel, what became of it? Who lost it? Was it destroyed? And by whom and when? Was it ever translated into Greek or into another foreign language? Why has not the Church preserved to us the original text of the real Gospel, or its translation? If the answer to these questions is in the negative, then we venture to ask another series of questions of equal importance; namely, Why did these Jewish Apostles and Evangelists write *not* in their own language but all of them in the Greek language? Where did the fisherman Shimon Kipha (Simon Peter), Yohannan (John), Yá'qūb (James), and the publican Mattai (Matthew) learn the Greek language in order to write a series of "holy Scriptures"? If you say the "Holy Ghost taught them," you simply make yourselves ridiculous. The Holy Ghost is not a teacher of grammar and languages. It would require another Revelation to expound the reason or wisdom why the Holy Ghost should make a revelation in the Jewish language to an Israelite in Nazareth, then cause it to be destroyed, and finally teach half a dozen Jews the Greek tongue and inspire each one to write in his own style and way a portion of the same Revelation!

If it be argued that the Gospels and the Epistles were written for the benefit of the Jews of Dispersion, who knew the Greek language, we venture to inquire: What benefit at all did those Jews of the Dispersion derive from the New Testament; and why a copy of it should not have been made for the Jews of Palestine in their own language, considering the fact that Jerusalem was the centre of the new Faith, and James, the "brother of the Lord" (Gal. i. 19), was the President or Head of the Church and residing there (Acts xv.; Gal. ii. 11-15, etc.).

It would be a desperately hopeless effort to find a single parable, oracle, or any revealed message of Jesus Christ in his own language. The Synod of Nicea must be for ever held criminally responsible as the sole cause of this irreparable loss of the Sacred Gospel in its original Aramaic text.

The reason why I so pertinently insist on the indispensable necessity of the intact preservation of the revealed message of Allah is obvious; it is because only such a document can be considered as reliable and valid. A translation, no matter how faithfully and ably it may have been made, can never maintain the *exact* force and the *real* sense as contained in the original words and expressions. Every version is always liable to be disputed and criticized. These four Gospels, for instance, are not even a translation, but the very original text in the Greek language; and the worst of it is that they are badly corrupted by later interpolations.

Now, we have before us a sacred song, undoubtedly sung in a Semitic dialect, but as it is, presented to us in a Greek version. Naturally we are very curious to know its words in the original language in which it was sung. Here

I draw the serious attention of the reader to the exact equivalent Semitic term rendered into the Greek language *eudokia* and translated into English "good will." The hymn is composed of three clauses. The subject of the first clause is Allaha (in Aramaic), rendered "Theos" in Greek. The subject of the second clause is Shlama (in Aramaic), and translated "Eiriny" into Greek. And the subject of the third clause is eudokia in Greek, and rendered "Bona voluntas" by the Vulgate and "Sobhra Tabha" (pronounced sōvrā ṭāvā) by the Pshittha (al-Băsíṭ).

Both these versions, which have been followed by all other versions, have failed to convey the exact meaning and the sense of the word "eudokia," and consequently the second and the third clauses remain meaningless and even senseless, if not altogether untrue. Disappointed as we may be for not having the exact words of this heavenly anthem in their original forms, yet we need not despair in our endeavour to find out and discover the true sense contained in it.

We shall therefore proceed to find out the true etymological significations of the Greek words "Eiriny" and "Eudokia," and the real sense and interpretation of the Angelical Doxology.

The Christian interpretation of the terms "Eiriny" and "Eudokia" is wrong and utterly untenable.

According to the interpretation of this hymn by all the Christian Churches and sects, the faith in the divinity of Jesus Christ, in the redemption from sin and hell-fire through his death upon the Cross, and in holding a continual communication with the Holy Ghost, brings "peace" and tranquillity to the heart, and makes the believers entertain towards each other "good will," benevolence, and mutual love. This interpretation, thus far, is commonly accepted by the Sacramentarian and the Evangelical groups. But they do not stop at these three principal points, and very discreetly too; for thus far no general peace, no reconciliation, no concord and union, no good will and mutual love is felt among them. Then they part with each other and try other means to ascertain this "peace" and this "good will." The Sacramentarians insist on the belief in seven sacraments and many dogmas which neither common sense nor the simple doctrine of Jesus could tolerate. The Church, having been cleansed by the blood of the Redeemer through the mysteriously sanctified waters of Baptism, has become the Bride of the Lamb and his body; the Church, being herself the body of the Lamb, feeds upon his body in the mysteriously hallowed bread and wine, and transubstantiated into the real flesh and blood of the Bridegroom. The Bride — Church — has particular devotions to the "sacred hearts" of Jesus, of Mary, and of St. Joseph; to the fourteen stages or mansions of the Crucifixion; to the statues and images of hundreds and hundreds of saints and martyrs; to thousands of authentic or fictitious bones and relics of the same; and adoration to the consecrated wafer *exactly* as to God the Almighty! Still there is no peace; all sins, grave or otherwise, must be confessed to the priest; and it is the absolution that the sinner obtains from that "spiritual father" that produces peace and tranquillity in his heart, and fills it with good will!!!

If we turn to the evangelical group of diverse creeds and tenets, we shall find them endeavouring to procure an internal peace by praying directly to the three persons of the deity individually — now to Jesus, now to the Spirit, then to the Father — with closed eyes, but with oratorical gestures and movements; by reading the Bible, and by other practices private or in public; and then they believe that they are filled with the Holy Spirit and are at peace! But I assure the reader that all these "penitent" Christians, who through their real

or artificial devotions pretend to have obtained "peace," and
to have possessed "good will" towards their neighbours, instead of becoming docile, meek, and peaceful like their pretended Master, become extremely bigoted and intolerant.
Whether an orthodox or a heterodox, when a Christian comes
out from the church where he has "shared" the "Lord's Com-
munion" which they call the "Institution of the Eucharist,"[1]
they become so hypocritically fanatical and unsocial as to
prefer to meet a dog rather than a Muslim or a Jew, because
these do not believe in the Trinity and in the "Lord's Supper."
I *know* it. *I* used to be of the same sentiments when I was
a Catholic priest. The more I thought myself spiritual, holy,
and sinless, the more I hated the heretics, especially the non-
believers in the Trinity.

When the Christians, especially their priests and pastors,
become fervent and zealous in their peculiar devotions and
practices, they become exceedingly excited, furious, and
offensive towards their religious adversaries! Show me a
single Catholic, Schismatic, or a heretical Saint after the
Nicene Council, who was not a tyrant, either in his writings,
or preachings, or in his deeds against those whom he considered "heretics." The Roman Inquisition is an immortal
witness to the fulfilment of this Angelical hymn of "Peace
upon earth and good will among men"!

It is apparent that the *true peace* cannot be acquired by
artificial means. There are only three means that can procure the true and perfect peace; namely, a firm belief in the
absolute oneness of Allah; a complete submission and resignation to His Holy Will; and frequent meditation and

---

1. I forgot to mention above that St. Luke, according to the ancient
    Pshittha Version, does not contain verses 17-19 of chapter xxii; nor
    are these so-called "essential words" existing in the Liturgy of the
    Nestorians.

contemplation on Him. He who has recourse to these three means is a real and practical Muslim, and the peace that he acquires thereby is *true* and *unartificial*. He becomes tolerant, honest, just, and compassionate; but at the same time quite equipped to *fight* heart and soul in defence of all that appertains to the glory of Allah and to his own honour when threatened or attacked. It is obvious that the acquisition of this *perfect* peace is accomplished by an inward faith and an inflexible submission to the Creator, and *not* by outward ostentatious practices and rituals. These latter will benefit us *only* when the faith is genuine, and the submission voluntary and unconditional.

But surely the angels did not sing in honour of private or individual peace, which is, after all, limited to a comparatively small number of godly men; nor did they do so in praise of an imaginary universal peace, which would mean a total disarmament of nations and a cessation of wars and hostilities. No; neither of these two specific peaces was the object of this melody. The spiritual peace is a tranquillity of heart and conscience granted by Allah as a grace and blessing only to those few believers who have made great progress in piety and spiritual life, and love Him, above all, and sacrifice every other love for His.

It was neither a social nor political peace for the people of Israel; for the history of the last twenty centuries shows the very contrary. The angels could not, therefore, sing and announce a peace which could never be realized or accomplished. We are forced, then, in face of the subsequent historical facts on the one hand, and by the importance of the occasion, as well as the quarter from which this remarkable announcement was made, on the other, to conclude that this "peace upon earth" was none other than the approaching establishment of the Kingdom of Allah upon earth, which is *Islam*. The Greek word "Eiriny" stands for the Semitic "Shalom," "Shlama," and "Islam." That is all!

The very mention of "a multitude of heavenly hosts" gives the hymn a martial or triumphal character. It is indeed a singular indication of joy on the part of the armies belonging to the Kingdom of Heaven, in favour of their future allies belonging to the Kingdom of God on earth, of which the newly born Babe of Bethlehem was the greatest Evangelist and Herald.

On various occasions, in the course of these articles, we have explained that Shalom, in its concrete and practical sense, has the signification of the religion that is good, sound, safe, salutary, and the way of peace, in opposition to the religion that is evil, bad, harmful, destructive, and the way that conducts towards misery and perdition. It was in this sense that Allah, in His Message through the prophecy of Isaiah (xlv.) to Cyrus, used the word Shalom, as synonymous with good in opposition to evil. This is precisely the literal, etymological, moral, and practical interpretation of Islam as the true religion, the powerful Kingdom of Allah on earth, with its permanent and sound laws and directions inscribed in the Holy Qur-án.

Beyond Islam, which literally signifies "making peace," any other interpretation or imaginary peace is irrelevant with the sense in which "Eiriny" is used in this triumphal angelic anthem. It was in this Islamic sense of the word that Jesus Christ, in his grand sermon on the Mount, said: "Blessed are the Muslims (literally, "the peacemakers"); for they shall be called the Children of God"[1] (Matt. v. 9). And it was precisely the imaginary peace which Sayyidiná Jesus Christ repudiated when he exclaimed: "Think not that I came to

---

1. The expression "children of God" will be treated later on.

establish peace upon earth; I did not come to set peace but a sword" (Matt. x. 34-6); or, as Luke declares: "I came to set fire on the earth ... Do you think that I came to establish peace? I tell you, no; but divisions ... " (Luke xii. 49-53).

Unless "Eiriny" be understood in the sense of the Religion of Islam, these two crucial and contradictory statements of Jesus must remain a riddle, if not an irretrievable injury which the Christian Church has committed in having accepted these Gospels as the "inspired Word of God."

II

"EUDOKIA" MEANS "AHMADIYEH"

[LUKE ii. 14]

To retranslate a masterpiece of an eminent author from a foreign version if he left other writings in his own language would not be very difficult. For thus the translator could study the mind, the technicalities, and the expressions in his works, and do his best to retranslate the book into its original language. But how far he would be successful is a question which only able translators can decide and determine. Similarly, if there were at least a couple of epistles or writings of St. Luke in the Hebrew, his Gospel could with comparatively less difficulty be translated into that tongue than it can now be done. But unfortunately even such is not the case. For nothing is extant of the ancient writings in the language of Jesus from which St. Luke translated the angelic hymn; nor has he himself left us another book in a Semitic dialect.

To make myself better understood, and in order to make the English readers better appreciate the extreme importance of this point, I venture to challenge the best scholar in English and French literature to retranslate from a French edition the dramatic work of Shakespeare into English without seeing the original English text, and to show the grace and the elegance of the original as well.

The great Muslim philosopher Ibn Sīnā (Avicenna) wrote in the Arabic, and some of his works were afterwards retranslated from the Latin into the Arabic because the originals were lost. Are these reproductions the exact texts of that Muslim Aristotle? Certainly not!

In the previous article in this series,[1] on "Eiriny," we discussed this translational point to a certain extent; and we had no difficulty in finding its equivalent Hebrew word "Shalom," because both are identical in the Septuagint and Hebrew texts. But the Greek compound word "Eudokia" does not occur, to the best of my knowledge, in the Septuagint Version, and it is extremely difficult to find out its equivalent or synonymous term in the original. St. Barnabas does not mention in his Gospel this angelic hymn and the story of the Shepherds of Bethlehem; nor do the other Synoptics or the Epistles in the New Testament.

The modern Greeks frequently adopt "Eudokia" and "Eudoxia" for their feminine proper nouns; and both these nouns are composed of two elements; "eu" and "dokeo," from the later being derived "doxa" which means "glory" or "praise" and so on.

In order to discover the original Semitic word in the song that the pious Shepherds heard and related, and which the evangelist Luke has formulated into "Eudokia," we are compelled to examine and trace it right from its Greek root and derivation. But before doing so, it is necessary to criticize

1. Vide *Islamic Review* for November, 1929.

and expose the erroneous versions which have eclipsed the true meanings of Eudokia and concealed its prophetical bearing upon Aḥmad or Muhammad.

There are two principal versions of the New Testament from the Greek text, one being in the so-called "Syriac" language, and the other in the Latin.   Both bear the same significant title of "Simplex" or "Simple," which both the "Pshiṭtha" and the "Vulgate" signify.   There is much new material of information about these two famous ancient versions which must embarrass the most erudite Christian historians and the most dogmatic theologians.   But for the present it may suffice to say that the Aramaic[1] Version, called the Pshiṭtha, is older than the Latin Vulgate.   It is common knowledge that the Church of Rome for the first four centuries had no Scriptures or Liturgy in the Latin but in the Greek. Before the Nicene Council in 325 A.C., the Canon of the books of the New Testament was not completed, or rather established.   There were dozens of Gospels and Epistles bearing the names of different Apostles and other companions of Jesus, which were held by various Christian communities as sacred, but they were rejected by the Nicene Council as spurious.

As the seat or centre of the Syriac language and learning was Orhai, i.e. Edessa, and *never* Antioch, it was here that the books of the New Testament were translated from the Greek, after the notorious Assembly of Nicea.

A profound examination and study of the early Christian literature and history will show that the first preachers of the Gospel were Jews who spoke Aramaic or the old Syriac language.   Whether this "Gospel" was a written document, or an unwritten doctrine or religion taught and propagated

1.   The Pshiṭtha Version of the Old Testament never uses the words "Syria" and "Syriac," but "Aram" and "Aramaic."

orally, is a question for itself and lies outside the sphere of our present subject. But one thing is certain and does really fall within the periphery of our subject — namely, the early Christians conducted their religious services in the Aramaic language. That was the common language spoken by the Jews, the Syrians, the Phœnicians, the Chaldeans, and the Assyrians. Now it is but clear that the Christians belonging to the Aramaic-speaking nationalities would certainly prefer to read and pray in their own language, and consequently various Gospels, Epistles, prayer-books, and liturgies were written in the Syriac. Even the Armenians, before the invention of their alphabet in the fifth century, had adopted the Syriac characters.

On the other hand, the proselytes from the non-Semitic "Gentiles" to the "new way" read the Old Testament in its Greek Version of the "Seventy." As a matter of course, the scholars of the Greek philosophy and the ex-ministers of the Greek mythology, once converted to the new faith and with the Septuagint before them, could have no difficulty in the production of a "New Testament" as a completion or a continuation of the old one.

How the simple Gospel of the Nazarene Messenger of Allah became a source of two mighty currents of the Semitic and the Hellenic thought; and how the Greek polytheistic thought finally overpowered the monotheistic Semitic creed under the most tyrannical Greco-Latin Emperors, and under the most intolerant and superstitious Trinitarian Bishops of Byzantium and Rome, are points of extreme moment for a profound study by the Muslim Unitarian savants.

Then there are the questions of the unity of faith, of doctrine, and of the revealed text. For more than three centuries the Christian Church had no New Testament as we see it in its present shape. None of the Semitic or Greek

Churches, nor did Antioch, Edessa, Byzantium, and Rome possess all the books of the New Testament, nor even the four Gospels before the Nicene Council. And I wonder what was or could be the belief of those Christians who were only in possession of the Gospel of St. Luke, or of St. Mark, or of St. John, concerning the dogmas of the Eucharist, Baptism, the Trinity, the miraculous conception of Christ, and of dozens of other dogmas and doctrines! The Syriac Version of the Pshiṭṭha does not contain the so-called "Essential" or "Institutional Words," now extant in St. Luke (xxii. 17, 18, 19). The last twelve verses of the sixteenth chapter of the Second Gospel are not to be found in the old Greek manuscripts. The so-called "Lord's prayer" (Matt. vi. 9; Luke xi. 2) is unknown to the authors of the Second and Fourth Gospels. In fact, many important teachings contained in one Gospel were unknown to the Churches which did not possess it. Consequently there could possibly be no uniformity of worship, discipline, authority, belief, commandments, and law in the Early Church, just as there is none now. All that we can gather from the literature of the New Testament is that the Christians in the Apostolical age had the Jewish Scriptures for their Bible, with a Gospel containing the true revelation made to Jesus, and that its substance was precisely the same as announced in this Seraphic Canticle — namely, ISLAM and AHMADIYEH. The special mission assigned by Allah to His Apostle Jesus was to revert or convert the Jews from their perversion and erroneous belief in a Davidic Messiah, and to convince them that the Kingdom of God upon earth which they were anticipating was not to come through a Messiah of the Davidic dynasty, but of the family of Ishmael whose name was AHMAD, the true equivalent of which name the Greek Gospels have preserved in the forms "Eudoxos" and "Periclytos" and *not* "*Paraclete*" as the Churches have shaped it. It goes without saying that the "Periclyte" will form one of the principal topics in this series of articles. But whatever be the signification of the "Paraclete" (John xiv. 16, 26; xv. 26, and xvi. 7) or its true etymological orthography, there still remains the shining truth that Jesus left behind him and unfinished religion to be completed and perfected by what John (*ubi supra*) and Luke (xxiv. 49) describe as *"Spirit."* This "Spirit" is not a god, a third of the three in a trinity of gods, but the holy Spirit of Aḥmad, which existed like the Spirits of other Prophets in Paradise (cf. the Gospel of Barnabas). If the Spirit of Jesus, on the testimony of an Apostle, John (xvii. 5, etc.), existed before he became a man, the Muslim Unitarians, too, are perfectly justified in believing in the existence of the Spirit of Muhammad on the testimony of another Apostle, Barnabas! And why not? As this point will be discussed in the course of the succeeding articles, for the present all I want to ask *all* the Christian Churches is this: Did all the Christian Churches in Asia, Africa, and Europe possess the Fourth Gospel before the Nicene Council? If the answer be in the affirmative, pray, bring your proofs; if it be in the negative, then it must be admitted that a large portion of the Christians knew nothing about St. John's "Paraclete," a barbarous word which does not mean either a "comforter" or "mediator" or anything at all! These are certainly very serious and grave charges against Christianity.

But to turn to the point. The Pshiṭtha had translated the Greek word "Eudokia" (the Greeks read the word "Ivdokia," or rather pronounce it "Ivthokia") as "Sobhra Tabha" (pronounced "Sovra Tava"), which signifies "good hope," or "good anticipation;" whereas the Latin Vulgate, on the other hand, renders "Eudokia" as "Bona Voluntas," or "good will."

I fearlessly challenge all the Greek scholars, if they dare, to contradict me when I declare that the translators of the Syriac and Latin Versions have made a serious error in their interpretation of "Eudokia." Nevertheless, I must confess that I cannot conscientiously blame those translators of having deliberately distorted the meaning of this Greek term; for I admit that both the Versions have a slight foundation to justify their respective translations. But even so, it must be remarked that they have thereby missed the prophetical sense and the true meaning of the Semitic vocabulary when they converted it into the Greek word "Eudokia."

The exact and literal equivalent of "good hope" in the Greek language is not "eudokia," but "eu elpis, or rather "euelpistia." This exposition of "evelpistia" (the proper Greek pronunciation) is enough to silence the Pshiṭtha. The precise and the exact corresponding term to the Latin "bona voluntas," or "good will," in the Greek tongue is *certainly not* "eudokia," but "euthelyma." And this short but decisive explanation again is a sufficient reprimand to the priests of the Vatican, of Phanar (Constantinople), and of Canterbury, who chant the "Gloria in Excelsis" when they celebrate Mass or administer other sacraments.

1. THE ETYMOLOGY AND SIGNIFICATION OF "EUDOKIA"

Now let us proceed to give the true meaning of "Eudokia."

The adjectival prefix "eu" signifies "good, well, more, and most," as in "eudokimeo" — "to be esteemed, approved, loved," and "to acquire glory"; "eudokimos" — "very esteemed, most renowned and glorious"; "eudoxos" — "most celebrated and glorious"; "eudoxia" — "celebrity, renown." The Greek substantive "doxa," used in the compound nouns "orthodox," "doxology," and so on, is derived from the verb "dokeo." Every student of English literature knows that "doxa" signifies "glory, honour, renown." There are numerous phrases in the classical Greek authors where "doxa" is used to signify "glory": "Peri doxis makheshai" — "to fight for glory." The famous Athenian orator Demosthenes "preferred glory to a tranquil life," "glory equal to that of the gods." I am cognizant of the fact that "doxa" is, although seldom, used to signify (a) opinion, belief; (b) dogma, principle, doctrine; and (c) anticipation or hope. But all the same, its general and comprehensive sense is "glory." In fact, the first portion of the Canticle begins with: "Doxa [Glory] be to Allah in the highest."

In the *Dictionnaire Grec-Français* (published in 1846 in Paris by R. C. Alexandre) the word "eudokia" is rendered "bienveillence, tendresse, volunté, bon plaisir," etc.; and the author gives "dokeo" as the root of "doxa," with its various significations I have mentioned above.

The Greeks of Constantinople, among whose teachers I have had several acquaintances, while unanimously understanding by "eudokia" the meaning of "delight, loveliness, pleasantness, and desire," also admit that it does signify "celebrity, renown, and honourability" in its original sense as well.

2. THE ETYMOLOGY OF THE HEBREW FORMS OF MaHMaD AND HiMDaH, AND THEIR SIGNIFICATIONS

I am convinced that the only way to understand the sense and the spirit of the Bible is to study it from an Islamic point of view. It is only *then* that the real nature of the

Divine Revelation can be understood, appreciated, and loved. It is only then, too, that the spurious, the false, and the heterogeneous elements interpolated in it can be discovered in their blackest features and eliminated. And it is from this point of view that I welcome this Greek word "eudokia," which in its true and literal signification admirably corresponds to the Hebrew "Mahmad, Mahamod, Himdah," and "Hemed" so frequently used in the Old Testament.

(a) *Hamad.* This verb, which is constituted of three essential consonants *hmd,* and common to all the Semitic dialects, *everywhere* in the Sacred Writ of the Hebrews signifies: "to covet, fall in love, long for, take pleasure and delight in," and "to desire ardently." Those who know Arabic will naturally understand the comprehensive sense of the word *Shahwat,* which is rendered in English as "lust, cupidity, ardent desire, and appetite." Well, this is the precise sense and signification of the verb "ḥamad" in the Hebrew Scriptures. One of the commands in the famous Decalogue of the Torah (Arabic "Taurāt") or the Law contains this clause: "Lo taḥmōd ish rëikha" — "Thou shalt not *covet* the wife of thy neighbour" (Exod. xx. 17.)

(b) *Hemed.*[1] The substantive in the masculine gender, and "Himdah" in the feminine, signifies: "lust, desire, pleasantness, delight, object of longing and of desire, loveliness" (Hag. ii. 7; Jerem. xxv. 34, etc.).

(c) MaHMaD, MaHaMoD (Lam. i. 7, 10; ii. 4, etc.). These participles forms are also derivatives from the verb "ḥamad" and mean: "most covetable, delightful, pleasant, delicious, charming, precious, beloved."

That the Arabic form MuHaMmaD and the Hebrew MaHMaD and MaHaMoD are derived from one and the

---

1. An article on "Himdah," by the learned Professor, was published in the *Islamic Review* for October, 1927.

same verb or root, and that they, notwithstanding the slight orthographic difference between the forms, have one common origin and signification, there cannot be a jot or iota of doubt. I have given the meanings of the Hebrew forms as the Jews and the lexicographers have understood them.

(d) It will therefore be observed that the Greek word "eudokia" must be a literal representation of the Hebrew substantive HiMDah, and that both signify: "delight, pleasantness, good pleasure (*bon plaisir*), desire, loveliness, preciousness," and some other synonymous words.

Now it would follow from the above that the corresponding equivalent to the Hebrew "Maḥamod" can be none other than "eudoxos" which was the object of desire and longing, the most delightful, pleasant, and coveted, and the most precious, approved, loved, and esteemed.

3

That among all the sons of Adam the name Muḥammad should be given for the first time alone to the son of 'Abdullah and Āmina in the town of Mecca, is a unique miracle in the history of religions. There could be no artificial device, attempt, or forgery in this respect. His parents and relatives were pagans and knew nothing of the prohecies in the Hebrew or Christian Scriptures concerning a great Prophet who was promised to come to restore and establish the religion of Islam. Their choice of the name Muhammad or Aḥmad could not be explained away as a coincidence or an accidental event. It was surely providential and inspired.

Whether the Arabian poets and men of letters had preserved the archaic signification of the Hebrew passive participle of the *pi'el* form of the verb *ḥamad,* or not, I have no means to prove one way or another. But the Arabic passive participle of the *pi'el* conjugation of the verb *hammida* is Muhammad, and that of the Hebrew *himmid* Mahmad or Mahamod.   The affinity between the similarity and the identity of the two forms is unquestionable.

I have faithfully reproduced the significations of the Hebrew forms as given by the lexicographers and translators. But the intrinsical or spiritual sense of "Himdah" and "Mahamod" is: "praise and praiseworthy, celebrity and celebrated, glory and glorious."   For among the created beings and things, what can be "more glorious, honourable, illustrious, and praised than that which is most coveted and desired."   It is in this practical sense that the Qur-án uses the word *hamdu* from which Ahmad and Muhammad are derivations, and *hamdu* is the same word as the Hebrew *hemed*.   The glory of Muhammad surpasses that of any other creatures, as illustrated by Daniel (vii.), and in the oracle of Allah: "Law lā ka lamā Khalaqna 'l-Aflāka" — "Were it not for thee, were is not for thee (O beloved Muhammad), We would not have created the worlds" (or heavens).   But the highest honour and glory granted by Allah to His most esteemed Apostle was that he was commissioned to establish and to perfect the true religion of Allah, under the name of "Islam," which, like the name of its founder Muhammad, has so very many consolating and salubrious significations; "peace, security, safety, transquillity, salvation," and "the Good" in opposition to "the Evil"; besides those of submission and resignation to the will of Allah.

4

The vision by which the pious Shepherds were honoured on the occasion of the birth of Jesus Christ was timely and opportune.   For a great Missioner of Allah, a holy Evangelist

of Islam was born on that night.   As Jesus was the Herald
of the Kingdom of Allah, so was his Gospel an Introduction
to the Qur-án.   The advent of Jesus was the beginning of a
new era in the history of religion and morals.   He himself
was not the "Maḥamod" who was to come afterwards to
destroy the Evil One and his Kingdom of Idolatry in the
Promised Lands.   The "Fourth Beast," the mighty Roman
Power, was still growing and expanding its conquests.   Jerusalem, with its gorgeous temple and priesthood, was to be
destroyed by that Beast.   Jesus "came to his own people;
but that people received him not."   And those among the
Jews who received him were made "children of the Kingdom," but the rest dispersed in the world.   Then followed
the ten terrible persecutions under the pagan Roman
Emperors which were to crown thousands with the diadem
of martyrdom; and Constantine the Great and his successors
were allowed to trample upon the true believers in the unity
of Allah.   And then it was that Muhammad — not a god or
son of a god, but "the glorious, the coveted, the most illustrious Son of Man, the perfect Barnasha" — was to come and
destroy the Beast.

III

JOHN THE BAPTIST ANNOUNCES A
POWERFUL PROPHET

John the Baptist, according to the narratives of the four
Evangelists, was a cousin and contemporary of Jesus, being
only about six months older than the latter.   The Qur-án
does not mention anything about the life and work of this
Prophet except that God, through the angels, announced to

his father Zachariah that he would have a son name Yaḥyā, who would bear witness to the word of Allah, and that he would be an honourable person, chaste, and one of the righteous prophets (Qur-án, iii. —). Nothing is known about his infancy, except that he was a Nazarite living in the wilderness, eating locusts and wild honey, covering his body with a cloth made of camel's hair, tied with a leather girdle. He is believed to have belonged to a Jewish religious sect called the "Essenes," from whom issued the early Christian "Ibionites" whose principal characteristic was to abstain from worldly pleasures. In fact, the Qur-ánic descriptive term of this hermit Prophet — "ḥaṣūra," which means "chaste" in every sense of the word — shows that he led a celibate life of chastity, poverty, and piety. He was not seen from his early youth until he was a man of thirty or more, when he began his mission of preaching repentance and baptizing the penitent sinners with water. Great multitudes were drawn to the wilderness of Judea to hear the fiery sermons of the new Prophet; and the penitent Jews were baptized by him in the water of the River Jordan. He reprimanded the educated but fanatical Pharisees and the Priests, and threatened the learned but rationalistic Saduqees (Saducees) with the coming vengeance. He declared that he was baptizing them with water only as a sign of purification of the heart by penance. He promulgated that there was coming after him another Prophet who would baptized them with the Holy Spirit and fire; who would gather together his wheat into his granaries and burn the chaff with an inextinguishable fire. He further declared that he who was coming afterwards was to such an extent superior to himself in power and dignity that the Baptist confessed to be unfit or unworthy to bow down to untie and loose the laces of his shoes.

It was on one of these great baptismal performances of

Hazrat Yahyā (St. John the Baptist) that Jesus of Nazareth also entered into the water of the Jordan and was baptized by the Prophet like everybody else.   Mark (i. 9) and Luke (iii. 21), who report this baptism of Jesus by John, are unaware of the remarks of John on this point as mentioned in Matthew (iii), where it is stated that the Baptist said to Jesus: "I need to be baptized by thee, and didst thou come to me?"   To which the latter is reported to have replied: "Let us fulfil the righteousness"; and then he baptized him.   The Synoptics state that the spirit of prophecy came down to Jesus in the shape of a dove as he went out from the water, and a voice was heard saying: "This is my beloved son, in whom I am well pleased."

The Fourth Gospel knows nothing about Jesus being baptized by John; but tells us that the Baptist, when he saw Jesus, exclaimed: "Behold the Lamb of God," etc. (John i). This Gospel pretends that Andrew was a disciple of the Baptist, and having abandoned his master brought his brother Simon to Jesus (John i) — a story flagrantly contradicting the statements of the other Evangelists (Matt. iv. 18-19, Mark i. 16-18).   In St. Luke the story is altogether different: here Jesus knows Simon Peter before he is made a disciple (Luke iv. 38, 39); and the circumstance which led the Master to enlist the sons of Jonah and of Zebedee in the list of his disciples is totally strange to the other Evangelists (Luke vi 1-11).   The four Gospels of the Trinitarian Churches contain many contradictory statements about the intercourse between the two cousin prophets.   In the Fourth Gospel we read that the Baptist did not know who Jesus was until after his baptism, when a Spirit like a pigeon came down and dwelt in him (John i); whereas St. Luke tells us that the Baptist, while a foetus in the womb of his mother, knew and worshipped Jesus, who was also a younger foetus in the womb of Mary (Luke i. 44). Then, again, we are told that the Baptist while in prison, where he was beheaded (Matt. xi. xiv), did not know the real nature of the mission of Jesus!

There is a mysterious indication hidden in the questions put to the Prophet Yaḥyā by the Priests and the Levites. They ask the Baptist: "Art thou Messiah? art thou Elijah?" And when he answers "No!" they say: "If thou art neither the Messiah, nor Elijah, and nor *that Prophet,* why then dost thou baptize?" (John i). It will therefore be noticed that, according to the Fourth Gospel, John the Baptist was neither the Messiah nor Elijah, nor *that Prophet*! And I venture to ask the Christian Churches, who believe that the inspirer of all these contradictory statements is the Holy Ghost — i.e. the third of the three gods — *whom* did those Jewish Priests and the levites mean by *"and that Prophet"*? And if you pretend not to know whom the Hebrew clergy meant, do your popes and patriarchs know who *"and that Prophet" is?* If not, than what is the earthly use of these spurious and interpolated Gospels? If, on the contrary, you *do* know who *that Prophet* is, then why do you keep silent?

In the above quotation (John i) it is expressly stated that the Baptist said he *was not* a Prophet; whereas Jesus is reported to have said that "no men born of women were ever greater than John" (Matt. xi). Did Jesus really make such a declaration? Was John the Baptist greater than Abraham, Moses, David, and Jesus himself? And in what did his superiority and greatness consist? If this testimony of Jesus about the son of Zachariah be authentic and true, then the greatness of the "Eater of the Locusts in the wilderness" can only consist in his absolute abnegation, self-denial, and refraining from the world with all its luxuries and pleasures; his ardent wish to invite the people to penance; and his good tidings about *"that Prophet."*

Or did his greatness consist — as the Churches will have it — in being a cousin, contemporary and witness of Jesus? The value and greatness of a man, as well as of a Prophet, can be determined and appreciated by his work. We are absolutely ignorant of the number of persons converted through the sermons and purified by the baptism of John. Nor are we informed with regard to the effect of that conversion upon the attitude of the penitent Jews towards the "Lamb of God!"

Christ is said to have declared that John the Baptist was the reincarnation of the Prophet Elijah (Matt. xi. 14, xvii. 12; Luke i. 17), whereas John expressly told the Jewish deputation that he was *not* Elijah, nor Christ, nor that Prophet (John i).

Now can one, from these Gospels full of statements opposing and denying each other, form a correct conclusion? Or can one try to find out the truth? The charge is exceedingly grave and serious, because the persons concerned are not ordinary mortals like ourselves, but two Prophets who were both created in the womb by the Spirit and born miraculously — one had no father, while the parents of the other were sterile and an impotent nonagenarian couple. The gravity of the charge is even more serious when we come to consider the nature of the documents in which these contradictory statements are written. The narrators are the Evangelists, persons alleged to be inspired by the Holy Spirit, and the record believed to be a revelation! Yet there is a lie, a false statement, or a forgery somewhere. Elijah (or Elias) is said to come before *"that Prophet"* (Mal. iv. 5, 6); Jesus says, "John is Elijah"; John says, "I am *not Elijah*", and it is the sacred Scripture of the Christians which makes both these affirmative and negative statements!

It is absolutely impossible to get at the truth, the true religion, from these Gospels, unless they are read and examined from an Islamic and Unitarian point of view. It is only *then* that the truth can be extracted from the false, and the authentic distinguished from the spurious. It is the spirit and the faith of Islam that can alone sift the Bible and cast away the chaff and error from its pages. Before proceeding farther to show that the Prophet foretold by the Baptist could be none other than Muhammad, I must draw the serious attention of my readers to one or two other important points.

It may, in the first place, be remarked that the Muslims have the highest reverence and veneration for all the Prophets, particularly for those whose names are mentioned in the Qur-án, like John ("Yaḥyā") and Jesus (" 'Isa"); and believe that the Apostles or Disciples of Jesus were holy men and inspired by Allah. But as we do not possess their genuine and unadulterated writings we consequently cannot for a moment imagine the possibility that either of these two great Servants of Allah could have contradicted each other.

Another important matter to be noted is the very significant silence of the Gospel of Barnabas about John the Baptist. This Gospel, which never mentions the name of Yaḥyā, puts his prophecy about the "more powerful Prophet" into the mouth of Jesus Christ. Therein Christ, while speaking of the Spirit of Muhammad as having been created before that of other Prophets, says that it was so glorious that when he comes Jesus would consider himself unworthy to kneel and undo the laces of his shoes.

The great "Crier" in the wilderness, in the course of his sermons to the multitudes, used to cry aloud and say: "I baptize you with water unto repentence and the forgiveness of sins. But there is one that comes after me who is stronger than I, the laces of whose shoes I am not worthy to untie; he will baptize you with the Spirit and with fire." These words are differently reported by the Evangelists, but all show the same sense of the highest respect and consideration in regard to the imposing personality and the majestic dignity of the Powerful Prophet herein foretold. These words of the Baptist are very descriptive of the Oriental manner of hospitality and honour accorded to a dignified visitor. The moment the visitor steps in, either the host or one of the members of the family rushes to take off his shoes, and escorts him to a couch or cushion. When the guest leaves the same respectful performance is repeated; he is helped to put on his shoes, the host on his knees tying the laces.

What John the Baptist means to say is that if he were to meet that dignified Prophet he would certainly consider himself unworthy of the honour of bowing to untie the laces of his shoes. From this homage paid beforehand by the Baptist one thing is certain: that the foretold Prophet was known to all the Prophets as their Adon, Lord, and Sultan; otherwise such an honourable person, chaste and sinless Messenger of Allah as Seyidna Yaḥyā, would not have made such a humble confession.

Now remains the task of determining the identity of *"that Prophet."* This article, therefore, must be divided into two parts, namely:

A.   The foretold Prophet was not Jesus Christ; and

B.   The foretold Prophet was Muhammad.

Everybody knows that the Christian Churches have always regarded John the Baptist as a subordinate of Jesus, and his herald. All the Christian commentors show Jesus as the object of John's witness and prophecy.

Although the language of the Evangelists has been distorted by interpolators to that direction, yet the fraud or error cannot for ever escape the searching eye of a critic and an impartial examiner. Jesus could not be the object of John's witness because:

(1)   The very preposition "after" clearly excludes Jesus from being the foretold Prophet. They were both contemporaries and born in one and the same year. "He that is coming after me" says John, "is stronger than I." This "after" indicates the future to be at some indefinite distance; and in the prophetical language it expresses one or more cycles of time. It is well known to the Sufees and those who lead a spiritual life and one of contemplation that at every cycle, which is considered to be equivalent of five or six centuries, there appears one great Luminary Soul surrounded by several satellites who appear in different parts of the world, and introduce great religious and social movements which last for several generations until another shining Prophet, accompanied by many disciples and companions, appears with prodigious reforms and enlightenment. The history of the true religion, from Abraham to Muhammad, is thus decorated with such epochmaking events under Abraham, Moses, David, Zorobabel, Jesus, and Muhammad. Each of these epochs is marked with special characteristic features. Each one makes a progress and then begins to fade away and decay until another luminary appears on the scene, and so on down to the advent of John, Jesus, and the satellite Apostles.

John found his nation already toiling under the iron yoke of Rome, with its wicked Herods and their pagan legions. He beheld the ignorant Jewish people misled by a corrupt and arrogant clergy, the Scriptures corrupted and replaced by a superstitious ancestral literature. He found that that people had lost all hope of salvation, except that Abraham, who was their father, would save them. He told them that Abraham did not want them for his children because they were unworthy of such father, but that "Allah could raise children for Abraham from the stones" (Matt. iii). Then they had a faint hope in a Messiah, a descendant from the family of David, whom they expected then, as they do to-day, to come and restore the kingdom of that monarch in Jerusalem.

Now when the Jewish deputation from Jerusalem asked, "Art thou the Messiah?" he indignantly replied in the negative to this as well as to their subsequent questions. God alone knows what rebukes and reprimands they did hear from those fiery utterings of the Holy Prophet of the Wilderness which the Church or the Synagogue have been careful not to let appear in writing.

Leaving aside the exaggerations, which have been evidently added to the Gospels, we fully believe that the Baptist introduced Jesus as the true Messiah, and advised the multitudes to obey him and follow his injunctions and his gospel. But he clearly told his people that there was another, and the last, great Luminary, who was so glorious and dignified in the presence of Allah that he (John) was not fit to undo the laces of his shoes.

(2) It was not Jesus Christ who could be intended by John, because if such were the case he would have followed Jesus and submitted to him like a disciple and a subordinate. But such was not the case. On the contrary, we find him preaching, baptizing, receiving initiates and disciples, chastizing King Herod, scolding the Jewish hierarchy, and foretelling the coming of another Prophet "more powerful" than himself, without taking the least notice of the presence of his cousin in Judea or Galilee.

(3) Although the Christian Churches have made of Jesus Christ a god or son of a god, the fact that he was circumcised like every Israelite, and baptized by St. John like an ordinary Jew, proves the case to be just the reverse. The words interchanged between the Baptist and the baptized in the River Jordan appear to be an interpolation or a commonalty, for they are contradictory and of a deceptive character. If Jesus were in reality the person whom the Baptist foretold as "more powerful" than himself, so much so that he was "not worthy to kneel and unloose his shoes," and that "he would baptize with the Spirit and fire," there would be no necessity nor any sense in his being baptized by his inferior in the river like an ordinary penitent Jew! The expression of Jesus, "It behoves us to fulfil all the justice," is incomprehensible. Why and *how* "*all the* justice" would be accomplished by them if Jesus were baptized? This expression is utterly unintelligible. It is either an interpolation or a clause deliberately mutilated. Here is another instance which presents itself to be solved and interpreted by the Islamic spirit. From a Muslim point of view the only sense in this expression of Jesus would be that John, through the eye of a Seer or "Sophi," perceived the prophetical character of the Nazarene, and thought him for a moment to be the Last Great Apostle of Allah, and consequently shrank from baptizing him; and that it was only when Jesus confessed his own identity that he consented to baptize him.

(4) The fact that John while in prison sent his disciples to Jesus, asking him: "Art thou *that* Prophet who is to come, or shall we expect another one?" clearly shows that the Baptist *did not know* the gift of prophecy in Jesus until he heard — *while in the prison* — of his miracles. This testimony of St. Matthew (xi. 3) contradicts and invalidates that of the Fourth Gospel (John i), where it is stated that the

Baptist, on seeing Jesus, exclaimed: "Behold the Lamb of God that taketh away [or bears] the sin of the world!" The fourth Evangelist knows nothing of the cruel martyrdom of John (Matt. xiv; Mark vi. 14-29).

From Muslim unitarian point of belief, it is a moral impossibility that a Prophet like the Baptist, whom the Holy Qur-án describes, *Sayyidan, wa Hasūran wa Nabiyyan mina 's-Sālihīna,"* should use such a paganish expression about Jesus Christ. The very nature and essence of John's mission was to *preach penance* — that is to say, every man is responsible for his sin and must *bear it,* or *take it away himself by repentance.* The baptism was only an outward ablution or washing as a sign of the remission of sins, but it is the contribution, the confession (to God, and to him who is injured by that sin — if absolutely necessary) and the promise not to repeat it, that can *take it away.* If Jesus were the "Lamb of God," to take away the sin of the world, then John's preaching would be — God forbid! — ridiculous and meaningless! Besides, John better than anyone else knew that such words from his lips would have caused — as has been the case — an irreparable error which would entirely disfigure and deform the Church of Christ. The root of the error which has soiled the religion of the Churches is to be sought and found out in this silly "vicarious sacrifice" business! Has the "Lamb of God" taken away the sin of the world? The dark pages of the "Ecclesiastical History" of any of the numerous hostile and "heretical" Churches will answer with a big No! The "lambs" in the confessional-boxes can tell you by their groanings under the tremendous weight of the multi-coloured sins loaded upon their shoulders that the Christians, notwithstanding their science and civilization, commit more horrible sins, murders thefts, intemperances, adulteries, wars, oppressions, robberies, and insatiable greed for conquest and money than all the rest of mankind put together.

(5) John the Baptist could not be the precursor of Jesus Christ in the sense in which the Churches interpret his mission. He is presented to us by the Gospels as a "voice crying aloud in the wilderness," as the fulfilment of a passage in Isaiah (xl. 3), and as a herald of Jesus Christ on the authority of the Prophet Malakhi (Mal. iii. 1). To assert that the mission or duty of the Baptist was to prepare the way for Jesus — the former in the capacity of a precursor and the latter in that of a triumphant Conqueror coming "suddenly to his temple," and there to establish his religion of "Shalom" and make Jerusalem with its temple more glorious than before (Hag. ii. 8) — is to confess the absolute failure of the whole enterprise.

Nevertheless one thing is as true as two and two make four — that the whole project, according to the extravagant view of the Christians, proves a total failure. For, from whatever point of view we examine the interpretations of the Churches, the failure appears to be obvious. Instead of receiving his prince in Jerusalem at the Gate of the Temple clad in diadem and purple, amidst the frantic acclamations of the Jews, the precursor receives him, naked like himself, in the middle of the River Jordan; and then to introduce him, after immersing or plunging his master into the water, to the crowds as "behold, this is the Messiah!" or "this is the Son of God!" or elsewhere "behold the Lamb of God!" would either be tantamount to simply insulting the people of Israel or to blaspheming; or to purely mocking Jesus as well as making himself ridiculous.

The true nature of the austere ascetic's mission, and the true sense of his preaching, is altogether misunderstood by the Churches, but *understood* by the Jewish priests and casuists who obstinately rejected it. I shall deal with this in my next article, and show that the nature of John's mission as well as the object of Christ's message to the Jews was quite different to what the Churches pretend to believe.

IV

THE PROPHET FORETOLD BY THE BAPTIST WAS CERTAINLY MUHAMMAD

There are two very significant remarks about John the Baptist made by Jesus Christ, but recorded in a mysterious way. The first remark about the Baptist is that in which John is presented to the world as the reincarnate Eliah (Elijah) the Old Testament. The mystery with which this appellation is enveloped consists in the significant silence of Christ about the identity of the person whom Eliah (*not* Elias) was expected to officially announce and introduce to the world as the Last Prophet. The language of Jesus in this respect is exceedinly obscure, ambiguous, and mysterious. If John was Eliah, as is expressly and fearlessly declared, why, then, is the person whose precursor was Eliah *not expressly* and *fearlessly mentioned?* If Jesus were the "Messenger of the Covenant" and the *Dominator* [as the Vulgate translates the Hebrew *Adon* (Mal. iii. 1).], why does he not openly say so? If he courageously declared that it was not he himself but *another* Prophet who was that "Dominator," it must, indeed, have been a criminal hand which erased and effaced the words of Jesus from the original Gospel. At all events, it is the Gospels that are responsible for this ambiguity and obscurity. It cannot but be described

as diabolical tampering with the text that has misled billions
of Christians for so many centuries. Jesus, whatever he
believed he represented, ought to have, to say the least,
shown himself straightforward, and to have frankly declared:
"John is the Eliah who was sent as a precursor to prepare
the way for me!" Or if such was not the case, then he could
have made the following declaration: "John is the Eliah who
was sent to prepare the way for Muhammad." Perhaps this is
due to the love of Jesus for ambiguity. There are, in fact,
several instances — as reported in the Gospels — where
Jesus give an answer or makes a statement which is obscure
and entirely unintelligible. Leaving his godhead aside, as a
Prophet, nay even as a teacher, he was expected to be a
straightforward teacher and leader.

The other remark is shrouded in still a thicker mystery.
"No man born of woman was ever greater than John the
Baptist," says Jesus, "but the least in the Kingdom of Heaven
is greater than John." Does Jesus Christ mean to teach us
that John the Baptist and all the Prophets and the righteous
men *were outside* the Kingdom of God? Who is the "least"
that was "greater" than John, and consequently than all the
people of God preceding the Baptist? Does *Jesus* mean by
the "least" *himself,* or the "least" among the baptized Christians? It cannot be himself, because in his time that Kingdom
was not yet established on earth; if it be, then he could not
be the "least" in it since he was its founder. The Churches —
rather each Church, orthodox or heterodox, from its own
peculiar point of view — have discovered a very abstruse or
a very absurd solution for this problem; and that solution
is that the "least" Christian washed with the blood of Jesus
— either through the Sacrament of Baptism, according to
the belief of the Sacerdotalists, or through the regeneration
of some kind, according to the superstition of the Evangeli-

cals — becomes "greater" than the Baptist and all the army
of the holy men and women, including Adam, Noah,
Abraham, Moses, David, Eliah, Daniel, and John the
Baptist! And the reason or proof of this marvellous claim is
that the Christian, however, sinful, ignorant, low, and poor
he may be, providing he has faith in Jesus as his Saviour,
has the privileges which the holy Prophets coveted to have
but did not enjoy. These privileges are innumerable; purification from original sin through the Christian Baptism; the
knowledge of the "Holy Trinity" (! ! ! *hāshā! astaghfiru
'llāh!* — Allah forbid and pardon this term); the feeding upon
the flesh and the blood of Jesus in the Sacrament of the
Eucharist; the grace of making the sign of a cross; the privilege of the keys of Heaven and of Hell delivered to the
Sovereign Pontiff; and the rapturous ecstasies of the Puritans,
Quakers, Brethren, and all other sects called Nonconformists
who, each in its own way, while claiming the same privileges
and prerogatives, all agree that each good Christian will
become on the day of resurrection a pure virgin and present
herself as a bride to the "Lamb of God"!

Do you not think, then, that the Christians are right to
believe that the "least" among them is "greater" than all the
Prophets? Do you not think, then, that a sturdy Patagonian
monk and a penitentiary Parisian nun are higher than Adam
and Eve, because the mystery of the Trinity is revealed to
these idiots and not to our first parents who lived with Allah
in Paradise before their fall? Or, don't you think that this
sort of belief is most unbecoming and undignified in these
lofty times of advanced science and civilization? To claim
that an English prince or an orphan negro is "greater" that
John the Baptist because they are Christians is, to say the
least, abominable!

Yet all these diverse beliefs and creeds are derived

from the New Testament and from the words put into the mouth of Jesus and of his Apostles. For us Muslim Unitarians, however, there are a few scintillating sparkles left in the Gospels; and they are enough for us to discover the truth about the real Jesus and his cousin, Yoḥannan Ma'mdānā (John-Baptist).

JOHN-BAPTIST FORETOLD MUHAMMAD

1. According to the testimony of Jesus, no man born of woman was ever greater than John the Baptist. But the "least" in the Kingdom of Heaven is greater than John. The comparison made by the "Spirit of Allah" (Rūḥu 'llāh, i.e. Jesus) is between John and all the preceding Prophets as the officers and administrators of the Kingdom of Heaven. Now in chronological order the *last* Prophet would be the *least* of them all, he would be their junior and their youngest. The word "z'īrā" in the Aramaic, like the Arabic "saghīr," signifies "little, small young." The Pshittha Version uses the word "z'īrā or "z'eīrā" in apposition to "rabba" for "great, old." Every Christian will admit that Jesus is *not* the "last" Prophet, and therefore he cannot be the "least." Not only were the Apostles themselves endowed with the gift of prophecy, but also many other holy men in the apostolic age were favoured with it (Acts xi. 27, 28; xiii. 1; xv. 32; xxi, 9, 10, etc).

And as we cannot determine *which* of these numerous Church Prophets was the "last, we are naturally forced to seek elsewhere a Prophet who is indisputably the Last and the Seal of the Prophetic List. Can we imagine a stronger and more brilliant evidence in favour of Muhammad than the fulfilment, in his holy person, of this wonderful prophecy of Jesus Christ?

In the long list of the prophetic family, certainly the "youngest," the "least" is Muhammad; he is the "Benjamin" of the Prophets; yet he is their Sultan, their "Adon" and their "Glory." To deny the prophetical and apostolical character and nature of Muhammad's mission is a fundamental denial of the whole Divine Revelation and all the Prophets who preached it. For all other Prophets put together had not accomplished the gigantic work which the Prophet of Mecca did alone in the short period of but twenty-three years of his apostolic mission.

The mystery of the pre-existence of the spirits of the Prophets has not been revealed to us, but every true Muslim believes it. It was that pre-existing spirit that by the power of the Word of Allah "Kun" ("Be!") a Sarah, a Hanna, and a Blessed Virgin Mary gave birth to Isaac, to the Baptist, and to Jesus. There are several other names as recorded in the Old Testament — for instance, Samson, Jeremiah.

The Gospel of Barnabas reports Jesus as speaking of the Spirit of Muhammad which he declares to have been created before everything else. Hence the Baptist's witness about the Prophet whom he foretold: "He who comes after me has become before me, for he was before me" (John i. 15).

It is useless to interpret these wonderful words of the Baptist about Muhammad as referring to Jesus as the author of the Fourth Gospel attempts to do.

There is a remarkable chapter about John the Baptist in the well-known book of Ernest Renan on *La vie de Jesu.* Long ago I carefully read this work. If the learned French writer had the least consideration for Muhammad's claim in the world of Prophets, I am sure his profound investigations and comments would have led him entirely to a different conclusion. He, like all other dissident and Biblical critics, instead of finding out the truth, criticizes religion adversely and leads his readers to scepticism.

I am happy to say that it is my privilege, by the grace of Allah, to solve the problem, to ring up the curtain of mystery which has covered the true sense and meaning of "the Least in the Kingdom of Heaven!"

2.   John the Baptist recognizes Muhammad as superior and more powerful than himself. That significant expression made to the Jewish multitudes, "He that cometh after me" reminded their Scribes, Pharisees, and lawyers of the ancient prophecy of their great anchestor Jacob, in which that patriarch uses the unique title of "Shīlokḥah" for the "Rasūl Allah," the epithet frequently used by Jesus for Muhammad as preserved in the Gospel of Barnabas. At the time of writing my article on the "Shiloh"[1] I said that the word might be a corruption of "shīlōūkh" or "Shīlokhah,"[2] which means the Apostle of Allah, but I did not then recollect that St. Jerome, as well, had understood the Hebrew form in that sense, for he has translated it as "qui mittendis est."

We have only an epitome of John's sermon in a few lines, written not by himself but by an unknown hand — at least not in his own original tongue — and much tampered with by transcribers and redactors who had already made his disciple Jesus an idol or a god. But when we come to compare this sermon preached in the wilderness of Judea and on the shores of the Jordan with the marvellous grace, elegance, eloquence, and power so manifest in every verse and page of the Holy Qur-án, we understand the sense of the words, "He is more powerful than I!"

1. Cf. *Islamic Review* for September, 1928, p. 313 *et seq.*
2. The Oriental Hebrews and Assyrians pronounce the word "Shilokha" or "Shīlōākh." It is very difficult to write or transliterate the Semitic languages in the Latin characters.

When I picture to myself the ascetic Baptist preaching aloud in the wilderness, or on the banks of the Jordan, to the masses of the Jewish believers, with a theocratic history of some four thousand years old behind them, and then make a brief review of the quiet, orderly, and dignified manner in which Muhammad proclaimed his celestial verses of the Qurán to the unbelieving Arab pagans; and, finally, when I examine and behold the effect of the two preachings upon the hearers and the final result, I understand the magnitude of the contrast between them, and of the significance of the words "He is more powerful than I!"

When I contemplate the seizure and imprisonment of the helpless Baptist by Herod Antipas[1] and his cruel decapitation — or when I peruse the confused but tragical accounts of the flagellation of Jesus (or Judah Ishariot) by Pilate, his coronation with a crown of thorns by Herod, and the catastrophe upon the Calvary — and then turn my eyes upon the triumphal entry of the great Adon — the Sultan of the Prophets — into Mecca, the total destruction of all the ancient idols and the purification of the Holy Ka'ba; upon the thrilling scene of the vanquished deadly enemy headed by Abū Sufyān at the feet of the victorious Shīlohah — the Apostle of Allah — begging his clemency and making the profession of faith; and upon the glorious worship, devotion, and the final sermon of the Seal of the Prophets in these solemn Divine words: "Al-yauma akmaltu lakum dīnakum" ("To-day I have completed for you your religion"), etc., then I fully understand the weight and value of the Baptist's confession, "He is more powerful than I!"

   3.   "The Coming Wrath." Have you ever met with a

1.   There is anachronism in the account of John's martyrdom concerning the family of Herod the Great in the Gospels (Matt. xiv, etc.); the reader can consult the *Antiquities* of Joseph Flavius.

sensible, judicious, and convincing interpretation of this phrase in any of the numerous commentaries on the Gospels? What does John mean, or wish his audience to understand, by his expression: "Behold the axe is already set at the root of the tree"? Or his remark: "He holds the van in his hand to purge out his threshing-floor"? Or when he reduced the title "Children of Abraham" to nothing?

I will not detain you on the vagaries of the commentators, for they are reveries which neither John nor his hearers had ever dreamed of. Could John ever teach those haughty Pharisees, and those rationalistic Saduqees[1] who denied the corporeal resurrection, that on the day of the last judgment Jesus of Nazareth would pour down upon them his wrath and burn them like the fruitless trees and like the chaff in the fire of hell? There is not a single word in all the literature of the Scriptures about the resurrection of bodies or about hell-fire. These Talmudistic writings are full of eschatological material very similar to those of the Zardushtees, but have no distinct origin in the canonical books.

The Prophet of repentance and of good tidings does not speak about the remote and indefinite wrath which certainly awaits the unbelievers and the impious, but of the near and proximate catastrophe of the Jewish nation. He threatened the wrath of Allah awaiting that people if they persisted in their sins and the rejection of his mission and that of his colleague, Jesus Christ. The coming calamity was the destruction of Jerusalem and the final dispersion of Israel which took place some thirty years afterwards during the lifetime of many among his hearers. Both he and Jesus announced the coming of the Great Apostle of Allah whom

---

1. This Hebrew name is wrongly written "Saducees."

the Patriarch Jacob had announced under the title of Shiloha, and that at his advent all prophetic and royal privileges and authority would be taken away from the Jews; and, indeed, such was the case some six centuries later, when their last strongholds in the Hijaz were razed to the ground and their principalities destroyed by Muhammad. The increasingly dominating power of Rome in Syria and Palestine was threatening the quasiautonomy of the Jews, and the emigration current among the Jews had already begun. And it was on this account that the preacher inquires, "Who has informed you to flee from the coming wrath?" They were warned and exhorted to bear good fruits and good harvest by repentance and belief in the true Messengers of God, especially in the Rasūl Allah, who was the true and the last powerful Commander.

4. The Jews and the Christians have always charged Muhammad of having established the religion of Islam by force, coercion, and the sword. The Muslim modernists have always tried to refute this charge. But this does not mean to say that Muhammad never wielded the sword. He had to use it to preserve the name of God. Every patience has limits, every favour has an end. It is not that Allah's patience or favour is finite; with Him all is settled, defined and fixed. The chance and the time graciously granted by Allah to the Jews, to the Arabs, and to the Gentiles lasted for more than four thousand years. It was only after the expiry of this period that Allah sends His beloved Muhammad with power and sword, with fire and spirit, to deal with the wicked unbelievers, with the ungrateful children of Abraham — both the Ishmaelites and the Israelites — and to deal with the power of the Devil, *once for all.*

The whole of the Old Testament is a tale of theocracy and of idolatry. Now and then a little sparkle of Islam —

that is, the religion of Allah — glittered in Jerusalem and in Mecca; but it was always persecuted by the power of the Devil. The four diabolical Beasts had to come and trample under their feet the handful of believers in Allah. Then comes Muhammad to crush and kill the Venemous Serpent and to give him the opprobrious title of "Iblīs" — the "Bruised" Satan. Certainly Muhammad was a fighting Prophet, but the object of that fighting was victory not vengeance, defeat of the enemy and not his extermination, and, in a word, to establish the religion of Islam as the Kingdom of God upon the earth. In fact, when the Crier in the desert shouted, aloud, "Prepare the way of the Lord, and make straight His paths," he was alluding to the religion of the Lord in the form of a Kingdom which was drawing nigh. Seven centuries before, the Prophet Isaiah had cried out and pronounced the same words (Isa. xl. 1-4); and a couple of centuries later Allah Himself paved the way for Cyrus by raising and filling up every valley, and by lowering every hill and mountain, in order to make the conquest easy and the march rapid (xlv. 1-3). History repeats itself, they say; the language and its meaning is the same in both cases, the former being a prototype of the latter. Allah had smoothed the path for Cyrus, subdued his enemies to the Persian conquerer because of His House in Jerusalem and His chosen people in the captivity. Now again He was repeating the same providence, but on a larger and wider scale. Before the preaching of Muhammad, idols and falsehood disappeared; before his sword empires tumbled down; and the children of the Kingdom of Allah became equals and formed a "people of the Saints of the Most High." *For it is only in Islam that all the believers are equal, no priest, no sacrament; no Muslim high as a hill, or low like a valley; and no caste or distinction of race and rank. All believers are one, except in virtue and piety, in which they can excel each other. It is only the religion of Islam that does not recognize any being, however great and holy, as an absolute mediator between Allah and man.*

V

THE BAPTISM OF JOHN AND JESUS ONLY A TYPE OF THE "SIBGHATU 'L-LĀH"[1]

It is a great pity that the Evangelists have not left us a complete and detailed account of the sermon of John the Baptist; and assuming they ever did, it is nothing short of a crime on the part of the Church not to have preserved its text.   For it is impossible to imagine the mysterious and enigmatic words of the Baptist in their present shape could have been understood even by the most erudite among his audience.   We know that the Jewish doctors and lawyers asked him to explain himself upon various points and to make his declarations more explicit and plain (John i. 19-23 and v. 33).   There is no doubt that he elucidated those vital points to his hearers, and did not leave them in obscurity; for he was "a burning and enlightening candle," who "gave witness concerning the truth" (John v. 33, 35). What was this witness, and what was the nature of the truth about which that witness was given?   And what makes it still more obscure is the fact that each Evangelist does not report the same points in identical terms.   There is no precision about the character of the truth; was it about the

---

1.   Holy Qur-àn ii. 138, Muhammad 'Alì's translation.

person of Christ and the nature of his mission, or was it about the Apostle of Allah as foretold by Jacob (Gen. xlix.)? What were the precise terms of John's witness about Jesus, and about the future Prophet who was his superior?

In the third article of this series[1] I offered ample proofs that the Prophet foretold by the Baptist was other than Jesus Christ; and in the fourth article[2] we find several arguments in favour of the Apostle of Allah as being a superior and more powerful Prophet than John. Those arguments, in my humble opinion, and in my solid conviction, are logical, true, and conclusive. Each of those arguments could be easily developed so as to make a voluminous book. I am fully conscious of the fact that these argumentations will present a jarring sound to the fanatical ears of many a Christian. But truth exalts itself and extols him who propagates it. The truth about which John gave witness, as quoted above, we unhesitatingly believe to be concerning Muhammad. John gave two witnesses, one about the "Shliha d'Allaha" — according to the then Palestinian dialect, which means the "Apostle of Allah" — and the other about Jesus, whom he declared to have been born of the Holy Spirit and not of an earthly father; to be the true Messiah who was sent by Allah as the last great Jewish Prophet to give a new light and spirit to the Law of Moses; and to having been commissioned to teach the Jews that their salvation rested on submitting to the great son of Ishmael. Like the old Jews who threw into disorder their Scriptures, the new Jews of the Christian Church, in imitation of their forefathers, have corrupted their own. But even these corruptions in the Gospels cannot conceal the truth.

1. Vide *Islamic Review* for March—April, 1930.
2. Ibid., May, 1930.

The principal point which constitutes the power and the superiority of the Prince of the Apostles of Allah is the baptism with the Holy Spirit and with fire. The admission by the author of the Fourth Gospel that Jesus and his disciples also used to baptize with water simultaneously with John the Baptist is an abrogation *de facto* of the parenthetical note that "Jesus did not baptize himself, but his disciples only" (John iii. 23 and iv. 1, 2). But granting that he himself did not baptize, the admission that his disciples did, while yet initiates and unlearned, shows that their baptism was of the same nature as that of John's. Considering the fact that Jesus during the period of his earthly mission administered that rite exactly as the Baptist was doing at the streams or pools of water, and that he ordered his disciples to continue the same, it becomes as evident and as clear as a barn door that he was not the person intended by the Crier in the Wilderness when he foretold the advent of a powerful Prophet with the baptism of the Spirit and fire. It does not require much learning or an extraordinary intelligence to understand the force of the argument — namely, Jesus during his lifetime baptized *not a single person* with the Holy Spirit and with fire. How, then, can he be regarded as the Baptizer with the Holy Spirit and with fire, or be identified with the Prophet foretold by John? If words, sermons, and prophecies *mean* anything, and are uttered in order to *teach* anything at all, then the words of the Baptist *mean* and *teach* us that the baptism with water would continue to be practised until the Appearance of the "Shilohah" or the Apostle of Allah, and then it would *cease* and give place to the exercise of the baptism with the Spirit and fire. This is the only logical and intelligible conclusion to be deduced from the preaching as recorded in the third chapter of the First Gospel. The

continuation of the Christian baptism and its elevation to
the dignity of a Sacrament is a clear proof that the Church
does not believe in a baptism other than that which is performed with water.   Logic, common sense, and respect for
any sacred writ ought to convince every impartial reader
that the two baptisms are quite different things.   The
Prophet of the desert does not recognize the baptism with
fire in the baptism with water.   The nature and the efficacy
of each baptism is distinctly stated and defined.   The one
is performed by immersing or washing the body with water
as a sign or mark of repentance; and the other is performed
no longer by water but by the Holy Spirit and the fire, the
effect of which is a *thorough change* of heart, faith, and
feeling.   One purifies the body, the other enlightens the
mind, confirms the faith, and regenerates the heart.   One is
outward, it is Judaism; the other is inward, it is Islam.
The baptism of John and Jesus washes the shell, but the
baptism of the Apostle of Allah washes the kernel.   In
short, the Judæo-Christian baptism is substituted by the
Islamic "Ghusl" and "Wodhu" — or the ablutions which
are performed, not by a prophet or priest, but *by the
believing individual himself*.   The Judæo-Christian baptism
was necessary and obligatory so long as the baptism of
Allah — the Qur-ánic "Sibghatu 'l-Lāh" — was anticipated;
and when Muhammad thundered the divine revelations of
the Qur-án, then it was that the former baptism vanished
as a shadow.

The extreme importance of the two baptisms deserves
a very serious consideration, and I believe the observations
made in this article must considerably interest both the
Muslims and other readers.   For the point under discussion, from a religious standpoint, is vital to salvation.   The
Christians, I honestly maintain, are not justified in perpe-

tuating their baptism with water *ad infinitum,* since their own Gospels foretell that it will be abrogated by *another one* which will *exclude* the use of water altogether.   I submit the following observations to the thoughtful and impartial judgment of my readers.

What Baptism Is and What it is Not

(*a*)   It is within our rights to agree or to disagree with a doctrine or a theory, but nothing can justify our conduct if we deliberately distort and misrepresent a doctrine in order to prove our own theory about it.   To distort the Scriptures is iniquitous and criminal; for the error caused in this respect is irreparable and pernicious.   Now the baptism of John and Jesus is plainly described and illustrated to us in the Gospels, and is entirely alien and opposed to the baptism of the Churches.

We are not positively certain about the original Hebrew or Aramaic word for the Greek baptism.   The Pshittha Version uses the word "ma'muditha" from the verb "aīmād" and "aa'mid," which means "to stand up like an *a'muda*" (a pillar or column), and its causative form "aa'mid" "to erect, set up, establish, confirm" and so on, but it has no signification of "to immerse, dip, wash, sprinkle, bathe," as the ecclesiastical baptism is supposed to mean.   The original Hebrew verbs "rahas" "to bathe", "tabhal" (read "ṭaval") "to dip, to immerse," might give the sense conveyed by the Greek word "baptizo" — "I baptize." The Arabic versions of the New Testament have adopted the Aramaic form, and call the Baptist "al-Mā'midān," and "ma'mudiyeh" for "baptism."   In all the Semitic languages, including the Arabic, the verb "a'mad" signifies in its simple or *qal* form "to stand erect like a pillar," and does not

contain the meaning of washing or immersion; and therefore it could not be the original word from which the Greek
"baptismos" is the translation.   There is no necessary to
argue that both John and Jesus never heard of the word
"baptismos" in its Greek form, but that there was evidently
another Semitic nomenclature used by them.

(b)   Considering the classical signification of the Greek
"baptismos" which means tincture, dye, and immersion,"
the word in use could not be other than "Saba," and the
Arabic "Sabagha," "to dye."   It is a well-known fact that
the Sabians, mentioned in the Qur-án and by the early
Christian Fathers — such as Epiphanus and others — were
the followers of John.   The very name "Sabians," according to the celebrated Ernest Renan (*La vie de Jesus,* ch.
vi), signifies "Baptists."   They practised baptism, and like
the old Hassayi (Essenians, or al-Chassaïtes) and Ibionayi
(Ebionites) led an austere life.   Considering the fact that
their founder, Budasp, was a Chaldean sage, the true
orthography of their name would be "Saba'ï," i.e. "Dyers"
or "Baptists."   A famous Chaldean or Assyrian Catholicos
of the fourth century, Mar Shimon, was called "Bar Saba'ï,"
"Son of the Dyers."   Probably his family belonged to the
Sabin religion.   The Qur-án writes this name "Sābi'īn" with
the *hamza* vowel instead of *ain* as it is in the original
Aramaic "Sābā'ī."   I am cognisant, however, of other
interpretations placed on the name "Sabian": some authors
suppose it to be derived from "Sābi'," the son of Sheth, and
others from the Hebrew "Sabā," which means "army,"
because they used to have a kind of special devotion to the
stars as the host of heaven.   Although they have nothing
in common with the Christian Churches, except their
peculiar 'Sab'utha," or Baptism, they are wrongly called
"the Christians of St. John-Baptist."   The Qur-án, as usual,

writes all foreign names as they were pronounced by the Arabs.

An extensive and deep research in the religion of the Sabians, who had almost overrun the Arab nation long before the light of Islam shone with the appearance of the Holy Apostle of Allah, will show us several truths. There were three forms of baptism practised by the Jews, the Sabians, and the Christians. The Jewish baptism, which had no origin in their sacred books, was invented chiefly for the proselytes. Each religion had its definite baptismal formula and a special ritual. The Jewish "Kohen" (priest) baptized his convert in the name of Allah; the Sabian in the name of Allah and of John; but the Christian "Qushīsha" (in Arabic "qassis" or presbyter) baptized in the name of the Father, of the Son, and of the Holy Ghost, in which the names of Allah and of Jesus are not directly recited. The diversity and the antagonism of the three baptismal systems is apparrent. The Jew, as a true Unitarian, could not tolerate the name of John to be associated with that of the Elohim; whereas the Christian formula was extremely repugnant to his religious taste. There is no doubt that the Christian baptism, with its sacramental character and polytheistic taint, was abhorred also by the Sabians. The symbol of the convenant between Allah and His people was *not* baptism but circumcision (Gen. xvii.), an ancient institution which was strictly observed, not only by the three religions, but also by many pagan Arab tribes. These diverse baptismal forms and rituals among the Semitic peoples in the East were not an essential divine institution, but only a symbol or sign, and therefore not strong and efficacious enough to supplant one another. They all used water for the material of their baptism, and, more or less, in similar form or manner. But each religion adopted a different name to distinguish its own practice from that of the other two. The original Aramaic "Sab'-utha" — properly and truly translated into the Greek "baptismos" — was faithfully preserved by the Saba'ïtes (Sabians). It appears that the Semitic Christians, in order to distinguish their sacramental baptism from that of the Sabaites, adopted the appellation of "ma'mudītha" which, from a linguistic point of view, has nothing whatever to do with baptism or *even* with washing or immersion. It is only an ecclesiastical coinage. Why "ma'mudītha" was adopted to replace "Sab'utha" is a question altogether foreign to our present subject; but *en passant*, I may add that this word in the Pshittha is used also for a pool, a basin for ablution (John v. 2). The only explanation which may lead towards the solution of this problem of the "ma'mudītha" is the fact that John the Baptist and his followers, including Jesus the son of Mary and his disciples, cause a penitent or a proselyte to stand straight like a pillar in a pool of water or in a river in order to be bathed with water; hence the names of "āa'mid" and "ma'mudītha."

(*c*) The Christian baptism, notwithstanding its fanfaronade definitions, is nothing more or less than an aspersion with water or an immersion in it. The Council of Trent anathematizes anyone who would say that the Christian baptism is the same as that of St. John's. I venture to declare that the Christian baptism has not only no spiritual character or effect, but is also even below the baptism of the Baptist. And if I deserve the anathema of the Church for my conviction, I shall deem it as a great honour before my Creator. I consider the pretentions of a Christian priest about the baptism as a means of purification of the soul from original sin and all the rest of it as of a piece with the claims of a sorceror. The baptism with water was *only* a symbol of baptism with the Holy Spirit and with fire, and after the establishment of Islam as the official kingdom of God all the three previous baptisms vanished and were abolished.

(*d*) From the meagre and scant account in the Gospels we cannot get a positive definition of the true nature of the baptism practised by John and Jesus. The claim that the Church is the depository of the divine revelation and its true interpreter is as absurd as is ridiculous the claim that the baptized infant or adult receives the Holy Spirit and becomes a child of God.

If the Greek word "baptismos" is the exact word for the Aramaic "Sab'utha" or "Sbhu'tha," which I am sure it is, then the Arabic "Sibghat" in the Qur-ān, not only does it solve the problem and uncover the veil hiding the mysterious prophecy of John the Baptist, but also is a marvellous proof that the sacred scripture of Islam is a direct revelation of Allah, and that His Apostle was inspired and the real person whom John predicted! The baptist ("Saba'ā") plunges or immerses his neophyte or an infant into a pond, as a dyer or a fuller plunges a cloth or garment into a kettle of dye. It is easily understood that baptism is not a "thāra," purification or washing, nor "tabhāla," an immersion, nor even a "rāhsa," a bathing or washing, but "sab'aitha," a dyeing, a colouring. It is extremely important to know these distinctions. Just as a "saba'a," a dyer, gives a new colour to a garment by dipping it into a kettle of tincture, so a baptist give his convert a new spiritual hue. Here we must make a fundamental distinction between a proselyte Gentile and a penitent Jew and Ishma-elite Arab. The former was formally circumcized, whereas the latter baptized only. By the circumcision a Gentile was admitted into the family of Abraham, and therefore into the fold of God's people. By baptism a circumcized believer was admitted into the society of the penitent and reformed believers. Circumcision is an ancient divine institution which was not abrogated by Jesus nor by Muhammad. The baptism practised by John and the Christ was only for the benefit of the penitent persons among the circumcized. Both these institutions indicated and presented a religion. The baptism of John and of his cousin Jesus was a mark of admission into the society of the purified penitents who promised loyalty and homage to the Apostle of Allah whose coming they both foretold.

It follows, therefore, that just as circumcision signified the religion of Abraham and his adherents (his slaves were also circumcized), so baptism signified the religion of John and Jesus, which was a preparation for the Jews and the Gentiles to accord a cordial reception to the Founder of Islam and to embrace his religion.

(e) According to the testimony of St. Mark (i. 1-8), the baptism of John had the character of the "remission of sins." It is stated that "all the country of Judæa and the inhabitants of Jerusalem went out to him and were all baptized by him in the River Jordan while confessing their sins." This is tantamount to saying that millions of the penitent Jews confessed their sins, were baptized by the Prophet, and then their sins were obliterated by the waters of baptism. It is generally admitted that St. Mark's Gospel is the oldest of the Four Gospels. All the ancient Greek manuscripts do not contain the last twelve verses added to chapter xvi. of this Gospel (verses 9-20). Even in these supplementary verses the formula "in the name of the Father, and of the Son and of the Holy Ghost" is not inscribed. Jesus simply says: "Go and preach my Gospel unto the whole world; he who believes and is baptized shall live, and he who does not believe shall be damned."

It is evident that the baptism of Jesus was the same as that of John's and a continuation of it. If the baptism of John was a sufficient means of the remission of sins, then the assertion that the "Lamb of God carries away the sins of the world" (John i.) is exploded. If the waters of the Jordan were efficacious enough to cleanse the leprosy of Naaman through the prayer of the Prophet Elisha (2 Kings v.), and to remit the sins of the myriads through that of the Prophet John, the shedding of the blood of a god would be superfluous and, indeed, incompatible with the divine justice.

There is no doubt that until the appearance of the Apostle Paul on the scene, the followers of Jesus Christ practised the baptismal ritual of John-Baptist. It is significant to note that Paul was a "Pharisee" belonging to a famous Jewish sect — like that of the Saducess — whom John and Jesus denounced as "the sons of the vipers." It is also to be observed that the author of the fifth book of the New Testament, called the "Acts of the Apostles," was a companion of this Paul, and pretends to show that those baptized by John the Baptist had not received the Holy Spirit "and therefore were rebaptized and then filled" with the Holy Spirit (Acts viii. 16, 17 and xix. 2-7), *not* through baptism in the name of Jesus, *but* through the "laying of hands." It is clearly stated in these quotations that the two baptisms were identical in their nature and efficacy, and that they did not "bring down" the Holy Spirit upon the person baptized whether by John, Jesus, or in the name of either of the two. By the "laying of their hands" of the Apostles upon a baptized person the Holy Spirit touched his heart, to fill it with faith and love of God. But this divine gift was granted only to the Apostles who were really prophets and inspired, and cannot be claimed by their so-called successors.

(f)   If the Gospels mean anything at all in their statements concerning baptism, they leave behind the impression that there was no difference between the two baptisms, except that they were administered in the name of one or other of the two Prophets.   The great Pharisee Paul or Saul of Tarsus has not a single kind word about John the Baptist, who had branded the sect of the Pharisees with the opprobrious epithet "the children of the vipers."   There is a tinge of grudge against John and against the value of his baptism in the remarks made by Luke in the "Acts of the Apostles."   And Luke was a disciple and companion of Paul.   The admission by Luke that the baptism in the name of Jesus, too, was not carried out by the Holy Spirit is a sure proof against the Church which has arbitrarily and wantonly transformed it into a sacrament or a mystery. The Church's baptism was a perpetuation of John's baptism and nothing more; but the baptism with the Holy Spirit and with fire was reserved only for Islam.   The expression that some twelve persons in Samaria "had not yet received the Holy Spirit, *because they were only baptized in the name of our Lord Jesus"* (Acts vii. 16, 17), is decisive to frustrate the pretentions of the Church.

The last three verses in the passage cited are held by many to be an interpolation.   They did not exist in the oldest existing MS., which is, of course, the origin of all subsequent versions of the Bible, including the Vulgate.   A document is absolutely unworthy of serious judicial notice if a portion of it is proved to be a forgery.   But here we go a step farther for the said addition to the original text

is admitted to be such even by those who speak of its
genuineness.

But let us take the prophecy as it stands.   I need not
say that it speaks of things at which ordinary common sense
can guess, seeing that the events foretold are always occurring from time to time in the course of Nature.   Pestilence
and war, famine and earthquakes have visited the world
so often that a mention of them in a prophecy as a sign
of its authenticity would deprive it of any importance it
might otherwise possess.   Besides, the first followers of a
new faith are sure to meet with persecution, especially if
they chance to be of inferior social position.   But apart
from this, the prophecy speaks in one strain of several
things, which may or may not occur together at any one
time.   They have never yet so occurred.   The persecution
of the disciples began immediately after the departure of
Jesus from Judæa.   They were "delivered up to the
synagogues and into prison, and brought before kings and
rulers" for his name's sake.   The prediction, however, did
not need a prophetic mind, since the persecution had started
even when Jesus was with his disciples.   These events were
the natural sequel of teachings distasteful to the Jews.   The
disciples no doubt bore every conceivable hardship and trial
with patience and courage, but they were sure of the return
of the Master in accordance with his promise: "Verily I say
unto you, that this generation shall not pass, till all these
things be done."   Belief in these words created a wonderful patience in the generation referred to.   But his words
passed away though the time did not come for the "heaven
and the earth to pass away."   Moreover, the days of the
disciples' persecution did not witness any unusual phenomena
in the form of earthquake, fighting, or pestilence.   Even in
the period immediately following, the prophesied four events

did not synchronize.   In the last two scores of years of the last two centuries we heard "of wars and commotions." "Nation" did "rise against nation and kingdom against kingdom."   "Great earthquakes" were experienced in divers places and famines and pestilence, but neither did the sun become darkened nor the moon fail to give its light, which things had to occur before "the coming of the Son of Man." These words may be taken in a metaphorical sense, but in that case, why should the Adventists look for the second coming in its literal sense?   Moreover, most of the above-mentioned phenomena have taken place at times when those who preached and taught in the name of Jesus were not likely, for political reasons, to be brought before kings and rulers for punishment.   On the contrary, they had obtained free access into lands that had long been closed against them.   All of which goes to prove that either the prediction is folklore or a legendary account of the things of which Jesus spoke on different occasions.   Either he himself had had but a hazy notion of coming events, or the recorders of his life, who wrote two centuries after, mixed up hopelessly different things dealing with different matters.

VI

THE "SIBGHATU 'L-LĀH," OR THE
BAPTISM WITH THE HOLY
SPIRIT AND WITH FIRE

One of the few religious phenomena I have not been able to explain is this: How is it that the well-known Saba'ītes (Sabians), so predominant in the Arabian peninsula

and Mesopotamia, did not embrace Christianity if the
Prophet John the Baptist had really and openly· declared
and presented Jesus as the "more powerful" Prophet than
himself, and the Messiah whose shoes he was not worthy
to unloose?   If, as foretold by John, Jesus was the Apostle
of Allah who came to baptize with the Holy Spirit and
with fire the myriads whom he "dyed" in the water of the
Jordan and elsewhere, why did not Jesus baptize them
instantly with the Spirit and with fire and then purge of
idolatry all the lands promised by Allah to the seed of
Abraham and establish the Kingdom of God by force and
fire?   It is absolutely inconceivable that the disciples and
the believers in the divine mission of John should not follow
Jesus if he had been presented to the public as his Lord
or Superior on the spot.   The followers of John might have
been excused for their refusal to enter into the Christian
Church if Jesus Christ had come, say, a century later than
the Baptist, but happily such was not the case.   They were
both contemporaries and born in the same year.   They both
baptized with water unto repentence, and prepared their
penitent converts for the Kingdom of God that was
approaching but not established in their time.

The Saba'ītes, the "Dyers" or "Baptists," were the
faithful adherents of John.   They may have fallen into
error and superstition; but they knew perfectly well that
it was not Jesus who was intended in the propphecy of their
Prophet.   They embraced Islam when Muhammad came.
The people of Harran in Syria are *not* — as they have
been supposed to be — the remnant of the old Saba'ītes.
In the promised lands only three non-Muslim religions were
recognized and tolerated by the Qur-án, namely, Judaism,
Christianity, and Sabianism.   It is stated that the Harranians
pretended to be the remnant of the old Saba'ītes, and they

were, therefore, permitted to practise their peculiar religion without molestation by the Turkish Government.

The Christian conception of the Holy Spirit is entirely different from the Islamic and the Jewish. The Holy Spirit is not a divine person with divine attributes and functions not belonging to this or that other divine persons of a triple god. The Christian belief that this same holy ghost, the third divine person, descends from his (or her, or its) heavenly throne at the bidding of every priest — in his daily celebration of some sacrament — to consecrate its elements and change their essence and qualities into some supernatural elements is extremely repugnant to the religious sentiments of every Unitarian, whether Jew or Muslim. Nothing could horrify a Muslim's feeling more than the belief that the Holy Spirit — always at the intervention of a priest — changes the water of baptism into the blood of a crucified god and blots out the so-called original sin; or a belief that the magic operation upon the material elements of the Eucharist transubstantiates them into the blood and body of an incarnate god. These beliefs were absolutely opposed to the teachings of the Old Testament and a falsification of the real doctrine of John and Jesus. The Christian assertion that the Holy Spirit at the incantations of a priest, fills certain individuals and sanctifies them, but does not guarantee their impeccability and ignorance, is meaningless. We are told that Hananiah (Ananias) and his wife Shapirah were baptized, which is to say filled with the Holy Ghost. They were thus inspired by the third divine person to sell their field and to place its price in cash at the feet of the Apostle Peter, but at the same time were seduced by the devil to conceal a portion of the money. The consequence was that the unfortunate communist couple were stricken dead miraculously (Acts v.).

Think of the belief that the Third Person of the Trinity descends upon men, sanctifies them, and then allows them to fall into error, heresy, and atheism, and abandons them to commit murderous wars and massacres. Is this possible? Can the devil seduce a man filled with and guarded by the Holy Ghost and change him into a demon? The Holy Qur-án is very expressive on this point. Allah says to the devil:

> "Verily thou shalt have no power over my servants, but over those only who shall be seduced and who shall follow thee" (chap. xv.).

We cannot believe, nor even imagine for a moment, that a servant of God, a righteous believer who has received the Spirit of sanctification, can fall into a deadly sin and perish in hell. Nay, a holy person, so long as he is in this material world, is to combat and struggle against sin and evil; he may fall, but he will rise again and shall never be abandoned by the pure Spirit that guards him. True repentance is the work of the good Spirit that lives in us. If a Christian be baptized with the Holy Spirit and fire, in the sense which the book of the "Acts of the Apostles" describes and the Churches accept, then every baptized Latin, Greek, or Abyssinian must not only become a sinless saint but also a linguist and a polyglot prophet!

The truth is that the Christians have not a definite or precise conception about the Holy Spirit filling a baptized Christian. If it be God, then how dare the devil approach, tempt, and seduce the hallowed or rather defied man? And, besides, what is more serious is: How can the devil chase away the Holy Ghost and settle himself in the heart of a baptized heretic or atheist? On the other hand, if the Holy Spirit means the Archangel Gabriel or some other angel, then the Christian Churches roam in a desert of superstition; for an angel is not omni-present. If this Spirit that purifies and fills a baptized Christian is *God Himself,* for such is their belief in the Third Person of the Trinity, then all the baptized Christians ought to claim themselves divine or deified.

Then there is a Protestant conception of the Holy Spirit, which (or who[1]) fills the hearts of those who, at the highest excitement and ecstasy during an inflammatory sermon of an ignorant or learned haranguer, believe themselves to become "new-born"; yet many among them slide back and become what they were before, rogues and swindlers!

Now before I come to explain, according to my humble understanding, the spiritual and fiery baptism, I wish to admit and confess that there are many pious and God-fearing persons among the Jews and the Christians. For however their religious views and beliefs may differ from ours, they love God and do good in His name. We cannot comprehend and determine the dealings of God with the peoples of different religions. The Christian conception of the Deity is only an erroneous definition of the true God in whom they believe and love. If they extol Jesus and deify him, it is not that they wish to dishonour God, but because they see His beauty in that Ruh-Allah (the "Spirit of God," i.e. Jesus). They certainly cannot appreciate the Apostleship of Muhammad, not, because they deny his unparalleled service to the cause of God by inflicting the greatest blow on the devil and his cult of idolatry, but because they do not understand as *he* did the true nature of the mission and person of Jesus Christ. Similar reasoning may be put forward

---

1. The Holy Spirit, in all the Christian literature of diverse languages, has not a fixed gender. He, she, it, are all commonly used as the personal pronouns for the Holy Ghost.

with regard to the attitude of the Jews towards Jesus and
Muhammad.   God is Merciful and Forgiving!

The Holy Spirit, with the definite article "the," means
a special angelic personality, Gabriel, or any one of the
numerous "pure" spirits created by Allah, and appointed to
perform some particular mission.   The descent of the Holy
Spirit upon a human person is to reveal to him the will and
the oracles of Allah, and to make him a prophet.   Such an
one can *never be* seduced by the satan.

The baptism with the Holy Spirit and fire which Muhammad brought is explained to us by the divine revelation only
in one verse of Al-Qur-án:

> "The Baptism of God (have we received), and
> who is better than God to baptize?   Him do we wor-
> ship" (chap. ii.).

This is the translation of Sale (cf. *The Koran*).

The Muslim commentators rightly understand the word
"Sibghat," not in its literal signification of "dyeing," but in
its spiritual or metaphorical sense of "religion."   This
Qur-ánic verse cancels and abolishes the religions of the
"Sab'utha" and of the "Ma'mudītha" or both the Saba'ites
and the Nasāra.   "Sibghatu 'l-Lāh" is the baptism of the
religion of Allah, not with water, but with the Holy Spirit
and fire!   The religion professed by any of the companions
of the Apostle of Allah in the first years of the Hijrat is
to-day professed in its entirety by every Muslim.   This cannot be said of the baptismal religion.   *More than sixteen
Œcumenical Councils have been summoned to define the religion of Christianity,* only to be discovered by the Synod of
the Vatican in the nineteenth century that the mysteries of
the "Infallibility" and the "Immaculate Conception" were
two of the principal dogmas, both unknown to the Apostle
Peter and the Blessed Virgin Mary!   Any faith or religion

dependent upon the deliberations and decisions of General Synods—holy or heretical—is artificial and human. The religion of Islam is the belief in one Allah and absolute resignation to His will, and this faith is professed by the angels in heaven and by the Muslims on earth. It is the religion of sanctification and of enlightenment, and an impregnable bulwark against idolatry. Let us develop these points a little further.

The spiritual baptism is the direct work of God Himself. As a fuller or a laundress washes the linen or any other object with water; as a dyer tints the wool or cotton with a tincture to give it a new hue; and as a baptist blots out the past sins of the true penitent believer, so does God Almighty baptize, *not* the body, but the spirit and the soul of him whom He mercifully directs and guides unto the Holy Religion of Islam. This is the "Sibghatu 'l-Lāh,," the Baptism of Allah, which makes a person fit and dignified to become a citizen of the Kingdom of Allah and a member of His religion.   When the Angel Gabriel communicated the Word of Allah for the first time to Muhammad, he (Mumammad) was invested with the gift of prophecy. His spirit was purified and magnified with the Holy Spirit to such a degree and extent that when he in his turn pronounced that Word to those whose spirit Allah pleased to guide were also purified, baptized.   They, too, thus became holy officers in the new army of the faithful Muslims.   This spiritual baptism does not make the Muslims prophets, sinless saints, or miracle-mongers.   For after the Revelation of the Will and Word of Allah in the Holy Qur-án there is the end of the prophecy and of revelation.   They are not made sinless saints because their piety and good works would not be the outcome of effort and struggle against evil, and therefore not justly meritorious.   They are not appointed to become workers of supernatural miracles because they have a firm and sound faith in their Lord.

Further, this "Sibghatu 'l-Lāh" makes the true Muslims grave, constant in their duties to Allah and towards their fellowmen, especially towards their families. *It does not move them to the folly of believing themselves holier than their co-religionists, and so to arrogate the post of pastorship to themselves over others as if they were their flocks and herds. Fanaticism, religious conceit, and the like are not operations of the Holy Spirit. Every Muslim receives at his creation the same "Sibghatu 'l-Lāh," the same religion and spiritual baptism, and has to run the race of his short earthly life to the best of his ability and effort in order to win the crown of glory in the next world. Every Muslim needs only education and religious training in accordance with the wisdom of the Word of God. But he needs not the intercession of a priest, sacrament, or saint. Every enlightened believer can become an Imām, a missionary, a preacher according to his learning and religious zeal, not for vain glory or lucrative gain.*

In short, every Muslim, whether at his birth or at his conversion, is baptized spiritually, and becomes a citizen of the Kingdom of God, a free man, and possesses equal rights and obligations, according to his ability, virtue, knowledge, wealth, rank.

St. John the Baptist asscribes this spiritual and igneous baptism to the Great Apostle of Allah, not as a divine being, God, or son of God, but as a holy agent, and as an instrument through which this divine baptismal sacrament was to be operated. Muhammad delivered the Message of Allah which was His Word; he led the prayers, administered the divine service, and fought the holy wars against the unbelievers and the idolators to defend his cause. But the success and the victory achieved was God's. In the same way John preached and baptized, but the contrition, penance, and the remission of sins could only be done by God. The Prophet John's prediction that "he who comes after me is more powerful than I; he will baptize you with the Spirit and with fire" is quite intelligible, because only through Muhammad this spiritual baptism was given and performed.

It is to be remarked that the *form* and *material* of this baptism is altogether divine and supernatural. We feel and see the effect of an invisible but real cause which accomplishes that effect. There is no longer water as the material, nor a baptist to officiate at the ritual or the form. It is God who, through the Spirit, works it out. The materials of the "Sibghatu 'l-Lāh" in the words of the Baptist are the Holy Spirit and fire. The form exclusively belongs to Allah. We cannot attribute to the Almighty any form of operation except His Word "Kun"—"Be!"—and His command is obeyed or created. The result is that a Muslim becomes sanctified, enlightened, and an equipped soldier to fight the Satan and his idolatry. These three effects of the "Sibghatu 'l-Lāh" deserve a serious consideration and study. Their exposition is but brief.

1. The Holy Spirit, whether the Archangel Gabriel or another of the created Superior Spirits, by the command of God sanctifies the spirit of a Muslim at his birth or conversion—as the case may be; and this sanctification means:

(a) Engraving a perfect faith in the one true God. The "Subghatu 'l-Lāh" makes the spirit of a true Muslim believe in the absolute unity of Allah, to rely upon Him, and to know He alone is his Master, Owner, and Lord. This faith in the true God is manifest in every person who professes himself a Muslim. The mark and the evidence of this ingrained faith in a Muslim shines brilliantly when he affirms,

"Anā muslim, Alḥamud li 'l-Lāhi ("I am Muslim; praised be Allah!"). What is more impressive and singularly obvious a sign of a holy faith than the hatred and repugnance which a Muslim feels against any other object of worship besides God? Which of the two is holier in the sight of God: he who worships his Creator in a simple building of the Mosque, or he who worships the fourteen pictures and images representing the scenes of the Crucifixion in a building whose walls and altars are adorned with the idolatrous statues, its ground covering the bones of the dead, and its dome decorated with the figures of angels and the saints?

(b) The sanctification by the Holy Spirit and fire which God works upon the spirit of a Muslim is that He impregnates and fills it with love for, and submission to, Him. An honourable husband would rather divorce his beloved consort than see her sharing his love with any other man. The Almighty will cast away any "believer" who associates any other object or being with Him. The Muslim's love for Allah is not theoretical or idealistic but practical and real. He will not hesitate for a moment to expel from his house his wife, son, or friend if he should blaspheme the Holy Name or Person. A pagan or a person of other religion may show a similar furious zeal for his object of worship. But that love which is shown for the One True God is holy and sanctified; and such love can only exist in the heart of a Muslim. Those auspicatory and doxological formulæ "Bismi 'l-Lāhi" and Alhamdu li 'l-Lāhi," which mean, respectively, "In the name of Allah" and "Praised be Allah" at the beginning and the end of every action or enterprise, are the most sincere expressions of the purified Muslim spirit impressed and inebriate with the "Love of God" that transcends and excels every other love. These ejaculations are not artificial or hypocritical expressions in the mouths of Muslims, but they are the prayer and the praise of the baptized spirit that resides in his body.   And if a Christian and a Jew are imbued with the same faith and devotion, and if their soul does effuse those expressions that the spirit of a Muslim does, then he is a Muslim though he knows it not.

(c) The baptismal sanctification which the "Sibghatu 'l-Lāh" inspires in the spirit of a Unitarian Muslim, besides faith and love, is a total submission and resignation to the holy will of God. This absolute submission emanates not only from faith and love, but also from a holy fear and from a deep respect so latent in the soul and spirit of every true believer.

Such are the principal characteristics of the spiritual baptism, and nowhere are they manifest but among the adherents of Islam.   John the Baptist, Jesus Christ and his apostles believed in, loved, and feared the same Allah as every Muslim does according to the degree of the divine grace and mercy. The Holy Spirit himself, too, is a creature and loves and fears the same Allah whom you and I do.

2. The second mark of the spiritual baptism is enlightenment. The true knowledge of Allah and of His will, so much as men are enable to possess, can only and exclusively be seen in Muslims. This knowledge sparkles dazzlingly in the countenance and the general behaviour of every Muslim. He may not comprehend the essence and the person of God, just as a child cannot understand the nature and the qualities of his parents; yet a baby recognizes its mother among all other women. The analogy is by far below the reality, and the comparison infinitely inferior between an enlightened good Muslim in relation to his Creator and a baby crying after its own good mother. Every Muslim, however ignorant, poor, and sinful, sees the signs of Allah in every phenomenon of the nature. Whatever befalls

him, in happiness or misery, Allah is in his mind. The Muslim call to prayer is a living witness of this enlightenment. "There is no object of worship besides Allah," is an eternal protest against all those who associate with Him other objects unworthy of worship. Every Muslim confesses: "I witness that God is the only Being worthy of worship."

In this respect I may hint at the fact that the human soul is quite different from the human spirit. It is this holy spirit that enlightens the soul and implants in it the knowledge of truth. It is again the evil spirit that induces the soul to error, idolatry, and ungodliness.

3. The "Sibghatu 'l-Lāh" is that divine baptism with fire which arms and equips the Muslim to become a bulwark against error and superstition, chiefly against idolatry of every kind. It is this baptismal fire that melts the soul and spirit of a Muslim, thus separating its golden substance from the rubbish and ordure. It is the power of God which strengthens and consolidates the union between Him and the believing servant, and arms him to fight for the religion of God. The fervour and the zeal of the Muslim for Allah and His religion is unique and holy. The savages also fight for their fetishes, the heathen for their idols, and the Christians for their cross; but what a contrast between these unworthy object of worship and the God of Islam!

In conclusion, I must draw the attention of my Muslim brethren to think who they are; to remember the favours of Allah; and to live accordingly.

VII

THE "PARACLETE" IS NOT THE
HOLY SPIRIT

In this article we can now discuss the famous "Paraclete" of the Fourth Gospel. Jesus Christ, like John-Baptist, announced the advent of the Kingdom of God, invited the people to repentance, and baptized them for the remission of their sins. He honourably accomplished his mission, and faithfully delivered the message of God to the people of Israel. He was not himself the founder of the Kingdom of God, but only its herald, and that is why he wrote nothing and authorized no one to write the Holy Gospel that was inscribed in his mind. He revealed the Gospel which meant the "good news" concerning the "Kingdom of God" and the "Pereiklitos" to his followers, not in writing, but in oral discourses, and in public sermons. These discourses sermons, and parables were transmitted by those who had heard them to those who had not. Later on it was that the sayings and teachings of the Master were reduced to writing. Jesus was no longer the Rabbi, but the Logos —the Divine Word; no longer the Forerunner of the Paraclete but his very Lord and Superior. His pure and true words were adulterated and mixed with myth and legend. For a time he was expected at any moment to come down from the clouds with legions of angels. The Apostles had all passed away; the second coming of Jesus Christ was delayed. His person and doctrine gave rise to a variety of religious and philosophical speculations. Sects succeeded one another; Gospels and Epistles under different names and titles appeared in many centres; and a multitude of the Christian scholars and apologists combated and criticized each other's theory. If there had been written a Gospel during the lifetime of Jesus, or even a book authorized by the College of the Apostles, the teachings of the Prophet of Nazareth would have preserved their purity and integrity until the appearance of the Periqlit—Aḥmad. But such was not the case. Each writer took a different view about the Master and his religion, and described him in his book —which he named Gospel or Epistle—according to his own imagination. The high-soaring flight of thought concerning the Word; the prophecy about the Periqlit; the inexplicable discourse of Jesus upon his flash and blood; and a series of several miracles, events, and sayings recorded in the Fourth Gospel were unknown to the Synoptics and consequently to a great majority of the Christians who had not seen it at least for a couple of centuries.

The Fourth Gospel, too, like every other book of the New Testament, was written in Greek and not in Aramaic, which was the mother-tongue of Jesus and his disciples. Consequently, we are again confronted with the same difficulty which we met with when we were discussing the "Eudokia" of St. Luke,[1] namely: What word or name was it that Jesus used in his native tongue to express that which the Fourth Gospel has translated as "the Paraclete" and which has been converted into "comforter" in all the versions of that Gospel?

Before discussing the etymology and the true signification of this unclassical or rather corrupt form of the Paraclete it is necessary to make a brief observation upon one particular feature of St. John's Gospel. The authorship and authenticity of this Gospel are questions which concern the Higher Biblical Criticism; but it is impossible to

1. Vide *Islamic Review* for January, 1930.

believe that the Apostle could have written this book as we
have it in its present shape and contents.   The author,
whether Yoḥannan (John) the son of Zebedee, or someone
else under that name, seems to be familiar with the doctrine
of the celebrated Jewish scholar and philosopher Philon
concerning the Logos (Word).   It is well known that the
conquest of Palestine and the foundation of Alexandria by
Alexander the Great opened up, for the first time, a new
epoch for culture and civilization.   It was then that the
disciples of Moses met with those of Epicurus, and the
mighty impact of the spiritual doctrines of the Bible on the
materialism of the Greek paganism took place.   The Greek
art and philosophy began to be admired and studied by
the Jewish doctors of the law both in Palestine and in
Egypt, where they had a very numerous community.   The
penetration of the Greek thought and *belles-lettres* into the
Jewish schools alarmed their priests and learned men.   In
fact, Hebrew was so much neglected that the Scriptures
were read in the Alexandrian Synagogues in the Septuagint
Version.   This invasion by a foreign knowledge, however,
moved the Jews to make a better study of their own law,
and to defend it against the inauspicious new spirit.   They
endeavoured, therefore, to find a new method for the interpretation of the Bible in order to enable the possibility
of a *rapprochement* and reconciliation of the Biblical truths
with the Hellenic thought.   For their former method of a
literal interpretation of the law was felt to be unworkable
and too weak to stand against the fine reasoning of Plato
and Aristotle.   At the same time the solid activities of the
Jews and their profound devotion to their religion often
aroused against themselves the jealousy and hatred of the
Greeks.   Already, under Alexander the Great, an Egyptian priest, Manetho, had written libels or calumnies against

Judaism.   Under Tiberius, too, the great orator Apion had resuscitated and envenomed the insults of Manetho. So that this literature poisoned the people who, later on, cruelly persecuted the believers in the one true God.

The new method was accordingly found and adopted. It was an Allegorical Interpretation of every law, precept, narration and even the names of great personages were considered to conceal in them a secret idea which it attempted to bring to light.   This Allegorical Interpretation soon arrogated to itself the place of the Bible, and was like an envelope enclosing in itself a system of religious philosophy.

Now the most prominent man who personified this science was Philon, who was born of a rich Jewish family in Alexandria in the year 25 before the Christian Era. Well versed in the philosophy of Plato, he wrote his allegorical work in a pure and harmonious Greek style.   He believed that the doctrines of the Revelation could agree with the highest human knowledge and wisdom.   What preoccupied his mind most was the phenomenon of the dealings of God, the pure Spirit, with the earthly beings. Following Plato's theory of the "Ideas," he invented a series of intermediary ideas called "the emanations of the Divinity," which he transformed into angles who unite God with the world.   The fundamental substance of these ideas, the Logos (Word), constituted the supreme wisdom created in the world and the highest expression of the Providential action.

The Alexandrian School followed the triumph of Judaism over Paganism.   "But," as rightly remarks the Grand-Rabin Paul Haguenauer in his interesting little book *Manuel de Littérature Juive* (p. 24). "mais d'elle surgirent, plus tard, des systèmes nuisibles á l'hébraïsme" indeed noxious systems, not only to Judaism but to Christendom too!

The origin of the doctrine of the Logos is to be traced, therefore, to the theology of Philon, and the Apostle John —or the author of the Fourth Gospel, whoever he be— only dogmatized the theory of the "ideas" which had sprung up first from the golden brain of Plato. As remarked in the first article of this series, the Divine Word means the Word of God, and *not* God the Word. The word is an attribute of a rational being; it belongs to any speaker, but it is not *the* rational being, the speaker. The Divine Word is not eternal, it has an origin, a *beginning;* it did not exist before the beginning except potentially. The word is not the essence. It is a serious error to substantialize any attribute whatever. If it be permitted to say "God the Word," why should it be prohibited to say, God the Mercy, God the Love, God the Vengeance, God the Life, God the Power, and so forth? I can well understand and accept the appellation of Jesus "the Divine Spirit" ("Rūhu 'l-Lāh"), of Moses "the Divine Word" ("Kalamu 'l-Lāh"), of Muhammad "the Divine Apostle" ("Rasūl Allah"), meaning the Spirit of God, the Word of God, the Apostle of God respectively. But I can never understand nor accept that the Spirit, or the Word, or the Apostle, is a Divine Person having divine and human natures.

Now we will proceed to expose and confute the Christian error about the Paraclete. In this article I shall try to prove that the Paraclete is not, as the Christian Churches believe, the Holy Ghost, nor does it at all mean the "comforter" or the "intercessor;" and in the following article, please God, I shall clearly show that it is not "Paraclete" but "Periclyte" which precisely signifies

"Aḥmad" in the sense of "the most Illustrious, Praised, and Celebrated."

1.—THE HOLY SPIRIT IS DESCRIBED IN THE NEW TESTAMENT AS OTHERWISE THAN A PERSONALITY

A careful examination of the following passages in the New Testament will convince the readers that the Holy Spirit, not only is it not the third person of the Trinity, but is not even a distinct person. But the "Paraclete" foretold by Jesus Christ is a distinct person. This fundamental difference between the two is, therefore, a decisive argument against the hypothesis of their being one and the same person.

(a) In Luke xi. 13 the Holy Spirit is declared to be a "gift" of God. The contrast between the "good gifts" which are given by wicked parents and the Holy Spirit which is bestowed upon the believers by God entirely excludes the idea of any personality of the Spirit. Can we conscientiously and positively affirm that Jesus Christ, when he made the above contrast, meant to teach his hearers that "God the Father" makes a gift of "God the Holy Spirit" to His earthly "children"? Did he ever insinuate that he believed the third person of the Trinity to be a gift of the first person of the Trinity? Can we conscientiously admit that the Apostles believed this "gift" to be God the Almighty offered by God the Almighty to mortals? The very idea of such a belief makes a Muslim shudder.

(b) In 1 Cor. ii. 12 this Holy Spirit is described in the neuter gender "the Spirit from God". St. Paul clearly states that as the Spirit which is in man makes him know the things that appertain to him so the Spirit of God makes a man know the things divine (1 Cor. 11). Consequently, the Holy Spirit here is not God but a divine issue, channel, or medium through which God *teaches, enlightens,* and *inspires* those whom He pleases. It is simply an action of God upon human soul and mind. The teacher, the enlightener, and the inspirer is not *directly the* Spirit but God Himself. I remarked that Philon was a student of Plato's philosophy. He had never seen Plato, but only learned Plato's philosophy and became a philosopher and a *Platonist.* In the same sense I say Peter the Apostle and 'Alī the Imām received the Holy Spirit of God and became inspired with the knowledge of God — they became *divine.* Just as the philosophy of Plato is *not the* Plato, and the Platonist Philon *not the* creator *of that* specific wisdom, so Peter and 'Alī were *not God.* They were divine because they were enlightened by the Spirit of God. St. Paul clearly sets forth, in the passage just quoted, that the human soul cannot discern the truths concerning God but only through His Spirit, inspiration, and direction.

(*c*)   Again, in 1 Cor. vi. 19 we read that the righteous servants of God are called "the temple of the Holy Spirit" which they "received from God." Here again the Spirit of God is not indicated to be a *person* or an *angel,* but His virtue, word, or power and religion. Both the body and the soul of a righteous believer are compared with a temple dedicated to the worship of the Eternal.

(*d*)   In the Epistle to the Romans (viii. 9) this same spirit that "lives" within the believers is called alternately "the Spirit of God" and the "Spirit of Christ." In this passage "the Spirit" means simply the faith and the true religion of God which Jesus proclaimed. Surely this spirit cannot mean to be the Christian ideal of the Holy Ghost, viz. another third of the three. We Muslims always wish and intend to regulate our lives and conduct ourselves in accordance with the spirit of Muhammad, meaning thereby that we are resolved to be faithful to the religion of God in much the same way as the Last Prophet was. For the holy Spirit in Muhammad, in Jesus, and in every other prophet was no other than the Spirit of Allah — praised be His Holy Name! This spirit is called "holy" to distinguish it from the impure and wicked spirit of the Devil and his fallen angels. This spirit is not a divine person, but a divine ray that enlightens and sanctifies the people of God.

(e) The Gospel formula, "In the name of the Father and of the Son and of the Holy Spirit," even if authentic and truly prescribed by Christ, may be legitimately accepted as a formula of faith before the formal establishment of Islam, which is the real Kingdom of God upon earth. God Almighty in His quality of Creator is *the* Father of all beings, things, and intelligences, but not the Father of one particular son. The Orientalists know that the Semitic word *"abb"* or *"abba,"* which is translated as "father," means "one who brings forth, or bears fruit" ("ibba" = fruit). This sense of the word is quite intelligible and its use legitimate enough. The Bible frequently makes use of the appellation "Father." God, somewhere in the Bible, says: "Israel is my first-born son"; and elsewhere in the book of Job He is called "the father of the rain." It is because of the abuse of this divine appellation of the Creator by Christendom that the Qur-án refrains from using it. From a purely Unitarian and Muslim point of belief the Christian dogma concerning the eternal birth or generation of the Son is a blasphemy.

Whether the Christian baptismal formula is authentic or spurious I believe there is a hidden truth in it. For it must be admitted that the Evangelists *never* authorize the use of it in any other ritual, prayer, or creed other than that of Baptism. *This point is extremely important.* St. John had foretold the Baptism with the Holy Spirit and fire by the Prophet Muhammad, as we saw in the preceding articles. The immediate Baptizer being God Himself, and the mediate the Son of Man or the Barnasha of the vision of Daniel, it was perfectly just and legitimate to mention those two names as the first and second efficient causes; and the name of the Holy Spirit, too, as the *causa materialis* of the Sibghatu 'l-Lah! Now the divine appellation "Father," before its abuse by the Church, was rightly invoked. In fact, the Sibghatu 'l-Lah is a new birth, a nativity into the Kingdom of God which is Islam. The Baptizer who causes this regeneration is directly Allah. To be born in the religion if Islam, to be endowed with the faith in the true God, is the greatest favour and gift of the "Heavenly Father" — to use the evangelistic expression. In this respect God is infinitely more beneficent than an earthly father.

As regards the second name in the formula, "the Son," one is at a loss to know who or what this "son" is? Whose son? If God be rightly addressed "Father," then one is curious, inquisitive, and anxious to know *which* of His innumerable "sons" is intended in the baptismal formula. Jesus taught us to pray "*Our* Father who art in heaven." If we are all His sons in the sense of His creatures, then the mention of the word "son" in the formula becomes somehow senseless and even ridiculous. We know that the name "the Son of Man" — or "Barnasha" — is mentioned eighty-three times in the discourses of Jesus. The Qur-án never calls Jesus "the son of man" but always "the son of Mary." He could not call himself "the son of man" because he was only "the son of woman." There is no getting away from the fact. You may make him "the son of God" as you foolishly do, but you can't make him "the son of man" unless you believe him to be the offspring of Joseph or someone else, and consequently fasten on to him the taint of illegitimacy.

I don't know exactly how, whether through intuition, inspiration, or dream, I am taught and convinced that the second name in the formula is an ill-fated corruption of "the Son of Man," viz. the Barnasha of Daniel (vii.), and therefore Ahmad "the Periqlytos" (Paraclete) of St. John's Gospel.

As to the Holy Spirit in the formula, it is not a person or an individual spirit, but an agency, force, energy of God with which a man is born or converted into the religion and knowledge of the One God.

2.—What the Early Fathers of the Nasara (Christianity) say about the Holy Spirit.

(a) Hermas (Similitude v. 5, 6) uderstands, by the "Holy Spirit," the divine element in Christ, namely the Son *created* before all things. Without entering into the useless or rather meaningless discussion whether Hermas confounds the Holy Spirit with the Word, or if it is a distinct element belonging to Christ, it is admitted that the latter was *created* before all things — that is to say, in the beginning — and that the Spirit in Hermas' belief is not a person.

(b) Justin — called the "Martyr" (100?-167? A.C.) — and Theophilus (120?-180? A.C.) understand by the Holy Spirit sometimes a peculiar form of the manifestation of the Word and sometimes a divine attribute, but never a divine person. It must be remembered that these two Greek fathers and writers of the second century A.C. had no definite knowledge and belief about the Holy Ghost of the Trinitarians of the fourth and the succeeding centuries.

(c)   Athenagoras (110-180 A.C.) says the Holy Spirit is an emanation of God proceeding from and returning to Him like the rays of the sun (*Deprecatio pro Christianis*, ix, x).   Irenæus (130?-202? A.C.) says that the Holy Spirit and the Son are two servants of God and that the angles submit to them.   The wide difference between the belief and the conceptions of these two early father about the Holy Spirit is too obvious to need any further comment. It is surprising that the two servants of God, according to the declaration of such an authority as Irenæus, should, two centuries afterwards, be raised to the dignity of God and proclaimed two divine persons in company with the one true God by whom they were created.

(d)   The most illustrious and learned of all the ante-Nicene fathers and the Christian apologists was Origen (185-254 A.C.).   The author of the *Hexepla* ascribes personality to the Holy Spirit, but makes it a creature of the Son.   The creation of the Holy Spirit by the Son cannot be even in the beginning when the Word — or the Son — was created by God.

The doctrine concerning this Holy Spirit was not sufficiently developed in 325 A.C., and therefore was not defined by the Council of Nicea.   It was only in 386 A.C. at the second Œcumenical Council of Constantinople that it was declared to be the Third Person of the Trinity, consubstantial and coeval with the Father and the Son.

3. — The "Paraclete" does not signify either "consoler" or "advocate"; in truth, it is not a classical word at all.   The Greek orthography of the word is *Paraklytos* which in ecclesiastical literature is made to mean "one called to aid, advocate, intercessor" (*Dict. Grec.-Francais,* by Alex-

andre). One need not profess to be a Greek scholar to know that the Greek word for "comforter or consoler" is not "Paraclytos" but "Paracalon". I have no Greek version of the Septuagint with me, but I remember perfectly well that the Hebrew word for "comforter" ("mnăhem") in the Lamentations of Jeremiah (i. 2, 9, 16, 17, 21, etc.) is translated into *Parakaloon,* from the verb *Parakaloo,* which means to call to, invite, exhort, console, pray, invoke. It should be noticed that there is a long *alpha* vowel after the consonant *kappa* in the "Paracalon" which does not exist in the "Paraclytos." In the phrase (He who consoles us in all our afflictions") "paracalon" and not "paraclytos" is used. ("I exhort, or *invite, thee to work*"). Many other examples can be cited here.

There is another Greek word for comforter and consoler, i.e. "Parygorytys" from "I console."

As to the other meaning of "intercessor or advocate" which is given in the ecclesiastical word "Paraclete," I again insist that "Paracalon" and *not* "Paraclytos" can convey in itself a similar sense. The proper Greek term for "advocate" is *Sunegorus* and for "intercessor" or "mediator" *Meditéa.*

In my next article I shall give the true Greek form of which *Paraklytos* is a corruption. *En passant,* I wish to correct an error into which the French savant Ernest Renan has also fallen. If I recollect well, Monsieur Renan, in his famous *The Life of Christ,* interprets the "Paraclete" of St. John (xiv. 16, 26; xv. 7; 1 John ii. 1) as an "advocate." He cites the Syro-Chaldean form "Peraklit" as opposed to "Ktighra" "the accuser" from *Kategorus.* The Syrian name for mediator or intercessor is "mis'aaya," but in law courts the "Snighra" (from the Greek *Sunegorus*) is used for an advocate. Many Syrians unfamiliar with the Greek language consider the "Paraqlita" to be really the Aramaic or the syriac form of the "Paraclete" in the Pshittha Version and to be composed of "Paraq," "to save from, to deliver from," and "lita" "the accursed." The idea that Christ is the "Saviour from the curse of the law," and therefore he is himself too "Paraqlita" (1 John ii. 1), may have led some to think that the Greek word is originally an Aramaic word, just as the Greek sentence "Maran atha" in Aramaic is "Mārān Āthī," i.e. "our Lord is coming" (1 John xvi. 22), which seems to be an expression among the believers regarding the coming of the Last Great Prophet. This 'Mārān Āthī," as well as, especially, the baptismal formula, contains points too important to be neglected. They both deserve a special study and a valuable exposition. They both embody in themselves marks and indications otherwise than favourable to charistianity.

I think I have sufficiently proved that the "Paraclytos," from a linguistic and etymological point of view, does *not* mean "advocate, consoler, or comforter." Elsewhere I have described this as "barbarous," but I retract that expression and will replace it by "corruption." Ignorance commits many errors. For centuries the ignorant Latins and Europeans have been writing the name of Muhammad "Mahomet," that of Mushi "Moses." Is it, therefore, small wonder that some sturdy Christian monk or scribe should have written the true name in the corrupted form of *Paraklytos?* The former means the "most Illustrious, Praiseworthy," but the corrupted form means nothing at all except a standing shame to those who have for eighteen centuries understood it to signify an advocate or a consoler.

VIII

"PERIQLYTOS" MEANS "AHMAD"

"And when Jesus, the Son of Mary, said, O children of Israel, verily I am the apostle of God sent unto you, confirming the law which was delivered before me, and bringing glad tidings of an apostle who shall come after me and whose name shall be Ahmad" (Qur-an, lxi).

"And I will ask the Father, and he shall give you another Periqlytos, that he may stay with you for ever" (John xiv. 16, etc.).

There is some incoherency in the words ascribed to Jesus by the Fourth Gospel.   It reads as if several Periqlytes had already come and gone, and that "another Periqlytos" would be given only at the request of Jesus.   These words also leave behind the impression that the Apostles were already made familiar with this name which the Greek text renders Periqlytos.   The adjective "another" preceding a foreign noun for the first time announced seems very strange and totally superfluous.   There is no doubt that the text has been tampered with and distorted.   It pretends that the Father will send the Periqlyte at the request of Jesus, otherwise the Periqlyte would never have come!   The word "ask," too, seems superficial, and unjustly displays a touch of arrogance on the part of the Prophet of Nazareth.   If we want to find out the real sense in these words we must correct the text and supply the stolen or corrupted words, thus:

"I shall *go* to the Father, and he shall *send* you another *apostle whose name shall be* Periqlytos, that he may remain with you for ever."   Now with the additional italicized words, both the robbed modesty of Jesus is restored and the nature of the Periqlyte identified.

We have already seen that the Periqlyte is not the Holy Spirit, that is to say, a divine person, Gabriel, or any other angel. It now remains to prove that the Periqlyte could not be a consoler nor an advocate between God and men.

1. The Periqlyte is not the "Consoler" nor the "Intercessor." We have fully shown the material impossibility of discovering the least signification of "consolation" or of "intercession". Christ does not use Paraqalon. Besides, even from a religious and moral point of view the idea of consolation and intercession is inadmissible.

(a) The belief that the death of Jesus upon the Cross redeemed the believers from the curse of original sin, and that his spirit, grace, and presence in the Eucharist would be for ever with them, left them in need of no consolation nor of the coming of a consoler at all. On the other hand, if they needed such a comforter, then all the Christian presumptions and pretentions concerning the sacrifice of Calvary fall to the ground. In fact, the language of the Gospels and that of the Epistles explicitly indicates that the second coming Jesus upon the clouds was imminent (Matt. xvi. 28; Mark ix. 1; Luke ix. 27; 1 John ii. 18; 2 Tim. ii. 1; 2 Thess. ii. 3, etc.).

(b) Consolation can never make restitution of the loss. To console a man who has lost his sight, wealth, son, or situation, cannot restore any of those losses. The promise that a consoler would be sent by God after Jesus had gone would indicate the total collapse of all hope in the triumph of the Kingdom of God. The promise of a consoler indicates mourning and lamentation and would naturally drive the Apostles into disappointment if not into despair. They needed, not a consoler in their distress and afflictions, but a victorious warrior to crush the Devil and his power, one who would put an end to their troubles and persecutions.

(c) The idea of an "intercessor" between God and man is even more untenable than that of the "consoler." There is no absolute mediator between the Creator and the creature.   The unity of Allah alone is our absolute intercessor.   The Christ who advised his audience to pray to God in secret, to enter the closet and shut the door and then to pray — for only under such a condition their heavenly "Father" would hear their prayer and grant them His grace and succour — could not promise them an intercessor.   How to reconcile this contradiction!

(d) All believers, in their prayers, intercede for each other, the prophets and angels do the same.   It is our duty to invoke God's mercy, pardon, and help for ourselves as well as for others.   But God is not bound or obliged to accept the intercession of anyone unless He pleases.   If Allah had accepted the intercession of His Holy Servant Muhammad, all men and women would have been converted to the religion of Islam.

I would be duly grateful to the person through whose intercession I obtained pardon, and relief.   But I shall always dread the judge or the despot who was delivering me into the hands of an executioner.   How learned these Christians are, when they believe that Jesus at the right hand of his Father intercedes for them, and at the same time believe in another intercessor — inferior to himself — who sits on the throne of the Almighty!   The Holy Qur-án strictly forbids the faith, the trust in a "shafi' " or intercessor.   Of course, we do not know for certain, but it is quite conceivable that certain angels, the spirits of the prophets and those of the saints, are permitted by God to render help and guidance to those who are placed under their patronage.   The idea of an advocate before the tribunal of God, pleading the cause of his clients, may be very admirable, but it is erroneous, because God is not a human judge subject to passion, ignorance, partiality, and all the rest of it. The Muslims, the believers, need only education and religious training; God knows the actions and the hearts of men infinitely better than the angels and prophets. Consequently there is no necessity for intercessors between the Deity and the creatures.

(e) The belief in intercessors emanates from the belief in sacrifices, burnt offerings, priesthood, and a massive edifice of superstition. This belief leads men into the worship of sepulchres and images of saints and martyrs; it helps to increase the influence and domination of the priest and monk; it keeps the people ignorant in the things divine; a dense cloud of the intermediary dead cover the spiritual atmosphere between God and the spirit of man. Then this belief prompts men who, for the pretended glory of God and the conversion of the people belonging to a different religion than theirs, raise immense sums of money, establish powerful and rich missions, and lordly mansions; but at heart those missionaries are political agents of their respective Governments. The real cause of the calamities which have befallen the Armenians, the Greeks, and the Chaldeo-Assyrians in Turkey and Persia ought to be sought in the treacherous and revolutionary instruction given by all the foreign missions in the East. Indeed, the belief in the intercessors has always been a source of abuse, fanaticism, persecution, ignorance, and of many other evils.

Having proved that the "Paraclete" of St. John's Gospel does not and cannot mean either "consoler" or "advocate," nor any other thing at all, and that it is a corrupted form of Periqlytos, we shall now proceed to discuss the real signification of it.

2. Periqlytos etymologically and literally means "the

most illustrious, renowned, and praiseworthy." I take for my authority Alexandre's *Dictionnaire Grec-Francais*=Periqlytos, "Qu'on peut entendre de tous les côtés; qu'il est facile à entendre. Très célèbre," etc.;"=Periqleitos, très célèbre, illustre, glorieux;=Periqleys, très célèbre, illustre, glorieux," from=Kleos, glorire, renommée, célébrité." This compound noun is composed of the prefix "peri," and "kleotis," the latter derived from "to glorify, praise." The noun, which I write in English characters Periqleitos or Periqlytos, means precisely what AHMAD means in Arabic, namely the most illustrious, glorious, and renowned. The only difficulty to be solved and overcome is to discover the original Semitic name used by Jesus Christ either in Hebrew or Aramaic.

(*a*) The Syriac Pshittha, while writing "Paraqleita," does not even in a glossary give its meaning. But the Vulgate translates it into "consolator" or "consoler." If I am not mistaken the Aramaic form must have been "Mhamda" or "Hamīda" to correspond with the Arabic "Muhammad" or "Ahmad" and the Greek 'Periqlyte."

The interpretation of the Greek word in the sense of consolation does not imply that the name Periqlyte *itself* is the consoler, but the belief and the hope in the promise that *he will come* "to console the early Christians. The expectation that Jesus would come down again in glory before many of his auditors had "tasted the death" had disappointed them, and concentrated all their hopes in the coming of the Periqlyte.

(*b*) The Qur-ánic revelation that Jesus, the son of Mary, declared unto the people of Israel that he was "bringing glad tidings of an apostle, who shall come after me and whose name shall be Ahmad," is one of the strongest proofs that Muhammad was truly a Prophet and that the Qur-án is really a divine revelation. He could never have known that the Periqlyte meant Ahmad, unless through inspiration and divine revelation. The authority of the Qur-án is decisive and final; for the literal signification of the Greek name exactly and indisputably corresponds with Ahmad and Muhammad.

Indeed, the Angel Gabriel, or the Holy Spirit, seems even to have distinguished the positive from the superlative form the former signifying precisely Muhammad and the latter Ahmad.

It is marvellous that this unique name, never before given to any other person, was miraculously preserved for the most Illustrious and Praiseworthy Apostle of Allah! We never come across any Greek bearing the name Periqleitos (or Periqlytos), nor any Arab bearing the name of Ahmad. True, there was a famous Athenian called Periqleys which means "illustrious," etc., but not in the superlative degree.

(c)   It is quite clear from the description of the Fourth Gospel that Periqlyte is a definite person, a created holy spirit, who would come and dwell in a human body to perform and accomplish the prodigious work assigned to him by God, which no other man, including Moses, Jesus, and any other prophet, had ever accomplished.

We, of course, do not deny that the disciples of Jesus did receive the Spirit of God, that the true converts to the faith of Jesus were hallowed with the Holy Spirit, and that there were numerous Unitarian Christians who led a saintly and righteous life.   On the day of the Pentecost — that is, ten days after the Ascension of Jesus Christ — the Spirit of God descended upon the disciples and other believers numbering one hundred and twenty persons, in the form of tongues of fire (Acts ii.); and this number, which had received the Holy Spirit in the form of one hundred and twenty tongues of fire, was increased unto three thousand souls who were baptized, but were not visited by the flame of the Spirit. Surely one definite Spirit cannot be divided into six-score of individuals. By the Holy Spirit, unless definitely described as a personality, we may understand it to be God's power, grace, gift, action, and inspiration. Jesus had promised this heavenly gift and power to sanctify, enlighten, strengthen, and teach his flock; but this Spirit was quite different from the Periqlyte who alone accomplished the great work which Jesus and after him the Apostles were not authorized and empowered to accomplish, as we shall see later.

(*d*) The early Christians of the first and second centuries relied more upon tradition than upon writings concerning the new religion. Papias and others belong to this category. Even in the lifetime of the Apostles several sects, pseucudochrists, Antichrists, and false teachers, tore asunder the Church (1 John ii. 18-26; 2 Thess. ii. 1-12; 2 Peter ii. iii. 1; John 7-13; 1 Tim. iv. 1-3; 2 Tim. iii. 1-13; etc.). The "believers" are advised and exhorted to stick to and abide by the *Tradition*, namely, the oral teaching of the Apostles. These so-called "heretical" sects, such as the Gnostics, Apollinarians, Docetæ, and others, appear to have no faith in the fables, legends, and extravagant views about the sacrifice and the redemption of Jesus Christ as contained in many fabulous writings spoken of by Luke (i. 1-4). One of the heresiarchs of a certain sect — whose name has escaped my memory — actually assumed "Periqleitos" as his name, pretending to be "the most praiseworthy" Prophet foretold by Jesus, and had many followers. If there were an authentic Gospel authorized by Jesus Christ or by *all* the Apostles, there could be no such numerous sects, all opposed to the contents of the books contained in or outside the existing New Testament. We can safely infer from the action of the pseudo-Periqlyte that the early Christians considered the promised "Spirit of Truth" to be a person and the final Prophet of God.

3. There is not the slightest doubt that by "Periqlyte," Muhammad, i.e. Ahmad, is intended. The two names, one in Greek and the other in Arabic, have precisely the same signification, and both mean the "most Illustrious and Praised," just as "Pneuma" and "Rūḥ" mean nothing more or less than "Spirit" in both languages. We have seen that the translation of the word into "consoler" or "advocate" is absolutely untenable and wrong. The compound form of Paraqalon is derived from the verb composed of the prefix-Para-qalo, but the Periqlyte is derived from the Peri-qluo. The difference is as clear as anything could be. Let us examine, then, the marks of the Periqlyte which can only be found in Ahmad — Muhammad.

(a) Muhammad alone revealed the *whole* truth about God, His unity, religion, and corrected the impious libels and calumnies written and believed against Himself and many of His holy servants.

Jesus is reported to have said about Periqlyte that he is "the Spirit of Truth," that he "will give witness" concerning the true nature of Jesus and of his mission (John xiv. 17; xv. 26). In his discourses and orations Jesus speaks of the pre-existence of his own spirit (John viii. 58. xvii. 5, etc.). In the Gospel of Barnabas, Jesus is reported to have often spoken of the glory and the splendour of Muhammad's spirit whom he had seen. There is no doubt that the Spirit of the Last Apostle was created long before Adam. Therefore Jesus, in speaking about him, naturally would declare and describe him as "the Spirit of Truth." It was this Spirit of Truth that reprimanded the

Christians for dividing the unity of God into a trinity of persons; for their having raised Jesus to the dignity of God and Son of God, and for their having invented all sorts of superstitions and innovations. It was this Spirit of Truth that exposed the frauds of both the Jews and Christians for having corrupted their Scriptures; that condemned the former for their libels against the chastity of the Blessed Virgin and against the birth of her son Jesus. It was this Spirit of Truth that demonstrated the birthright of Ishmael, the innocence of Lot, Solomon, and many other prophets of old and cleared their name of the slur and infamy cast upon them by the Jewish forgers. It was this Spirit of Truth, too, that gave witness about the true Jesus, man, prophet, and servant of God; and has made it absolutely impossible for Muslims to become idolaters, magicians, and believers in more than the one only Allah.

(b) Among the principal marks of Periqlyte, "the Spirit of Truth," when he comes in the person of the "Son of Man"—Ahmad—is "he will chastise the world for sin" (John xvi. 8, 9). No other servant of Allah, whether a king like David and Solomon or a prophet like Abraham and Moses, did carry on this chastisement for sin to the extreme end, with resolution, fervour, and courage as Muhammad did. Every breach of the law is a sin, but idolatry is its mother and source. We sin against God when we love an object more than Him, but the worship of any other object or being besides God is idolatry, the evil and the total negligence of the Good—in short, sin in general. All the men of God chastised their neighbours and people for sin, but not "the *world*," as Muhammad did. He not only rooted out idolatry in the peninsula of Arabia in his lifetime, but also he sent envoys to the Chosroes Parviz and to Heraclius, the sovereigns of the two greatest

empires, Persia and Rome, and to the King of Ethiopia,
the Governor of Egypt, and Several other Kings and emirs,
inviting them all to embrace the religion of Islam and to
abandon idolatry and false faiths.   The chastisement by
Muhammad began with the delivery of the word of God
as he received it, namely, the recital of the verses of the
Qur-án; then with preaching, teaching, and practising the
true religion; but when the Power of Darkness, idolatry,
opposed him with arms he drew the sword and *punished*
the unbelieving enemy. This was in fulfilment of the decree
of God (Dan. vii.).   Muhammad was endowed by God
with power and dominion to establish the Kingdom of God,
and to become the first Prince and Commander-in-Chief
under the "King of Kings and the Lord of Lords."

(*c*) The other characteristic feature of the exploits
of Periqlyte — Ahmad — is that he will reprove the world
of righteousness and justice (*loc. cit.*).   The interpretation
"of righteousness, because I am going to my Father" (John
xvi. 10) put into the mouth of Jesus is obscure and
ambiguous.   The return of Jesus unto his God is given as
one of the reasons for the chastisement of the world by the
coming Periqlyte. Why so? And *who did* chastise the
world on that account? The Jews believed that they
crucified and killed Jesus, and did not believe that he was
raised and taken up into heaven.   It was Muhammad who
chastised and punished them severely for their infidelity.
"Say, O Muhammad, to the unbelieving Jews: They did
not really kill him; but God took him up unto Himself"
(Qur-án, iv. 158).   The same chastisement was inflicted
upon the Christians who believed and still believe that he
was really crucified and killed upon the Cross, and imagine
him to be God or the son of God.   To these the Qur-án
replied: "Yet they [the Jews] slew him not, nor crucified

him, but the matter was made dubious to them." *Several believers in Jesus in the very beginning of Christianity denied that Christ himself suffered upon the Cross, but maintained that another among his followers, Judas Iscariot or another very like him, was seized and crucified in his stead.* The Corinthians, the Basilidians, the Corpocratians and many other sectaries held the same view. I have fully discussed this question of the Crucifixion in my work entitled *Injīl wa Salīb* ("The Gospel and the Cross"), of which only one volume was published in Turkish just before the Great War. I shall devote an article to this subject. So the justice done to Jesus by Ahmad was to authoritatively declare that he was "Rūhu 'l-Lāh," the Spirit of God that he was not himself crucified and killed, and that he was a human being but a beloved and holy messenger of God. This was what jesus meant by justice concerning his person, mission, and transportation into heaven, and this was actually accomplished by the Apostle of Allah.

(*d*) The most important mark of Periqlyte is that he would chastise the world on account of Judgment "because the prince of this world is to be judged" (John xvi. 11). The King or Prince of this world was Satan (John xii. 31, xiv. 30), because the world was subject to him. I must draw the kind attention of my readers to the seventh chapter of the Book of Daniel written in Aramaic or Babylonian dialect. There it illustrates how the "thrones" ("Kursawan") and the "Judgment" ("dīna") were set up, and the "books" ("siphrin") were opened. In Arabic, too, the word "dīnu," like the Aramaic "dīna," means judgment, but it is generally used to signify religion. That the Qur-án should make use of the "Dina" of Daniel as an expression of judgment and religion is more than significant. In my humble opinion this is a direct sign and evidence of the truth revealed by

the same Holy Spirit or Gabriel to Daniel, Jesus, and
Muhammad. Muhammad could not forge or fabricate this
even if he were as learned a philosopher as Aristotle. The
judgment described with all its majesty and glory was set
up to judge the Satan in the form of the fearful fourth
Beast by the Supreme Judge, the Eternal. It was then that
someone appeared "like a son of man" ("kbar inish") or
"barnasha," who was presented to the Almighty, invested
with power, honour, and kingdom for ever, and appointed
to kill the Beast and to establish the Kingdom of the People
of the Saints of the Most High.

Jesus Christ was not appointed to destroy the Beast;
he abstained from political affairs, paid tribute to Cæsar,
and fled away when they wanted to crown him King. He
clearly declares that the Chief of this world is coming; for
the Periqlyte will root out the abominable cult of idolatry.
All this was accomplished by Muhammad in a few years.
Islam is Kingdom and Judgment, or religion; it has the
Book of Law, the Holy Al-Qurán; it has God as its Supreme
Judge and King, and Muhammad as its victorious hero of
everlasting bliss and glory!

(e) "The last but not the least mark of the Periqlyte
is that he will not speak anything of himself, but whatsoever
he hears that will he speak, and he will show you the future
things" (John xv. 13). There is not one iota, not a single
word or comment of Muhammad or of his devoted and holy
companions in the text of the glorious Qur-án. All its
contents are the revealed Word of Allah. Muhammad
uttered, pronounced the Word of God as he *heard it* read
to him by the Angel Gabriel, and was reduced to writing
by the faithful scribes. The words, sayings, and teachings
of the Prophet, though sacred and edifying, are not the
Word of God, and they are called Ahādith or Traditions.

Is he not, then, even in this description, the true Periqlyte? Can you show us another person, besides Ahmad, to possess in himself all these material, moral, and practical qualities, marks, and distinctions of Periqlyte? You *cannot*.

I think I have said enough on the Periqlyte and shall conclude with a sacred verse from the Qur-án: "I follow no other than what is revealed unto me; nor am I more than a Public Warner" (xlvi.).

IX

"THE SON OF MAN," WHO IS HE?

The Holy Qur-án presents to us the true Jesus Christ as "the Son of Mary;" and the Holy Gospels, too, present him to us as "the Son of Mary;" but that Gospel which was written on the white tablets of the heart of Jesus and delivered to his disciples and followers orally, alas! was soon adulterated with a mass of myth and legend. "The Son of Mary" becomes "the Son of Joseph," having brothers and sisters.[1] Then he becomes "the Son of David;"[2] "the Son of Man;"[3] "the Son of God;"[4] "the Son" only;[5] "the

1. Matt. xiii. 55, 56; Mark vi. 3; iii. 31; Luke ii. 48; viii. 19—21; John ii. 12; vii. 3, 5; Acts i. 14; I Cor. ix. 5; Gal. i. 19; Jude i.
2. Matt. xxii. 42; Mark xii. 35; Luke xx. 41, Matt. xx. 30; ix. 27; xxi. 9; Acts xiii. 22, 23; Apoc. v. 5; Rom. xv. 12; Heb. vii. 14, etc.
3. About eighty-three times in the discourses of Jesus this appellation is repeated.
4. Matt. xiv. 32, xvi. 16; John xi. 27; Acts ix. 20; 1 John iv. 15; v. 5; Heb. i. 2, 5, etc.
5. John v. 19, 20, 21, 23, 24, 26, etc.; and in the Baptismal formula, Matt. xxviii. 19; John i. 34, etc.

Christ;"[6] and "the Lamb."[7]

Many years ago, one day I visited the Exeter Hall in London; I was a Catholic priest then; *nolens volens* I was conducted to the Hall where a young medical gentleman began to preach to a meeting of the Young Men's Christian Association. "I repeat what I have often said," exclaimed the doctor, "Jesus Christ must be either what he claims to be in the Gospel or he must be the greatest impostor the world has ever seen!" I have never forgotten this dogmatizing statement. What he wanted to say was that Jesus was either the Son of God or the greatest impostor. If you accept the first hypothesis you are a Christian, a Trinitarian; if the second, then you are an unbelieving Jew. But we who accept neither of these two propositions are naturally Unitarian Muslims. We Muslims cannot accept either of the two titles given to Jesus Christ in the sense which the Churches and their unreliable Scriptures pretend to ascribe to those appellations. Not alone is he "the Son of God," and not alone "the Son of Man," for if it be permitted to call God "Father," then not only Jesus, but every prophet and righteous believer, is particularly a "son of God." In the same way, if Jesus were really the son of Joseph the Carpenter, and had four brothers and several married sisters as the Gospels pretend, then why alone should he assume this strange appellation of "the Son of Man" which is common to any human being?

It would seem that these Christian priests and pastors, theologians and apologists have a peculiar logic of their own for reasoning and a special propensity for mysteries and absurdities. Their logic knows no medium, no

6.   Matt. xvi. 16, and frequently in the Epistles.
7.   John i. 29, 36; and often in the Revelation.

distinction of the terms, and no definite idea of the titles and appellations they use. They have an enviable taste for irreconcilable and contradictory statements which they alone can swallow like boiled eggs. They can believe, without the least hesitation, that Mary was both virgin and wife, that Joseph was both spouse and husband, that James, Jossi, Simon, and Judah were both cousins of Jesus and his brothers, that Jesus is perfect God and perfect man, and that "the Son of God," "the Son of Man," "the Lamb," and "the Son of David" are all one and the same person! They feed themselves on heterogeneous and opposed doctrines which these terms represent with as greedy an appetite as they feel for bacon and eggs at breakfast. They never stop to think and ponder on the object they worship; they adore the crucifix and the Almighty as if they were kissing the bloody dagger of the assassin of their brother in the presence of his father!

I do not think there is even one Christian in ten millions who really has a precise idea or a definite knowledge about the origin and the true signification of the term "the Son of Man." All Churches and their commentators without exception will tell you that "the Son of God" assumed the appellation of "the Son of Man" or "the Barnasha" out of humility and meekness, never knowing that the Jewish Apocalyptical Scriptures, in which Jesus and his disciples heart and soul believed, foretold *not* a "Son of Man" who would be meek, humble, having nowhere to lay his head, and be delivered into the hands of the evildoers and killed, *but* a strong man with tremendous power and strength to destroy and disperse the birds of prey and the ferocious beasts that were tearing and devouring his sheep and lambs! The Jews who heard Jesus speaking of "the Son of Man" full well understood *to whom* he was alluding.

Jesus did not invent the name "Barnasha," but borrowed it from the Apocalyptical Jewish Scriptures: the Book of Enoch, the Sibylline Books, the Assumption of Moses, the Book of Daniel, etc. Let us examine the origin of this title "the Barnasha" or "the Son of Man."

1. "The Son of Man" is the Last Prophet, who established "the Kingdom of Peace" and saved the people of God from servitude and persecutions under the idolatrous powers of Satan. The title "Barnasha" is a symbolical expression to distinguish the Saviour from the people of God who are represented as the "sheep," and the other idolatrous nations of the earth under various species of the birds of prey, ferocious beasts, and unclean animals. The Prophet Hezekiel is almost always addressed by God as "Ben Adam," that is "the Son of Man" (or of Adam) in the sense of a Shepherd of the Sheep of Israel. This Prophet has also some Apocalyptical portions in his book. In his first vision with which he begins his prophetic book he sees besides the sapphire throne of the Eternal the appearance of "the Son of Man."[1] This "Son of Man" who is repeatedly mentioned as always in the presence of God and above the Cherubim is not Hezekiel (or Ezekiel) himself.[2] He is the prophetical "Barnasha," the Last Prophet, who was appointed to save the people of God from the hands of the unbelievers *here* upon *this earth,* and *not elsewhere!*

(a) "The Son of Man" according to the Apocalypse of Enoch (or Henoh).

There is no doubt that Jesus Christ was very familiar with the Revelation of Enoch, believed to be written by the

1. Ezek. i. 26.
2. Ezek. x. 2.

seventh patriarch from Adam.   For Judah, "the brother of
James" and the "servant of Jesus Christ," that is the brother
of Jesus, believes that Enoch was the real author of the
work bearing his name.[1]   There are some dispersed frag-
ments of this wonderful Apocalypse preserved in the
quotations of the Early Christian writers.   The book was
lost long before Photius.   It was only about the beginning
of last century that this important work was found in the
Canon of the Scriptures belonging to the Abyssinian Church,
and translated from the Ethiopic into the German language
by Dr. Dillmann, with notes and explanations.[2]   The book
is divided into five parts or books, and the whole contains
one hundred and ten chapters of unequal length.   The
author describes the fall of the angels, their illicit commerce
with the daughters of men, giving birth to a race of giants
who invent all sorts of artifices and noxious knowledge.
Then vice and evil increase to such a pitch that the Almighty
punishes them all with the Deluge.   He also relates his
two journeys to the heavens and across the earth, being
guided by good angels, and the mysteries and wonders he
saw therein.   In the second part, which is a description of
the Kingdom of Peace, "the Son of Man" catches the kings
in the midst of their voluptuous life and precipitates them
into hell.[3]   But this second book does not belong to one
author, and assuredly it is much corrupted by Christian
hands.   The third book (or part) contains some curious and
developed astronomical and physical notions.   The fourth
part presents an Apocalyptical view of the human race from
the beginning to the Islamic days, which the author styles

1.   Judah i. 14.   In the Gospels he is mentioned as one of the four
      brothers of Jesus, Matt. xiii. 55, 56, etc.
2.   It has also been translated into English by an Irish Bishop,
      Laurence.
3.   Enoch xlvi. 4 — 8.

the "Messianic" times, in two symbolical parables or rather allegories. A white bull comes out of the earth; then a white heifer joins him they give birth to two calves: one black, the other red; the black bull beats and chases away the red one; then he meets a heifer and they give birth to several calves of black colour, until the mother cow leaves the black bull in the search the red one; and, as she does not find him, bawls and shrieks aloud, when a red bull appears, and they begin to propagate their species. Of course, this transparent parable symbolizes Adam, Eve, Cain, Abel, Sheth, etc., down to Jacob whose offspring is represented by a "flock of sheep" — as the Chosen People of Israel; but the offspring of his brother Esau, i.e. the Edomites, is described as a swarm of boars. In this second parable the flock of sheep is frequently harassed, attacked, dispersed, and butchered by the beasts and birds of prey until we come to the so-called Messianic times, when the flock of sheep is again attacked fiercely by ravens and other carnivorous animals; but a gallant "Ram" resists with great courage and valour. It is then that "the Son of Man," who is the real master or owner of the flock, comes forth to deliver his flock.

A non-Muslim scholar can never explain the vision of a Sophee — or a Seer. He will — as all of them do — bring down the vision to the Maccabees and the King Antiochus Epiphanes in the middle of the second century B.C., when the Deliverer comes with a tremendous truncheon or sceptre and strikes right and left upon the birds and the beasts, making a great slaughter among them; the earth, opening its mouth, swallows them in; and the rest take to flight. Then swords are distributed among the sheep, and a white bull leads them on in perfect peace and security.

As to the fifth book, it contains religious and moral

exhortations. The whole work in its present shape exhibits indications which show that it was composed as late as 110 B.C., in the original Aramaic dialect, by a Palestinian Jew. At least such is the opinion of the *French Encyclopaedia.*

The Qur-án only mentions Enoch under his surname "Idrīs" — the Arabic form of the Aramaic "Drīsha" being of the same category of simple nouns as "Iblis" and "Blīsa."[1] "Idris" and "Drīsha" signify a man of great learning, a scholar and an erudite, from "darash" (Arabic "darisa"). The Qur-ánic text says: "And remember Idris in *the same* book; for he was a just person *and* a prophet; and We exalted him to a high place" (xix.).

The Muslim commentators, Al-Baydhāwi and Jalālu 'd-Dīn, seem to know that Enoch had studied astronomy, physics, arithmetic, that he was the first who wrote with the pen, and that "Idris" signifies a man of much knowledge, thus showing that the Apocalypse of Enoch had not been lost in their time.

After the close of the Canon of the Hebrew Scriptures in the fourth century or so B.C. by the "Members of the Great Synagogue," established by Ezra and Nehemiah, all other sacred or religious literature besides those included within the Canon was called Apocrypha and excluded from the Hebrew Bible by an assembly of the learned and pious Jews, the last of whom was the famous "Simeon the Just," who died in 310 B.C. Now among these Apocryphal books are included the Apocalypses of Enoch, Barukh, Moses, Ezra, and the Sibyline books, written at different epochs between the time of the Maccabees and after the destruction of Jerusalem by Titus. It seems to be quite *à la mode* with

---

1. "Iblis," the Arabic form of the Aramaic "Blisa," an epithet given to the devil which means the "Bruised One."

the Jewish Sages to compose Apocalyptical and religious literature under the name of some celebrated personage of antiquity. The Apocalypse at the end of the New Testament which bears the name of John the Divine is no exception to this old Judæo Christian habitude. If "Judah the brother of the Lord" could believe that "Henoh the Seventh from Adam" was really the author of the one hundred and ten chapters bearing that name, there is no wonder that Justin the Martyr, Papias, and Eusebius would believe in the authorship of Matthew and John.

However, my aim is not to criticize the authorship of, or to extend the comments upon these enigmatic and mysterious revelations which were compiled under the most painful and grievous circumstances in the history of the Jewish nation; but to give an account of the origin of this surname "the Son of Man" and to shed some light upon its true signification. The Book of Enoch too, like the Apocalypse of the Churches and like the Gospels, speaks of the coming of "the Son of Man" to deliver the people of God from their enemies and confuses this vision with the Last Judgment.

(b) The Sibylline Revelation, which was composed after the last collapse of Jerusalem by the Roman armies, states that "the Son of Man" will appear and destroy the Roman Empire and deliver the Believers in one God. This book was written at least fourscore years after Jesus Christ.

(c) We have already given an exposition of "the Son of Man" when we discussed the vision of Daniel,[1] where he is presented to the Almighty and invested with power to destroy the Roman Beast. So the visions, in the

---

1. Dan. vii. See the article, "Muhammad in the Old Testament," in the *Islamic Review* for November, 1938.

"Assumption of Moses," in the Book of Baruch (or Barukh), more or less similar in their views and expectations to those described in the above-mentioned "Revelations," all unanimously describe the Deliverer of the people of God as "Barnasha" or "the Son of Man," to distinguish him from the "Monster;" for the former is created in the image of God and the latter transformed into the image of Satan.

2. The Apocalyptic "Son of Man" could not be Jesus Christ.

This surname, "Son of Man," is absolutely inapplicable to the son of Mary. All the pretensions of the so-called "Gospels" which make the "Lamb" of Nazareth to "catch the kings in the midst of their voluptuous life and hurl them down into the Hell;"[1] lack every bit of authenticity, and the distance separating him from "the Son of Man" marching with the legions of angels upon the clouds towards the Throne of the Eternal is more than that of our globe from the planet of Jupiter. He may be *a* "son of man" and *a* "messiah," as every Jewish king, prophet, and high priest was, but he was *not* "*the* Son of Man" *nor* "the Messiah" whom the Hebrew prophets and apocalyptists foretold. And the Jews were perfectly right to refuse him that title and office. They were certainly wrong to deny him his prophethood, and criminal to have shed his innocent blood — as they and the Christians believe. "The Assembly of the Great Synagogue," after the death of Simeon the just in 310 B.C., was replaced by the "Sanhedrin," whose president had the surname of "Nassi" or Prince. It is astonishing that the "Nassi" who passed the judgment against Jesus, saying: "It is more profitable that one man should die rather than the whole nation should be

1. Enoch xlvi. 4 — 8.

destroyed,"[1] was a prophet![2] If he were a prophet, how was it that he did not recognize the prophetic mission or the Messianic character of *"the Messiah"*?

Here are, then the principal reasons why Jesus was not "the Son of Man" nor the Apocalyptic Messiah:

(*a*) A messenger of God is not commissioned to prophesy about himself as a personage of some future epoch, or to foretell his own reincarnation and thus present himself as the hero in some great future drama of the world. Jacob prophesied about "the Apostle of Allah,"[3] Moses about a prophet who would come after him with the Law, and Israel was exhorted to "obey him;[4] Haggai foretold Ahmad;[5] Malachi predicted the coming of the "Messenger of the Covenant" and of Elijah;[6] but none of the prophets ever did prophesy about his own sscond coming into the world. What is extremely abnormal in the case of Jesus is that he is made to pretend his identity with "the Son of Man," yet he is unable to do in the least degree the work that the foretold "Son of Man" was expected to accomplish! To declare to the Jews under the grip of Pilate that he was "the Son of Man," and then to pay tribute to Cæsar; and to confess that "the Son of Man had nowhere to lay his head;" and then to postpone the deliverance of the people from the Roman yoke to an indefinite future, was practically to trifle with his nation; and those who put all these incoherences as sayings in the mouth of Jesus only make idiots of themselves.

(*b*) Jesus knew better than everybody else in Israel *who* "the Son of Man" was and what was his mission. He was to dethrone the profligate kings and to cast them into

1. John xi. 50.   2. Idem, 51.   3. Gen. xlix. 10.
4. Deut. xviii. 15   5. Hag. ii. 7.   6. Mal. iii. 1, iv. 5.

the hell-fire. The "Revelation of Baruch" and that of Ezra—the Fourth Book of Esdras in the Vulgate—speak of the appearance of "the Son of Man" who will establish the powerful Kingdom of Peace upon the ruins of the Roman Empire. All these Apocryphal Revelations show the state of the Jewish mind about the coming of the last great Deliverer whom they surname "the Son of Man" and "the Messiah." Jesus could not be unaware of and unfamiliar with this literature and this ardent expectation of his people. He could not assume either of those two titles to himself in the sense which the Sanhedrin—that Supreme Tribunal of Jerusalem—and Judaism attached to them; for he was *not* "the Son of Man" and "the Messiah," because he had no political programme and no social scheme, and because he was himself the precursor of "the Son of Man', and of "the Messiah"—the Adon, the Conquering Prophet, the Anointed and crowned Sultan of the Prophets.

(c) A critical examination of the surname "Son of Man" put three and eighty times in the mouth of the master will and must result in the only conclusion that he never appropriated it to himself; and in fact he often uses that title in the third person. A few examples will suffice to convince us that Jesus applied that surname to someone else who was to appear in the future.

(i) A Scribe, that is a learned man, says: "I will follow thee wheresoever thou goest." Jesus answers: "The foxes have their holes; the birds of heaven their own nests; but the Son of Man has no place where to lay his head."[1] In the verse following he refuses one of his followers permission to go and bury his father! You will find not a single saint, father, or commentator to have troubled his

---

1. Matt. viii. 20.

head or the faculty of reasoning in order to discover the
very simple sense embodied in the refusal of Jesus to allow
that learned Scribe to follow him.   If he had place for
thirteen heads he could certainly provide a place for the
fourteenth too.   Besides, he could have registered him
among the seventy adherents he had.[1]   The Scribe in
question was not an ignorant fisherman like the sons of
Zebedee and of Jonah; he was a scholar and a practised
lawyer.   There is no reason to suspect his sincerity; he was
led to believe that Jesus was the predicted Messiah, the Son
of Man, who at any moment might summon his heavenly
legions and mount upon the throne of his ancestor David.
Jesus perceived the   erroneous notion   of   the   Scribe,
and plainly let him understand that he who had not two
square yards of ground on earth to lay his head could
naturally not be " *the* Son of Man"!   He was not harsh to
the Scribe; he benevolently saved him from wasting his time
in the pursuit of a futile hope!

(ii)   Jesus Christ is reported to have declared that the
Son of Man "will separate the sheep from the goats."[2]   The
"sheep" symbolize the believing Israelites who will enter
into the Kingdom but the "goats" signify the unbelieving
Jews who had joined with the enemies of the true religion
and were consequently doomed to perdition.   This was
practically what the Apocalypse of Enoch had predicted
about the Son of Man.   Jesus simply confirmed the revelation of Enoch and gave it a Divine character.   He himself was sent to exhort the sheep of Israel[3] to remain faithful to God and await patiently the advent of the Son of
Man who was coming to save them for ever from their

1.   Luke x. 1.
2.   Matt. xxv. 31 — 34.
3.   Matt. xv. 24.

enemies; but he himself was *not* the Son of Man, and had nothing to do with the political world, nor with the "sheep" and "goats" which both alike rejected and despised him, except a very small number who loved and believed in him.

(iii)   The Son of Man is said to be "the Lord of the Sabbath day," that is, he had the power to abrogate the law which made it a holy day of rest from labour and work. Jesus was a strict observer of the Sabbath, on which day he used to attend the services in the Temple or in the Synagogue.   He expressly commands his followers to pray that the national collapse at the destruction of Jerusalem should not happen on a Sabbath day.   How could, then, Jesus claim to be the Son of Man, the Lord of the Sabbath day, while he was obliged to observe and keep it like every Jew? How could he venture to claim that proud title and then predict the destruction of the Temple and of the Capital City?

These and many other examples show that Jesus could never appropriate the surname of "Barnasha" to himself, but he ascribed it to the Last Powerful Prophet, who really saved the "sheep," i.e. the believing Jews; and either destroyed or dispersed the unbelievers among them; abolished the day of Sabbath; established the Kingdom of Peace; and promised that this religion and kingdom will last to the day of the Last Judgment.

We shall in our next essay turn our attention to find all the marks and qualities of the Apocalyptic "Son of Man" which are literally and completely found in the last Apostle of Allah, upon whom be peace and the blessing of God!

X

BY THE APOCALYPTICAL "SON OF MAN," MUHAMMAD IS INTENDED

In my previous article I showed that "the Son of Man" foretold in the Jewish Apocalypses was not Jesus Christ, and that Jesus never assumed that appellation for himself, for thus he would have made himself ridiculous in the eyes of his audience.

There were only two courses open to him: either to denounce the Messianic prophecies and the Apocalyptical visions about the Barnasha as forgeries and legends, or to confirm them and at the same time to fill, if he were that lofty personage, the office of the "Son of Man." To say: "The Son of Man came to serve and not to be served,"[1] or "The Son of Man shall be delivered unto the hands of the Chief Priests and the Scribes"[2] or "The Son of Man came eating and drinking [wine]" with the sinners and the publicans,[3] and at the same time to confess that he was a beggar living on the charity and hospitality of others, was to insult his nation and its nation and its holiest religious sentiments! To boast that he was the Son of Man and had come to save and recover the lost sheep of Israel,[4] but had to leave this salvation to the Last Judgement, and even then to be cast into the eternal flames, was to frustrate all the hopes of that persecuted people, who alone in all mankind had the honour of being the only nation that professed the faith and religion of the true God; and it was to scorn their prophets and Apocalypses.

Could Jesus Christ assume that title? Are the authors

1. Matt. xx. 28.
2. Ibid. xx. 18.   3. Ibid. xi. 18.   4. Ibid. vxiii. 11.

of the four Gospels Hebrews? Could Jesus conscientiously believe himself to be what these spurious Gospels allege? Could a Jew conscientiously write such stories which are purposely written to disconcert and foil the expectation of that people? Of course, other than a negative answer cannot be expected from me to these questions. Neither Jesus nor his apostles would ever use such an extravagant title among a people already familiar with the legitimate owner of that surname. It would be analogous to putting the crown of the king upon the head of his ambassador, the latter having no army to proclaim him king. It would be simply an insane usurpation of the rights and privileges of the legitimate Son of Man. Consequently, such an unjustifiable usurpation on the part of Jesus would be equivalent to the asumption of the epithet of "the Pseudo Son of Man" and of the Antichrist! The very imagination of a similar act of audacity on the part of the Holy Christ Jesus makes my whole nature revolt. The more I read these Gospels the more I become convinced to believe that they are a production—at least in their present shape and contents— of authors other than the Jews. These Gospels are a counterpoise to the Jewish Revelations—particularly as a counter-project against the Sibyllian Books. This could only be done by Greek Christians who had no interest in the claims of the children of Abraham. The author of the Sibyllian Books places side by side with the Jewish prophets Enoch, Solomon, Daniel, and Ezra, the names of the Greek sages Hermes, Homer, Orpheus, Pythagoras, and others, evidently with the object of making propaganda for the Hebrew religion. These books were written when Jerusalem and the Temple were in ruins, some time before or after the publication of St. John's Apocalypse. The purport of the Sibyllian Revelation is that the Hebrew[1] Son of Man or the Messiah will come to destroy the power of Rome and to establish the religion of the true God for all men.

We can produce many sound arguments to prove the identity of "the Son of Man" with Muhammad only, and shall divide these arguments as follows:

ARGUMENTS FROM THE GOSPELS, AND FROM THE APOCALYPSES

In the most coherent and significant passages in the discourses of Jesus where the appellation "Barnasha" — or "the Son of Man"—appears, only Muhammad is intended, and in him alone the prediction contained therein is literally fulfilled. In some passages wherein Jesus is supposed to have assumed that title for himself, that passage becomes incoherent, senseless, and extremely obscure. Take for instance the following passages: "The Son of Man came eating and drinking, and they said, Behold. . ."[2] John-Baptist was a teetotaller, he fed himself only on water, locusts, and wild honey; they said he was a demoniac; but "the Son of Man," *id est* Jesus (?), who ate and drank wine, was branded as "the friend of publicans and sinners"! To blame a prophet for his fastings and abstinence is a sin of infidelity or of gross ignorance. But to reproach a person who claims to be a Messenger of God of frequenting the banquets of publicans and sinners, and for being fond of wine, is quite natural and a very serious

---

1. The name "Hebrew" in its wider sense is applied to all the descendants of Abraham, who afterwards assumed the names of their respective ancestors, such as the Ishmaelites, Edomites Israelites, etc.
2. Matt. xi. 19.

charge against the sincerity of that person who pretends to be a spiritual guide of men. Can we Muslims believe in the sincerity of a Khwaja or Mullah when we see him mixing with drunkards and prostitutes? Could the Christians bear with a curate or parson of a similar conduct? Certainly not. A spiritual guide may have intercourse with all sorts of sinners in order to convert and reform them, providing that he is sober, abstemious, and sincere. According to the quotation just mentioned, Christ admits that his behaviour had scandalized the religious leaders of his nation. True, the officers of the Custom-house, called "publicans," were hated by the Jews simply because of their office. We are told only two "publicans"[1] and one "harlot"[2] and one "possessed" woman[3] were converted by Jesus; but all the clergy and the lawyers were branded with curses and anathemas.[4] All this looks awkward and incredible The idea or thought that a Holy Prophet, so chaste and sinless like Jesus, was fond of wine, that he changed six barrels of water into a most intoxicating wine in order to render crazy a large company of guests already tipsy in the wedding-hall at Cana,[5] is practically to depict him an impostor and sorcerer! Think of a miracle performed by a thaumaturge before a rabble of drunkards! To describe Jesus as a drunkard, and gluttonous, and a friend of the ungodly, and then to give him the title of "the Son of Man" is to deny all the Jewish Revelations and religion.

Again, Jesus is reported to have said that "The Son of Man came to seek and recover that which was lost."[6]

1. Matthew and Zacchæus (Matt. ix. 9; Luke xix. 1 — 11).
2. John iv.
3. Mary Magdalene (Luke viii. 2).
4. Matt. xiii., etc.
5. John ii.
6. Matt. xiii. 11, Luke ix. 56; xix. 10, etc.

The commentators of course interpret this passage in a spiritual sense only. Well, it is the mission and the office of every prophet and the preacher of the religion to call the sinners to repent of their inquity and wickedness. We quite admit that Jesus was sent only to the "lost sheep of Israel," to reform and convert them from their sins; and especially to teach them more plainly concerning "the Son of Man" who was to come with power and salvation to restore what was lost and to reconstruct what was ruined; nay, to conquer and destroy the enemies of the true believers. Jesus could not assume for himself that Apocalyptic title "the Barnasha," and then not be able to save his people except Zacchæus, a Samaritan woman, and a few other Jews, including the Apostles, who were mostly slain afterwards on his account. Most probably what Jesus said was: "The Son of Man *will* come to seek and recover what is lost." For in Muhammad alone the believing Jews as well as the Arabs and other believers found all that was irremediably lost and destroyed — Jerusalem and Mecca, all the promised territories; many truths concerning the true religion; the power and kingdom of God; the peace and blessing that Islam confers in this world and in the next.

We cannot afford space for further quotations of the numerous passages in which "the Son of Man" occurs as either the subject or the object or the predicate of the sentence. But one more quotation will suffice, namely: "The Son of Man shall be delivered unto the hands of men,"[1] etc., and all the passages where he is made the subject of passion and death. Such utterances are put into the mouth of Jesus by some fraudulent non-Hebrew writer with the object of perverting the truth concerning "the Son of Man" as understood and believe by the Jews, and of

1.   Matt. xvi. 21; xvii. 12, etc.

making them believe that Jesus of Nazareth was the Apocalyptical triumphant Saviour, but he would only appear on the Day of the Last Judgment. It was a policy and a cunning propaganda of dissuasion, and then of persuasion, made purposely for the Jews. But the fraud was discovered, and the Jewish Christians belong to the Church which held these Gospels to be divinely revealed. For nothing could be more repugnant to Jewish national aspiration and religious sentiment than to present to them the expected Messiah, the great Barnasha, in the person of Jesus whom the Chief Priests and the Elders condemned to be crucified as a seducer! It is quite evident, therefore, that Jesus *never* appropriated the title of "the Son of Man;" but he reserved it only for Muhammad. Here are a few of the arguments:

(*a*) The Jewish Apocalypses ascribe the titles "the Messiah" and "the Son of Man" exclusively to the Last Prophet, who will fight with the Powers of Darkness and vanquish them, and then will establish the Kingdom of Peace and of Light on earth. Thus the two titles are synonymous; to disown either of them is to disown altogether the claim to being the Last Prophet. Now we read in the Synoptics that Jesus categorically denied his being the Christ and forbade his disciples to declare him "the Messiah"! It is reported that Simon Peter, in reply to the question put by Jesus: "Whom say you that I am?" said: "Thou art the Christ [Messiah] of God."[1] Then Christ commanded his disciples not to say to anybody that he is the Christ.[2] St. Mark and St. Luke know nothing about the "power of the keys" given to Peter; they, not being there, had not heard

---

1. Luke ix. 20.
2. Luke (ix. 21) says: "He rebuked them and commanded them not to say that he was the Messiah." Cf. Matt. xvi. 20; Mark viii. 30.

of it.   John has not a word about this Messianic conversation; probably he had forgotten it!   St. Matthew reports[1] that when Jesus told them not to say that he was the Christ he explained to them how he would be delivered and killed. Thereupon Peter began to reprove and admonish him not to repeat the same words about his passion and death. According to this story of St. Matthew, Peter was perfectly right when he said: "Master, be it far from thee!"   If it be true that his confession, "Thou art the Messiah," pleased Jesus, who conferred the title of "Sapha" or "Cepha" on Simon, then to declare that "the Son of Man" was to suffer the ignominious death upon the Cross was neither more nor less than a flat denial of his Messianic character.   But Jesus became more positive and indignantly scolded Peter, saying: "Get thee behind me, Satan!"   What follows this sharp rebuke are most explicit words of the Master, leaving not a modicum of doubt that he was *not* "the Messiah" or "the Son of Man."   How to reconcile the "faith" of Peter, recompensed with the glorious title of "Sapha" and the power of the keys of Heaven and of Hell, with the "infidelity" of Peter punished with the opprobrious epithet of "Satan," within half an hour's time or so?   Several reflections present themselves to my mind, and I feel it my bounden duty to put them in black and white.   If Jesus were "the Son of Man" or "the Messiah" as seen and foretold by Daniel, Ezra, Enoch, and the other Jewish prophets and divines, he would have authorized his disciples to proclaim and acclaim him as such; and he himself would have supported them.   The fact is that he acted the very reverse. Again, if he were the Messiah, or the Barnasha, he would have at once struck his enemies with terror, and by the aid

1.   Loc. cit., 21—28.

of his invisible angels destroyed the Roman and Persian powers, then dominant over the civilized world. But he did nothing of the sort; or, like Muhammad, he would have recruited some valiant warriors like 'Alī, Omar, Khālid, etc., and not like Zebedees and Jonahs, who vanished, like a frightened spectre when the Roman police came to arrest them.

There are two irreconcilable statements made by Matthew (or corrupted by his interpolator), which logically destroy each other. Within an hour Peter is "the Rock of Faith," as Catholicism will boast, and, 'the Satan of Infidelity," as Protestanism will scout him! Why so? Because when he believed Jesus to be the Messiah he was rewarded; but when he refused to admit that his master was not the Messiah he was convicted! There are no two "Sons of Man," the one to be the Commander of the Faithful, fight sword in hand the wars of God, and uproot idolatry and its empires and kingdoms; the other to be an Abbot of the poor Anchorites on the summit of Calvary, fight the wars of God cross in hand, and be martyred ignominiously by idolatrous Romans and unbelieving Jewish Pontiffs and Rabbis! "The Son of Man," whose hands were seen under the wings of the Cherubs by the Prophet Ezekiel (ii), and before the throne of the Almighty by the Prophet Daniel (vii), and described in the other Jewish Apocalypses, was not predestined to be hanged upon Golgotha, but to transform the thrones of the pagan kings into their own crosses; to change their palaces into calvaries, and to make sepulchres of their capital cities. Not Jesus, but Muhammad, had the honour of this title, "the Son of Man"! The facts are more eloquent than even the Apocalypses and the visions. The material and moral conquests achieved by

Muhammad the Holy Apostle of Allah over the enemy are unrivalled.

(b)   "The Son of Man" is called by Jesus "the Lord of the Sabbath day."[1]   This is very remarkable indeed. The sanctity of the seventh day is the theme of the Law of Moses.   God accomplished the work of creation in six days, and on the seventh He rested from all work.   Men and women, children and slaves, even the domestic animals were to repose from all labour under the pain of death.   The Fourth Commandment of the Decalogue orders the people of Israel: "Thou shalt remember the Sabbath day to sanctify it."[2]   The students of the Bible know how jealous God is reported to be concerning the strict observation of the Day of Rest.   Before Moses there was no special law about this; and the nomad Patriarchs do not seem to have observed it.   It is very likely that the Jewish Sabbath had its origin in the Babylonian *Sabattu*.

The Qur-án repudiates the Jewish anthropomorphous conception of the Deity, for it means to say, as if like man, God laboured six days, got fatigued, reposed and slumbered. The sacred verse of the Qur-án thus runs: "And verily We have created the heavens and the earth, and whatever is between them in six days; and no weariness affected Us" (1. 38).

The Jewish idea about the Sabbath had become too material and insidious.   Instead of making it a day of comfortable rest and a pleasant holiday, it had been turned into a day of abstinence and confinement.   No cooking, no walk, and no work of charity or beneficence were permitted.   The priests in the temple would bake bread and offer sacrifices on the Sabbath-day, but reproached the Prophet of Nazareth

1. Matt. xii. 7.
2. Exod. xx.

when he cured miraculously a man whose arm was withered.[1] To this Christ said that it was the Sabbath which was instituted for the benefit of man, and not man for the sake of the Sabbath. Instead of making it a day of worship and *then* a day of recreation, of innocent pleasure and real repose, they had made it a day of imprisonment and weariness. The least breach of any precept concerning the seventh day was punished with lapidation or some other penalty. Moses himself sentences a poor man to lapidation for having picked up a few sticks from the ground on a Sabbath day; and the disciples of Jesus were reproached for plucking some ears of corn on a Sabbath day, although they were hungry. It is quite evident that Jesus Christ was not a Sabbatarian and did not adhere to the literal interpretation of the draconic ordinances regarding the Sabbath. He wanted mercy or acts of kindness and not sacrifices. Nevertheless, he never thought of abrogating the Sabbath, nor could he have ventured to do so. Had he ventured to declare the abolition of that day or to substitute the Sunday for it, he would have been undoubtedly abandoned by his followers, and instantly mobbed and stoned. But he observed, so to say, the Law of Moses to its title. As we learn from the Jewish historian, Joseph Flavius, and from Eusebius and others, James the "brother" of Jesus was a strict Ibionite and the head of the Judaistic Christians who observed the Law of Moses and the Sabbath with all its rigours. The Hellenistic Christians gradually substituted first the "Lord's Day," i.e. the Sunday; but the Eastern Churches until the fourth century observed both days.

Now if Jesus were the Lord of the Sabbath day he would have certainly either modified its rigorous law or

1. Matt. xii. 10—13.

entirely abolished it. He did neither the one nor the other. The Jews who heard him understood perfectly well that he referred to the expected Messiah as the Lord of the Sabbath, and that is why they kept their silence. The Redactor of the Synoptics, here as everywhere, has suppressed some of the words of Jesus whenever "the Son of Man" forms the subject of his discourse, and this suppression is the cause of all these ambiguities, contradictions, and misunderstandings. Unless we take the Holy Qur-án as our guide, and the Apostle of Allah as the object of the Bible, all attempts to find the truth and to arrive at a satisfactory conclusion will end in failure. The Higher Biblical Criticism will guide you as far as the gate of the sacred shrine of truth, and there it stops, stricken with awe and incredulity. It does not open the door to enter inside and search for the eternal documents therein deposited. All research and erudition shown by these "impartial" critics, whether Liberal Thinkers, Rationalists, or indifferent writers, are, after all, deplorably cold, sceptical, and disappointing. Lately I was reading the works of the French savant Ernest Renan, *La vie de Jesus, Saint Paul,* and *L' Antichrist.* I was astonished at the extent of works, ancient and modern, which he has examined; he reminded me of Gibbon and others. But, alas, what is the conclusion of their inexhaustible research and study? Zero or negation! In the domain of science the marvels of Nature are discovered by the Positivists; but in the domain of Religion these Positivists make hay of it and poison the religious sentiments of their readers. If these learned critics were to take the spirit of the Qur-án for their guidance and Muhammad as the literal, moral, and practical fulfilment of Holy Writ, their research could not be so desultory and destructive. Religious men want a *real* and not an *ideal* religion; they want a "Son of Man"

who will draw his sword and march at the head of his valiant
army to pulverize the enemies of God and to prove by word
and deed that he is the "Lord of the Sabbath day," and to
abrogate it altogether because it was abused by the Jews
as the "Fatherhood" of God was abused by the Christians.
Muhammad *did* this!   As I have often repeated in these
pages, we can only understand these corrupted scriptures
when we penetrate, with the help of the light of Al-Qur-án,
into their enigmatic and contradictory statements, and it is
only *then* that we can sift them with the sieve of truthfulness
and separate the genuine from the spurious.   When, for
example, speaking about the priests continually dissolving
the Sabbath in the Temple, Jesus is reported to have said:
"Behold, here is one that is greater than the Temple."[1]   I
can guess of no sense in the existence of the adverb "here"
in this clause, unless we supply and attach to it an additional
"t," and make it read "there."   For, if Jesus or any other
prophet before him should have had the audacity of declaring
himself "greater than the Temple," he would have been
instantly lynched or stoned by the Jews as a "blasphemer,"
unless he could prove himself to be the Son of Man, invested
with power and greatness, as the Apostle of Allah was.

The abrogation of Saturday by the Prince of the
Prophets — Muhammad — is hinted at in the LXII Sura of
the Qur-án entitled "Al-Jumu'a" or "The Assembly."
Before Muhammad the Arabs called Friday "al A'ruba," the
same as the Syriac Pshitta "A'rubta" from the Aramaic
"arabh" — "to set down (the sun)."   It was so called
because after the setting of the sun on Friday the Sabbath
day commenced.   The reason given for the sacred character
of Saturday is that on that day God "rested" from His

1.   Matt. xii. 6.

work of creation. But the reason for the choice of Friday,
as it can easily be understood, is of a double nature. First,
because on this day the great work of the creation, or of
the universal formation of all the innumerable worlds, beings
and things visible and invisible, planets, and microbes was
completed. This was the first event that interrupted eternity,
when time, space, and matter came into being. The com-
memoration, the anniversary, and the sanctity of such a
prodigious event on the day on which it was achieved is
just, reasonable, and even necessary. The second reason
is that on this day prayers and worship are conducted by
the faithful unanimously, and for this reason it is called the
"jumu'a," that is to say, the congregation or assembly; the
divine verse on this subject characterizes the nature of our
obligation on Friday as: "O true believers! when ye are
called to prayer on Friday, hasten to the remembrance of
God and leave merchandise," etc.

The faithful are called to join in the divine service
together in a house dedicated to the worship of God, and
to leave off at that time any lucrative work; but after the
congregational prayers are over they are not forbidden to
resume their usual occupations. A true Muslim within
twenty-four hours worships his Creator three or five times
in prayer and devotion.

(c) We have already made a few remarks on the
passage in St. Matthew (xviii. 11) where the mission of the
"Son of Man" is "to seek and recover what was lost."
This is another important prediction — though undoubtedly
corrupted in form — about Muhammad, or the Apocalyptical
Barnasha. These "lost things" which the Barnasha would
seek and restore are of two categories, religious and
national. Let us examine them in detail:

(1) The mission of the Barnasha was to restore the

purity and the universality of the religion of Abraham which was lost. All the peoples and tribes descended from that patriarch of the believers were to be brought into the fold of the "Religion of Peace," which is no other than the "Dina da-Shlama," or the Religion of Islam. The religion of Moses was national and particular, and therefore its hereditary priesthood, its Levitical sacrifices and pompous rituals, its Sabbaths, jubilees, and festivals, and all its laws and corrupted scriptures would be abolished and substituted by new ones having a universal character , force, and durability. Jesus was a Jew; he could not have accomplished such a gigantic and stupendous undertaking because it was materially impossible for him to do it. "I came not to change the law or the prophets,"[1] said he. On the other hand, the rank idolatry, with all its abominable pagan practices, superstition, and sorcery, to which the Arab nationalities were addicted, had entirely to be wiped out, and the unity of the Deity and of religion to be restored under the flag of the Apostle of Allah bearing the Holy Inscription: "I bear witness that there is no object of Worship beside God; and I bear witness that Muhammad is the Apostle of God."

(2) The unification of the nations descended from Abraham, and their dependencies were to be restored and accomplished. Of the many corrupted, selfish, and unjustifiable silly notions the Hebrew Scriptures contain there is the indiscriminate bias they entertain against the non-Israelite nations. They never honour the other descendants of their great progenitor Abraham; and this antipathy is shown against the Ishmaelites, Edomites, and other Abrahamite tribes even when Israel had become the worst idolator and

1.   Matt. v. 17—19.

heathen. The fact that besides Abraham and Ishmael about three hundred and eleven male slaves and warriors in his service were circumcised[1] is an incalculably forcible argument against the Jewish attitude towards their cousin nationalities. The kingdom of David hardly extended its frontiers beyond the territory which in the Ottoman Empier formed only two adjacent "Vilayets," or Provinces. And the "Son of David," whom the Jews anticipate to come with the attribute of the "final Messiah," may or may not be able to occupy *even* those two provinces; and besides, *when* will he come? He was to have come to destroy the Roman "Beast." That "Beast" was only mutilated and slaughtered by Muhammad! What else is expected? When Muhammad, the Apocalyptic Barnasha, founded the Kingdom of Peace (Islam), the majority of the Jews in Arabia, Syria, Mesopotamia, etc., voluntarily rushed to the greatest shepherd of mankind when he appeared with the terrific blows which he struck at the "Brute" of paganism. Muhammad founded a universal Brotherhood, the nucleus of which is certainly the family of Abraham, including among its members the Persians, the Turks, the Chinese, the Negroes, the Javanese, the Indians, the Englishmen, etc., all forming one "ummat" (Arabic) or "Umtha da-Shlama," i.e. the Islamic Nation!

(3) Then the recovery of the promised lands, including the land of Canaan and all the territories from the Nile to the Euphrates, and gradually the extension of the Kingdom of Allah from the Pacific Ocean to the eastern shores of the Atlantic, is a marvellous fulfilment of all the prophecies about the Holiest and the Greatest of the Sons of Man!

Considering the stupendous work accomplished by

1. Gen.

Muhammad for the One True God, the brief time spent by him and his brave and devoted companions in its accomplishment, and the ineffaceable effects that the work and the religion of Muhammad have left upon all the kingdoms and the thinkers of mankind, one is at a loss to know what tribute to pay to this Prophet of Arabia, except the wish to behold him shining in redoubled glory before the Throne of the Eternal as Daniel saw in his vision!

XI

THE SON OF MAN ACCORDING TO THE JEWISH APOCALYPSES

From what has been already discussed in these pages it will have been that the appellation "Barnasha," or "the Son of Man," is not a title like "Messiah," that could be applied to every prophet, highpriest, and legally anointed king; but that it is a *proper noun*, belonging exclusively to the Last Prophet. The Hebrew Seers, Sophees, and the Apocalyptists describe the Son of Man, who is to come in due time as appointed by the Almighty to deliver Israel and Jerusalem from the heathenish oppression and to establish the permanent kingdom for "the People of the Saints of the Most High." The Seers, the Sophees, foretell the advent of the Powerful Deliverer; they see him — *only* in a vision, revelation, and faith — with all his might and glory. No Prophet or Sophee *ever* said that he *himself* was "*the* Son of Man," and that he would "come again on the Last Day to judge both the quick and the dead," as the Nicene Creed puts it on the pretended authority of the Sayings of Jesus Christ.

The frequent use of the appellation in question by the evangelists indicates, most assuredly, their acquaintance with the Jewish Apocalypses, as also a firm belief in their authenticity and divine origin. It is quite evident that the Apocalypses bearing the names of Enoch, Moses, Baruch, and Ezra were written long before the Gospels; and that the name "Barnasha" therein mentioned was borrowed by the authors of the Gospels; otherwise its frequent use would be enigmatic and an incomprehensible — if not a meaningless — novelty. It follows, therefore, that Jesus either believed *himself* to be the Apocalyptic "Son of Man," or that he knew the Son of Man to be a person distinctly other than himself. If he believed *himself* to be the Son of Man, it would follow that either *he* or the *Apocalyptists* were in error; and in either case the argument goes most decidedly against Jesus Christ. For his error concerning his own personality and mission is as bad as the erroneous predictions of the Apocalyptists, whom he believed to be divinely inspired. Of coure, this dilemmatic reasoning will lead us to a final conclusion unfavourable to himself. The only way to save Jesus from this dishonour is to look upon him as the Qur-án pictures him to us; and accordingly to attribute all the contradictory and incoherent statements about him in the Gospels to their authors or redactors.

Before discussing further the subject, "the Son of Man" as depicted in the Jewish Apocalypses, a few facts must be carefully taken into consideration. First, these Apocalypses not only do not belong to the canon of the Hebrew Bible, but also they are not even included among the Apocrypha or the so-called "Deutro-canonical" books of the Old Testament. Secondly, their authorship is not known. They bear the names of Enoch, Moses, Baruch, Ezra, but their real authors or editors seem to have known the final destruction of Jerusalem and the dispersion of the Jews under the Romans. These pseudonyms were chosen, not for fraudulent purposes, but out of a pious motive by the Sophees or Seers who composed them. Did not Plato put his own views and dialectics into the mouth of his master, Socrates? Thirdly, "these books," in the words of the Grand Rabbin Paul Haguenauer, "in an enigmatical, mystical, supernatural form, try to explain the secrets of the nature, the origin [sic] of God, the problems of good and evil, justice and happiness, the past and the future. The Apocalypse makes upon all these questions some revelations which surpass human understanding. Their principal personages are Enoch, Moses, Baruch, Ezra. These writings are evidently the product of the painful and disastrous epochs of Judaism."[1] Consequently they cannot be fully understood any more than the Apocalypse which bears the name of St. John the Apostle. Fourthly, these Apocalypses have been interpolated by the Christians. In the Book of Enoch "the Son of Man" is also called "the Son of Woman" and "the Son of God," thus interpolating the Church theory of Incarnation; surely no Jewish Seer would write "Son of God." Fifthly, it would be noticed that the Messianic doctrine is a later development of the old prophecies concerning the Last Apostle of Allah, as foretold by Jacob and other Prophets. It is only in the Apocrypha and the Apocalypses, and especially in the Rabbinical writings, that this "Last Deliverer" is claimed to descend from David. True, there are prophecies after the Babylonian captivity, and even after the deportation of the Ten Tribes into Assyria, about a "Son of David" who would come to gather together the dispersed Israel. But these predictions were fulfilled only partly under Zorobabel — a descendant of

1. *Munuel de Litterature Juive.* Nancy, 1927.

King David. Then after the Greek invasion the same predictions were preached and announced, and we only see a Judah Maqbaya fighting with a slight success against Antiochus Epiphanes. Besides, this success was temporary and of no permanent value. The Apocalypses, which carry their visions down to the time after the destruction of Jerusalem by Titus and Vespasian, foretell "the Son of Man" who will appear with great power to destroy the Roman power and the other enemies of Israel. Twenty centuries had to elapse before the Rome Empire was destroyed in the fifth century A.D. by a Turkish Emperor, Atilla — a pagan Hun — and finally by a Muslim Turk, the Fatih Muhammad II. But that power was completely destroyed, and for ever, in the lands promised to Ishmael by the Sultan of the Prophets, Muhammad al-Mustapha.

There remain two other observations which I cannot ignore in this connection. If I were a most ardent Zionist, or a most learned Rabbi, I would once more study this Messianic question as profoundly and impartially as I could. And then I would vigorously exhort my co-religionist Jews to desist from and abandon this hope for ever. Even if a "Son of David" should appear on the hill of Zion, and blow the trumpet, and claim to be the "Messiah," I would be the first to tell him boldly: "Please, Sire! You are too late! Don't disturb the equilibrium in Palestine! Don't shed blood! Don't let your angels meddle with these formidable aeroplanes! Whatever be the successes of your adventures, I am afraid they will not surpass those of your ancestors David, Zorobabel, and Judah Maccabaeus (Maqbaya)!" The great Hebrew conqueror was not David but Jesus bar Nun (Joshuah); he was the first Messiah, who instead of converting the pagan tribes of the Canaan that had shown so much hospitality and goodness to Abraham, Isaac, and Jacob, mercilessly massacred them wholesale. And Joshuah was, of course, a Prophet and the Messiah of the time. Every Israelite Judge during a period of three centuries or more was a Messiah and Deliverer.   Thus we find that during every national calamity, especially a catastrophe, a Messiah is predicted, and as a rule the deliverance is achieved always subsequent to the disaster and quite in an inadequate degree. It is a peculiar characteristic of the Jews that they alone of all the national aspire, through the miraculous conquests by a Son of David, after a universal domination of the inhabitants of the globe. Their slovenliness and inertia are quite compatible with their unshaking belief in the advent of the "Lion of Judah." And that is, perhaps the reason why they never attempt to concentrate all, their national resources, energy, and force and make a united effort to become a self-governing people·

Now to the Christians who claim Jesus to be the prophetical Son of Man, I would venture to say: If he were the expected Deliverer of Israel he would have delivered that people from the Roman yoke, no matter if the Jews had believed in him or not. Deliverance *first*, gratitude and loyalty *after*; and not *vice versa.* A man must *first* be liberated from the hands of his captors by killing or frightening them, and *then* be expected to show his permanent attachment and devotion to the liberator. The Jews were not inmates of a hospital to be attended by physicians and nurses; they were practically prisoners in bonds and needed a hero to set them free. Their faith in God and in His Law was as perfect as was that of their ancestors at the foot of Mount Sinai when He delivered it to Moses. They were not in need of a thaumaturgical prophet; all their history was interwoven with wonders and miracles. The raising to life of a dead Lazarus, the opening of the eyes of a blind Bartimaeus, or the cleansing of an outcaste leper, would neither strengthen their faith nor satiate their thirst for independence and liberty. The Jews rejected Jesus, not because he was not the Apocalyptic "Son of Man" or the Messiah—not because he was not a Prophet, for they knew very well that he did not claim to be be the former, and that he was a Prophet—but because they hated him for his words: Messiah was not the Son of David, but his Lord.[1] This admission of the Synoptics confirms the statement in the Gospel of Barnabas, where Jesus is reported to have added that the Covenant will be fulfilled with the "Shiloah"—the Apostle of Allah—who will come from the family of Ishmael. For this reason the Talmudists describe Jesus as "the second Balaam"—that is, the Prophet who prophesies for the benefit of the heathen at the expense of the "chosen people."

It is quite clear, therefore, that the Jewish reception to, or their rejection of, Jesus was not the condition *sine qua non* to determine the nature of his mission. If he were the Final Deliverer he would have made the Jews submit to him, *nolens volens,* as Muhammad did. But the contrast between the circumstances in which each of those two Prophets found himself, and their work, knows no dimensions and no limits. Suffice it to say that Muhammad converted about ten million pagan Arabs into most sincere and ardent believers in the true God, and utterly uprooted idolatry in the lands where it had struck root. This he did, because he held in one hand the Law and in the other the Sceptre; the one was the Holy Qur-án and the other the emblem of power and government. He was hated, despised, persecuted by the noblest Arab tribe to which he belonged, and forced to flee for his

1. Matt. xxii. 44—46; Mark xii. 35—37; Luke xx. 41—44.

life; but by the power of Allah he accomplished the greatest work for cause of the true religion which no other Prophet before him had ever been able to do.

I shall now proceed to show that the Apocalyptic Son of Man was no other than Muhammad al-Mustapha.

1. The most cogent and important proof that the Apocalyptic *Barnasha* is Muhammad is given in a wonderful description in the vision of Daniel (vii.) already discussed in a previous article. In no way whatever the Barnasha therein described can be identified with any of the Maccabees' heroes or with Jesus; nor can the terrible Beast which was utterly killed and destroyed by that Son of Man be a prototype of Antiochus Epiphanes or the Roman Caesar, Nero. The culminating evil of that dreadful Beast was the "Little Horn," which uttered blasphemies against the Most High by associating with His essence three co-eternal divine persons and by its persecution of those who maintained the absolute oneness of God. Constantine the Great is the person symbolized by that hideous Horn.

2. The Apocalypse of Enoch[1] foretells the appearance of the Son of Man at a moment when the small flock of the sheep, though vigorously defended by a ram, will be fiercely attacked by the birds of prey from above and by the carnivorous beast on land. Among the enemies of the little flock are seen many other goats and sheep that had gone astray. The lord of the flock, like a good shepherd, suddenly appears and strikes the earth with his rod or sceptre; it opens its mouth and swallows up the assailing enemy; chases and drives away from the pastures the rest of the pernicious

1. I regret to say that the "Jewish Apocalypses" are inaccessible to me. The Encyclopædias given only a compendium of each book, which does not satisfy my purpose of examining the text. I know that the Irish Archbishop Laurence has translated this Apocalypse into English, but it is, unfortunately, beyond my reach.

birds and brutes. Then a sword is given to the flock as an emblem of power and the weapon of destruction. After which the flock is no longer headed by a ram but by a white bull with two large black horns.

This parabolical vision is transparent enough. From Jacob downwards the "chosen people" is represented symbolically by the flock of sheep. The descendants of Esau are described as boars. Other heathen people and tribes are represented in the vision, according to their respective characteristics, as ravens, eagles, vultures, and different species of brutes, all thirsty to suck the blood of the sheep or hungry to devour them. Almost all Biblical scholars agree that the vision indicates the painful period of the Maccabees and their bloody struggles with the armies of Antiochus Epiphanes until the death of John Hurcanus in 110(?) B.C. This method of interpreting the vision is totally erroneous, and reduces the value of the whole book to nothing. That an antediluvian Prophet or a Seer should illustrate the history of the human race from a religious point of view, beginning with Adam, under the symbol of a White Bull, and ending with John Hurcanus or his brother Judah Maccabaeus (Maqbaya) as the Last White Bull, and then leave the flock of the "Believers" to be devoured again by the Romans, the Christians, and the Muslims to this very day, is ridiculous and shocking! In fact, the wars of the Maccabees and their consequence are not of such great significance in the history of the religion of God as to be the terminus of its development. None of the Maccabees was a Prophet, nor the founder of the so-called "Messianic reign" which the Gospels name the "Kingdom of God." Besides, this interpretation of the vision is inconsistent with the characters represented in the drama under the figurative symbols of the master of the flock, sceptre in hand, the Ram, and the White Bull; and

then with the large sword given to the shepherds with which
they kill or drive away the impure animals and birds. Fur-
thermore, this Christian interpretation of Enoch's Apocalypse
does not explain the mystical transplantation or the transportation of the terrestrial Jerusalem into a country farther
to the south; and what meaning can be given to the new
House of God built on the spot of the old one, larger and
higher than the former sacred edifice, to which flock not only
the believing sheep—the faithful Jews—but also the various
pagan nationalities that have embraced the religion of the
Son of Man who destroyed the enemies with his Sceptre or
Rod! For all these particular acts and representations are
seen and described in this dramatic vision. The chain that
links together the events depicted in this figurative language
begins with Adam and ends in the person of the Prophet
of Mecca! There are several cogent arguments to prove
this assertion.

(a) The two divisions of the sheep indicate the people
of the Scriptures, whether Jews or Christians, among whom
were those who were believers in the unity of God, and
those who made Jesus and the Holy Spirit also equal and
consubstantial with God. The Seer distinguishes the believers from the apostates. The Gospels report that on the
day of the Last Judgment "the sheep will be separated from
the goats,"[1] which indicates the same view. As to the
symbolical Ram, we may understand thereby Arius or some
spiritual Unitarian leader for the true Nassara and the chief
Rabbi for the faithful Jews—because they both had the same
common enemy. If we identify Constantine with the evil
Horn, we may justly identify Arius with the Ram. In fact,
Arius is entitled to this dignity because he headed the larger

1. Matt. xxv. 32—46, etc.

group in the Council of Nicea and vigorously defended the true religion against the monstrous doctrines of Trinitarian and Sacramentarian Churches.   From a strictly Muslim point of view the Jews, from the moment they rejected and condemned Jesus Christ to death, ceased to be the "chosen people," and that honourable title was given only to those who believed in his apostleship.

(b)   The Son of Man who saved the flock of sheep from its various enemies whom he sent down into the bosom of the earth by striking vehemently his pastoral staff on it, and gave a strong sword to the sheep to slaughter the impure brutes and birds of prey, was decidedly Muhammad. The sceptre (in Hebrew "shebet"—rod, staff) is the emblem of sovereignty, jurisdiction, and administration. The little sceptre accorded by God to the tribe of Judah[1] was taken away, and a stronger and larger one was given to the Apostle of Allah (the "Shiloah") in its place.   It is indeed marvellous how this prophetical vision of the Seer was literally fulfilled when Muhammad's sceptre became the emblem of the Muslim sovereignty over all the countries—in Egypt, Assyria, Chaldea, Syria, and Arabia—where the people of God were persecuted by the pagan powers of those countries and by the foreign heathen powers of the Medo-Persians, Greeks, and Romans!   What a glorious fulfilment of the vision it is when the flock of sheep, for many centuries having been exposed to the merciless beaks and claws of the birds of prey and to the sharp and terrible teeth and claws of the beasts, was now equipped with a large sword to defend which every Muslim carried until the blood of the Saints and Martyrs[2] was equitably avenged.

1. Gen. xlix. 10.
2. Rev. vi. 9 — 11.

(c) *The White Bull.*   Until Ishmael, all the Prophets are represented as white bulls; but from Jacob downwards the princes of the chosen people appear in the form of rams. The universal religion had been reduced to a national one; and the Emperor had become a petty chief.   Here is again another amazing fulfilment of the vision in the Mohammedan era.   The leaders or the patriarchs of the ancient international religion are represented as white bulls, and those of the Muslim Commanders of the Faithful also as white bulls, with the only distinction that the latter have large black horns, emblem of twofold power, spiritual and temporal.   Among all clean quadrupeds there is nothing more beautiful and noble than the white bull, and more so especially when it is crowned with a pair of large black horns.   It looks most majestic and full of grace!   It is very remarkable that the Imām of the believers, whether a Khalipha or a Sultan, or possessing both titles, is distinguished and perceived day and night by the purity of his faith and actions and by the solidity of his power and majesty at the head of the vast and innumerable hosts of the faithful composed of all races and languages!   The vision expressly avows the entrance and admission of the apostates and unbelievers into the flock.   Jews—thousands of Jews—Christians, and Sabians, as well as millions of Arabs and other heathen nationalities, believed in the oneness of Allah and embraced Islam.   In this connection it is worthy of note that all the blood shed in the wars of Badr, Ohud, and other campaigns led personally by the Prophet Muhammad, could not exceed one-hundredth of the blood shed by Joshua.   Yet not a single instance of cruelty or injustice can be proved against the Apostle of Allah. He was clement, noble, magnanimous, and forgiving.   This is why he is *alone* among all the human race represented in all prophetical visions "the Son of Man," like the first man before his fall!

(d) The Son of Man founds the Kingdom of Peace, the capital of which is no longer the old Jerusalem, but the new Jerusalem—the "Dāru 's-Salām," the "city or court of Peace." The Sophee or Seer in this wonderful vision narrates how the terrestrial Jerusalem is lifted up and transplanted in a southern country; but a new Temple, larger and higher than the first one, is built upon the ruins of the old edifice! Gracious God! how wonderfully all this was accomplished by Thy most Illustrious and Holy Servant Muhammad! The new Jerusalem is none other than Mecca, for it is in a southern country, its two hills, the "Marwa" and "Sapha," bear the same names as those of Moriah and Zion, of the same root and signification but originally earlier. "Irushalem" or "Uishalem" of old becomes a city of "Light and Peace." It is for this reason, too, that Mecca as the seat of the sacred ka'aba became the "Qibla" — the direction towards which the Muslims turn their faces at prayer. Here every year tens of thousands of pilgrim from all Muslim countries assemble, visit the Holy Ka'aba, offer sacrifices, and renew their fidelity to Allah and promise to lead a new life worthy of a Musulman. Not only Mecca, but also Medina and the territory surrounding them, has become sacred and inviolable, and forbidden to any non-Muslim man or woman! It was in fulfilment of his vision of Idris or Enoch, too, that the second Khalipha, Omar, rebuilt the Sacred Mosque at Jerusalem on the hill of Moriah, on the spot of the Temple of Solomon! All these marvellously prove that the vision was seen by a Seer inspired by God, who saw the Muslim events in a far-distant future. Could Rome or Byzantium claim to be the New Jerusalem? Can the Pope or any schismatic Patriarch claim to be the

Apocalyptic White Bull with two large horns? Can Christianity claim to be the Kingdom of Peace (Islam = "Shalom") while it makes Jesus and the Holy Ghost coeval and consubstantial with the Absolute One God? Most decidedly not.

(e) In those chapters dealing with the Kingdom of Peace, the Messiah is called Son of Man, but in the description of the Last Judgment which follows at the end of this Reign of Islam or Peace he is called "Son of Woman" and "Son of God," and made to share with God in the Judgment of the World. It is admitted by all scholars that these extravagant and foolish statements are *not* of Jewish origin but belong to the Christian imaginations, inserted and interpolated by them.

The other Apocalypses, those which bear the names of Moses, Baruch, Ezra, the Jubilees, and the Oracula Sibylliana, should be studied impartially, for it is then that they, like those of Daniel and Enoch, will not only be understood but also prove to be fulfilled in Muhammad and Islam.